VOLUME 511

SEPTEMBER 1990

THE ANNALS

of The American Academy *of* Political
and Social Science

RICHARD D. LAMBERT, *Editor*
ALAN W. HESTON, *Associate Editor*

FOREIGN LANGUAGE IN THE WORKPLACE

Special Editors of this Volume

RICHARD D. LAMBERT

National Foreign Language Center
Johns Hopkins University
Washington, D.C.

SARAH JANE MOORE

Philadelphia
Pennsylvania

Ⓢ **SAGE** PUBLICATIONS   *NEWBURY PARK   LONDON   NEW DELHI*

THE ANNALS

ERICA GINSBURG, *Assistant Editor*

Editorial Office: 3937 Chestnut Street, Philadelphia, PA 19104.

For information about membership* (individuals only) and subscriptions (institutions), address:

SAGE PUBLICATIONS, INC.
2455 Teller Road
Newbury Park, CA 91320

From India and South Asia,	*From the UK, Europe, the Middle*
write to:	*East and Africa, write to:*
SAGE PUBLICATIONS INDIA Pvt. Ltd.	SAGE PUBLICATIONS LTD
P.O. Box 4215	28 Banner Street
New Delhi 110 048	London EC1Y 8QE
INDIA	ENGLAND

SAGE Production Editors: KITTY BEDNAR and LIANN LECH
*Please note that members of The Academy receive THE ANNALS with their membership.
Library of Congress Catalog Card Number 89-64474
International Standard Serial Number ISSN 0002-7162
International Standard Book Number ISBN 0-8039-3874-8 (Vol. 511, 1990 paper)
International Standard Book Number ISBN 0-8039-3847-0 (Vol. 511, 1990 cloth)
Manufactured in the United States of America. First printing, September 1990.

The articles appearing in THE ANNALS are indexed in *Book Review Index, Public Affairs Information Service Bulletin, Social Sciences Index, Current Contents, General Periodicals Index, Academic Index, Pro-Views,* and *Combined Retrospective Index Sets.* They are also abstracted and indexed in *ABC Pol Sci, Historical Abstracts, Human Resources Abstracts, Social Sciences Citation Index, United States Political Science Documents, Social Work Research & Abstracts, Sage Urban Studies Abstracts, International Political Science Abstracts, America: History and Life, Sociological Abstracts, Managing Abstracts, Social Planning / Policy & Development Abstracts, Automatic Subject Citation Alert, Book Review Digest, Work Related Abstracts,* and/or *Family Resources Database.*

Information about membership rates, institutional subscriptions, and back issue prices may be found on the facing page.

Advertising. Current rates and specifications may be obtained by writing to THE ANNALS Advertising and Promotion Manager at the Newbury Park office (address above).

Claims. Claims for undelivered copies must be made no later than three months following month of publication. The publisher will supply missing copies when losses have been sustained in transit and when the reserve stock will permit.

Change of Address. Six weeks' advance notice must be given when notifying of change of address to ensure proper identification. Please specify name of journal. Send address changes to: THE ANNALS, c/o Sage Publications, Inc., 2455 Teller Road, Newbury Park, CA 91320.

The American Academy of Political and Social Science

3937 Chestnut Street   Philadelphia, Pennsylvania 19104

Origin and Purpose. The Academy was organized December 14, 1889, to promote the progress of political and social science, especially through publications and meetings. The Academy does not take sides in controverted questions, but seeks to gather and present reliable information to assist the public in forming an intelligent and accurate judgment.

Meetings. The Academy holds an annual meeting in the spring extending over two days.

Publications. THE ANNALS is the bimonthly publication of The Academy. Each issue contains articles on some prominent social or political problem, written at the invitation of the editors. Also, monographs are published from time to time, numbers of which are distributed to pertinent professional organizations. These volumes constitute important reference works on the topics with which they deal, and they are extensively cited by authorities throughout the United States and abroad. The papers presented at the meetings of The Academy are included in THE ANNALS.

Membership. Each member of The Academy receives THE ANNALS and may attend the meetings of The Academy. Membership is open only to individuals. Annual dues: $36.00 for the regular paperbound edition (clothbound, $48.00). Add $9.00 per year for membership outside the U.S.A. Members may also purchase single issues of THE ANNALS for $9.95 each (clothbound, $14.95).

Subscriptions. THE ANNALS (ISSN 0002-7162) is published six times annually—in January, March, May, July, September, and November. Institutions may subscribe to THE ANNALS at the annual rate: $96.00 (clothbound, $120.00). Add $9.00 per year for subscriptions outside the U.S.A. Institutional rates for single issues: $15.95 each (clothbound, $22.95).

Second class postage paid at Philadelphia, Pennsylvania, and at additional mailing offices.

Single issues of THE ANNALS may be obtained by individuals who are not members of The Academy for $13.95 each (clothbound, $22.95). Single issues of THE ANNALS have proven to be excellent supplementary texts for classroom use. Direct inquiries regarding adoptions to THE ANNALS c/o Sage Publications (address below).

All correspondence concerning membership in The Academy, dues renewals, inquiries about membership status, and/or purchase of single issues of THE ANNALS should be sent to THE ANNALS c/o Sage Publications, Inc., 2455 Teller Road, Newbury Park, CA 91320. *Please note that orders under $25 must be prepaid.* Sage affiliates in London and India will assist institutional subscribers abroad with regard to orders, claims, and inquiries for both subscriptions and single issues.

THE ANNALS

of The American Academy *of* Political
and Social Science

RICHARD D. LAMBERT, *Editor*
ALAN W. HESTON, *Associate Editor*

FORTHCOMING

THE NORDIC REGION: CHANGING PERSPECTIVES
IN INTERNATIONAL RELATIONS
Special Editor: Martin O. Heisler

Volume 512   November 1990

JAPAN'S EXTERNAL ECONOMIC RELATIONS:
JAPANESE PERSPECTIVES
Special Editors: Solomon B. Levine
Koji Taira

Volume 513   January 1991

ELECTRONIC LINKS FOR LEARNING
Special Editors: Vivian M. Horner
Linda G. Roberts

Volume 514   March 1991

See page 3 for information on Academy membership and
purchase of single volumes of **The Annals.**

CONTENTS

BOOK DEPARTMENT CONTENTS

PREFACE

The United States is experiencing a minor surge of interest in foreign language instruction at all levels of our formal education system. While we have had no hard data since 1986, enrollments seem to be up—spottily and with various strength in different languages, but, in general, up. Colleges and universities are reinstituting entrance and graduation requirements for foreign language study. Secondary and even primary schools are experimenting with new teaching strategies, new program organizational styles, and the spread of Chinese-, Russian-, and especially Japanese-language instruction into more and more schools and at more and more levels. It is not surprising, therefore, that the primary focus of national attention has been on different aspects of school- and college-based foreign language instruction, what its goals should be, and how to improve it.

This issue of *The Annals* takes a somewhat different cut. It starts not with the formal educational system but with the utilization of foreign languages by adults. It shares the premise expressed at the outset in Richard Lambert's article herein: "The greatest barrier to the expansion of foreign language competences in the United States is the low value placed on such competences by American society as a whole." It proceeds on the assumption that a major contributor to that low evaluation, one that must change if America's devout monolingualism is to be cured, is the low demand for and use of foreign language competences in key occupations. This is not to denigrate the general educational value of foreign language learning or the value of the study of a foreign language in producing a more cosmopolitan perspective. It does, however, focus on a particular goal of some of our language instruction, language for occupational use.

Most of the articles in this volume are concerned with foreign language competences. One article looks at other aspects of language in the workplace, however. Written by Mary McGroarty, it covers the problems of dealing with bilingualism in the workplace. General issues of bilingualism have been dealt with at greater length in another *Annals* volume, Courtney Cazden and Catherine Snow's *English Plus: Issues in Bilingual Education.*[1]

All of the other articles are concerned with foreign language competences, here and abroad. They concern what might be called the demand side of language competences: who wants them, who needs them, who uses them. In particular, they are concerned with occupations where either the foreign language competence itself is the primary skill being employed or it is an ancillary skill required for the successful execution of other duties. An example of the former is the translator described in Deanna Hammond's

1. Courtney B. Cazden and Catherine E. Snow, *English Plus: Issues in Bilingual Education,* vol. 508, *The Annals* of the American Academy of Political and Social Science (Mar. 1990).

article, the conference interpreters in Wilhelm Weber's article, and government positions designated as "linguists." There are, of course, other skills required of such people—indeed, both authors rightly insist that those who bring only language competences to such jobs are ineffective—but the other skills needed on the job are themselves language related.

The rest of the articles are concerned with the use of foreign languages as a supplemental skill in a variety of other occupations. Here the demand for foreign language competences is much less certain. Wakeland describes some experiments in the training of engineers, with less of an emphasis on the demand for foreign-language-competent engineers or the utilization of such skills in their employment. Garfield and Welljams-Dorof describe the ambivalent needs of scientists, particularly as they are reflected in the scientific literature. Clifford and Fischer discuss what in the United States is probably the largest organized market for foreign language competences, the federal government. The various agencies of the federal government both employ those with foreign language competences and maintain their own extensive training system almost entirely outside the formal education system.

A number of the articles deal with the demand for and utilization of foreign language competences in business. Crane and Reeves describe both increased demand and training in foreign languages in recent years in Europe, with particular reference to the effects of the coming unification of the European market. Tung describes the deliberate steps taken by the Japanese in providing their internationally oriented executives with foreign language competence. In contrast, the American situation is much less clear. Cramer describes the ambivalence of American business executives in Japan toward Japanese-language competence among Americans. Fixman describes a similar ambivalence for American business more generally. In Lambert's article, he examines the effects of what is essentially a supply-side experiment. What happens when American business majors certified to have a high level of foreign language competence are placed in the job market? Is that skill a factor in their hiring and placement? How does it affect what they do? What does their experience say about the potential for expansion of the demand for foreign language competences in American business?

It is hoped that, in general, the articles in this volume will contribute to a national discussion of what our occupational needs are for foreign language competence and what effective demand and utilization are and should be in particular occupations. Following such a discussion, a fresh examination of language instruction in our formal educational system may be in order, but that is the topic for another time.

RICHARD D. LAMBERT
SARAH JANE MOORE

Language Use in International Research:
A Citation Analysis

By EUGENE GARFIELD and ALFRED WELLJAMS-DOROF

ABSTRACT: The fact that English is the internationally accepted language of research communication raises the issue of a language barrier in two senses. First, those whose native language is not English risk being unaware of—and overlooked by—mainstream international research unless they learn to read, write, and publish in English. Second, native English-speaking researchers risk being ignorant of significant findings reported in foreign languages, especially the Japanese and Russian literature, unless they become proficient in at least one other language. The Institute for Scientific Information (ISI) data base is used to answer three basic questions bearing on this issue: (1) who writes in what languages; (2) who cites what languages; and (3) who cites what nations.

Eugene Garfield is founder and president of the Institute for Scientific Information. He earned a master's degree at Columbia University and a Ph.D. in structural linguistics from the University of Pennsylvania. He has authored over 1000 essays in ISI's Current Contents, *collected with other works in the now 11-volume book series* Essays of an Information Scientist.*

Alfred Welljams-Dorof is director of editorial services at ISI. He received his bachelor's degree at the University of Pennsylvania and has completed work toward a master's degree at Penn's Annenberg School of Communications.

F EW would argue with the claim that English is the lingua franca of international science. Previous studies by the Institute for Scientific Information (ISI) have demonstrated that most of the world's scientific literature is written and published in English and that the English-language literature is by far the most cited.[1]

The ISI data base offers unique perspectives on language use in the research literature. Each year it monitors thousands of journals for three major indexes to the research literature: *Science Citation Index (SCI)*; *Social Sciences Citation Index (SSCI)*; and *Arts & Humanities Citation Index (A&HCI)*.

Full bibliographic data are entered for every indexed source item; source items include original research articles, literature reviews, letters, notes, editorials, book reviews, and other items. These data include authors' names, institutions, and addresses; source-item title; journal title, volume, issue, year, and page numbers; language of publication; and other information.

All cited references are also indexed, which provides innovative capabilities for literature analysis and retrieval. These unique citation data have been used to develop quantitative indicators for bibliometric analysis of the research literature. Increasingly, the ISI data base is being utilized by policymakers and analysts for comparative evaluation of multinational scientific performance.

Previous ISI studies of language use have reported on the publication output of different nations in various languages and on their respective impacts, or the average number of citations received over a given time period. ISI has now developed a citation-based method to reveal interlingual and international links in the scientific literature. The data presented here identify not just who writes in what languages but also who cites what languages and what nations.

METHODS AND DEFINITIONS

The year 1984 was selected as a base year for analysis. The ISI file for that year allows us to track citations to 1984 source items over a five-year period, from 1984 through 1988. The analysis includes nearly 900,000 source items from 6100 journals indexed in the 1984 *SCI, SSCI,* and *A&HCI.* These source items received almost 3 million citations from 1984 to 1988. Book citations have been purposefully omitted from this analysis.

The nationality of a source item is defined here by the institutional affiliation of the first author. If a U.S. address is listed, the source item is credited to the United States, even if the first author is a British or French citizen, for example, or if he or she is a visiting researcher from another country working at a U.S. lab while

1. Eugene Garfield, "La science française est-elle trop provinciale?" (Is French science too provincial?), *La recherche*, 7:757-60 (Sept. 1976), reprinted in Eugene Garfield, *Essays of an Information Scientist* (Philadelphia: ISI Press, 1980), 3:89-94; idem, "Latin American Research. Part 1. Where It Is Published and How Often It Is Cited," *Current Contents*, 7 May 1984, pp. 3-8, reprinted in idem, *Essays*, 1985, 7:138-43; idem, "Is Japanese Science a Juggernaut?" *Current Contents*, 16 Nov. 1987, pp. 3-9, reprinted in idem, *Essays*, 1989, 10:342-48.

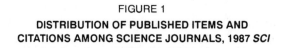

FIGURE 1
DISTRIBUTION OF PUBLISHED ITEMS AND
CITATIONS AMONG SCIENCE JOURNALS, 1987 *SCI*

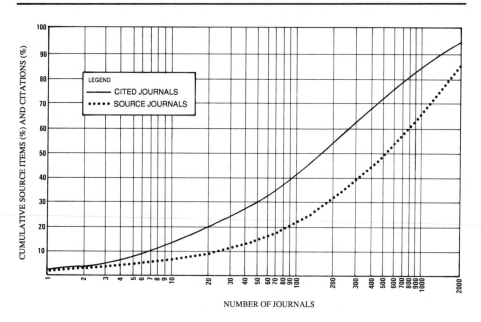

on sabbatical or other leaves of absence.

Also, this definition does not account for multinational collaborations —source items by researchers based in different nations. This may be a shortcoming in particular specialties, such as high-energy physics. Currently, the number of such source items is small. Their overall number is growing, however, accounting for about 4.4 percent of 570,000 source items indexed in the 1984 *SCI,* compared to 2.4 percent in the 1975 *SCI.*

Obviously, ISI-covered journals are only a sample of the international scientific literature, not an inventory of the entire universe. But we are confident they represent the major international research publications.

ISI data indicate that a relatively small proportion of the world's journals account for the majority of source items and citations. This is illustrated in Figure 1, which presents the distribution of source items and citations in the 1987 *SCI* file. The dotted line shows that 500 journals published about half of all source items that year. Only 200 journals received over 50 percent of the references cited in 1988, indicated by the solid line. ISI's coverage of more than 6000 journals goes well beyond what is necessary to capture the core of the international research literature.

TABLE 1

**LANGUAGE DISTRIBUTION OF 1984 ISI SOURCE ITEMS,
LISTING THE TOP 15 LANGUAGES OF PUBLICATION BY TOTAL ITEMS**

Language	Items		Citations, 1984-88		Cited Items	Total Impact	Cited Impact
	Number	% of total	Number	% of total			
English	759,753	84.7	2,841,591	97.4	362,602	3.74	7.84
German	43,533	4.9	27,745	1.0	9,989	0.64	2.78
French	35,050	3.9	17,081	0.6	6,707	0.49	2.55
Russian	30,578	3.4	26,284	0.9	11,238	0.86	2.34
Spanish	7,161	0.8	945	—	549	0.13	1.72
Japanese	5,743	0.6	2,809	0.1	1,354	0.49	2.07
Italian	5,626	0.6	201	—	156	0.04	1.29
Czech	1,847	0.2	449	—	295	0.24	1.52
Dutch	1,206	0.1	100	—	52	0.08	1.92
Portuguese	1,096	0.1	176	—	125	0.16	1.41
Swedish	780	0.1	12	—	10	0.02	1.20
Polish	710	0.1	163	—	114	0.23	1.43
Hungarian	686	0.1	178	—	102	0.26	1.75
Chinese	682	0.1	219	—	131	0.32	1.67
Ukrainian	622	0.1	169	—	100	0.27	1.69
16 other languages	1,667	0.2	136	—	87	0.08	1.56
Total	896,740	100.0	2,918,258	100.0	393,611	3.25	7.41

THREE BASIC QUESTIONS

In this article, the ISI data base will be used to answer three questions bearing on the issue of language use in science.

The first is, who writes in what languages? This will be answered by examining the number and impact of source items from a particular nation that were in English, German, French, Russian, Spanish, Japanese, and other major languages of publication in the 1984 ISI data base.

Second, who cites what languages? This will be examined by identifying the nationality of source items citing the literatures of various languages.

Finally, who cites what nations? Interlingual citation data may indicate a nation's awareness of research reported in various languages. For example, it will be shown that the ISI-covered Japanese- and Russian-language literature is cited primarily by source items from Japan or the USSR. This is not to say, however, that the scientific world is largely unaware of research from Japan or the USSR. International citation links will be examined to indicate the extent of a nation's awareness of literature from other countries.

LANGUAGE AND AUTHOR DISTRIBUTION

Table 1 presents the top 15 languages in the 1984 ISI data base, ranked by total number of source items. English clearly predominates, with about 760,000, or 85 percent of the total, written in English. Of these, 362,602, or 48 percent, were cited over 2.8 million times from 1984 to 1988. Dividing citations by total source items gives a five-year total impact of 3.74 citations, which is more than four times greater than that of other languages shown in Table 1. Dividing instead by cited source items gives a cited impact of 7.84, at least three times higher than that of other languages.

Thirty other languages are represented in the 1984 ISI data base, accounting for 15 percent of all source items. German is the second most frequent language of publication, with 43,500 source items, or 5 percent of the total. French is third with 35,000 source items, or 4 percent. German has the second highest cited impact, 2.78, followed by French, 2.55. While Russian-language source items in the ISI data base rank fourth in sheer numbers, they rank second on total impact, with 0.9 citations per source item.

Table 2 presents the top 17 nations in the 1984 ISI data base, ranked by number of source items. Source items with first authors based at U.S. institutions lead the list, accounting for 42 percent of the 722,295 addressed source items. The United Kingdom, with 9.3 percent, is second, followed by West Germany, 5.7 percent; the USSR, 5.6 percent; and Japan, 5.5 percent.

Switzerland's source items rank first in total impact (5.89) and cited impact (10.28). While Sweden shows the second highest total impact (5.81), its cited impact of 8.42 is third after that of the United States (9.28).

The Netherlands comes in third and fourth in total (5.13) and cited impact (7.98), respectively, followed by the United Kingdom at 4.14 and 7.69.

About 175,000 source items did not list an address. These include editorials, correction notes, commemorations, obituaries, and other anonymous source items. Their impact is rather low compared to that of all ISI items.

WHO WRITES IN WHAT LANGUAGES?

One measure of a nation's language use is the number of source items it produces in various languages. Table 3 lists nations by the number of source items written in English, German, French, Russian, Spanish, and Japanese. Also shown are the proportions that these numbers represent of a given nation's and language's total source items and the impact of the source items.

Not surprisingly, the leading nations within each language are the native speakers, nations in which the language is spoken. For example, over half of the English-language source items were written by first authors from the United States, the United Kingdom, Canada, and Australia. West and East Germany account for 49.8 percent of all German-language items. France takes 43.2 percent of all French source items while the Soviet Union, with 98.9 percent of the Russian-language items, and Japan with 98.8 percent of the Japanese-language items, are virtually the only nations writing in Russian and Japanese, respectively.

TABLE 2

NATIONAL DISTRIBUTION OF 1984 ISI SOURCE ITEMS,
LISTING 17 COUNTRIES WITH AT LEAST 6000 ITEMS

Nation	Items		Citations, 1984-88		Cited Items	Total Impact	Cited Impact
	Number	% of addressed items	Number	% of addressed items			
United States	303,613	42.0	1,495,949	51.6	161,126	4.93	9.28
United Kingdom	67,439	9.3	279,260	9.6	36,295	4.14	7.69
Federal Republic of Germany	41,147	5.7	160,682	5.5	22,240	3.91	7.22
USSR	40,295	5.6	43,325	1.5	14,327	1.07	3.02
Japan	39,840	5.5	162,842	5.6	25,343	4.09	6.43
Canada	32,181	4.5	120,950	4.2	17,775	3.76	6.80
France	31,621	4.4	119,516	4.1	17,184	3.78	6.96
Italy	15,421	2.1	48,089	1.7	8,740	3.12	5.50
Australia	15,058	2.1	57,643	2.0	8,873	3.83	6.50
India	14,346	2.0	19,586	0.7	6,755	1.37	2.90
Netherlands	11,136	1.5	57,145	2.0	7,162	5.13	7.98
Sweden	9,662	1.3	56,090	1.9	6,660	5.81	8.42
Switzerland	8,316	1.2	48,941	1.7	4,760	5.89	10.28
German Democratic Republic	7,055	1.0	10,520	0.4	3,000	1.49	3.51
Israel	6,734	0.9	26,704	0.9	4,109	3.97	6.50
Spain	6,231	0.9	15,026	0.5	3,094	2.41	4.86
Belgium	6,002	0.8	22,896	0.8	3,370	3.81	6.79
149 other nations	66,198	9.2	152,354	5.3	33,203	2.30	4.59
Addressed source items	722,295	80.5*	2,896,888	99.3*	384,016	4.01	7.54
Unaddressed source items	174,445	19.5*	21,370	0.7*	9,595	0.12	2.23
Grand total	896,740	100.0*	2,918,258	100.0*	393,611	3.25	7.41

*Percentage of grand total, not of addressed items.

Regardless of its native language, a nation's English-language publications have the highest impact. For example, 59 percent of West Germany's 41,000 source items were in English and 41 percent in German. Its English-language publications had a cited impact of 8.87 and a total impact of 5.83, compared to 3.08 and 1.16, respectively, for German. Switzerland's exceptional citation record, discussed earlier, is even better in English. Its cited impact of 11.71 and total impact of 7.67 are well above the second-ranked United States, at 9.29 and 4.95, respectively.

UNILINGUAL AND
BILINGUAL NATIONS

English is virtually the exclusive language of publication for the United States, the United Kingdom, and Australia. This is shown in the

TABLE 3

WHO WRITES IN WHAT LANGUAGES, LISTING NATIONS IN ORDER OF THEIR PUBLICATIONS IN THE TOP SIX LANGUAGES IN THE 1984 ISI DATA BASE

Source Language Author Nation	Items	Citations, 1984-88	% of Total Items	% of a Nation's Total Items in a Given Language	Total Impact	Cited Impact
English	759,753	2,841,591	100.0		3.74	7.84
United States	302,225		39.8	99.5	4.95	9.29
United Kingdom	67,232		8.8	99.7	4.15	7.70
Japan	36,571		4.8	91.8	4.38	6.65
Canada	31,040		4.1	96.5	3.88	6.86
Federal Republic of Germany	24,231		3.2	58.9	5.83	8.87
France	16,301		2.1	51.6	6.45	8.93
Australia	15,017		2.0	99.7	3.84	6.50
India	14,320		1.9	99.8	1.37	2.70
USSR	13,980		1.8	39.0	1.25	4.46
Italy	13,547		1.8	87.9	3.53	5.59
Netherlands	10,751		1.4	96.5	5.30	8.05
Sweden	9,432		1.2	97.6	5.94	8.46
152 other nations	205,106		27.0			
German	43,533	27,745	100.0		0.64	2.78
Federal Republic of Germany	16,737		38.4	40.7	1.16	3.08
German Democratic Republic	4,902		11.3	69.5	0.74	2.34
Austria	1,799		4.1	44.7	0.69	2.25
Switzerland	1,632		3.7	19.6	0.03	1.62
United States	400		0.9	—	0.36	2.51
63 other nations	18,063		41.5			
French	35,050	17,081	100.0		0.49	2.55
France	15,156		43.2	47.9	0.94	2.66
Canada	1,049		3.0	3.3	0.37	2.06
Belgium	976		2.8	16.3	0.60	2.12
Switzerland	554		1.6	6.7	0.65	2.26
United States	406		1.2	—	0.33	2.60
86 other nations	16,909		48.2			
Russian	30,578	26,284	100.0		0.86	2.34
USSR	30,247		98.9	75.1	1.10	2.34
Bulgaria	104		0.3	7.9	0.34	1.67
German Democratic Republic	47		0.2	0.7	0.19	1.27
United States	27		0.1	—	0.30	1.33
Hungary	17		0.1	0.5	0.47	1.60
Federal Republic of Germany	13		—	—	0.31	4.00
Poland	10		—	0.2	0.90	2.25
23 other nations	113		0.4			

(continued)

TABLE 3 Continued

Source Language Author Nation	Items	Citations, 1984-88	% of Total Items	% of a Nation's Total Items in a Given Language	Total Impact	Cited Impact
Spanish	7,161	945	100.0		0.13	1.72
Spain	2,044		28.5	32.8	0.26	1.81
Chile	632		8.8	55.3	0.22	1.86
Argentina	550		7.7	28.6	0.17	1.63
United States	415		5.8	0.1	0.05	1.18
Mexico	166		2.3	15.1	0.20	1.62
Venezuela	129		1.8	24.0	0.20	1.18
Brazil	68		1.0	2.3	0.18	1.71
34 other nations	3,157		44.1			
Japanese	5,743	2,809	100.0		0.49	2.07
Japan	5,671		98.8	7.9	0.83	2.15
People's Republic of China	29		0.5	1.0	0.24	1.75
Taiwan	17		0.3	2.1	0.00	0.00
Italy	12		0.2	0.1	0.00	0.00
5 other nations	14		0.2			

fourth column of data in Table 3: the percentage of a nation's total 1984 source items that were in English. Over 99.5 percent of U.S., U.K., and Australian source items were in English.

These nations are essentially unilingual in the sense that they write almost only in English and their foreign language publication is comparatively insignificant. The same is true of ISI-indexed publications from Sweden (97.6 percent are in English), Canada and the Netherlands (96.5 percent for both countries), and Japan (91.8 percent).

For West Germany, France, and Italy, English represents a smaller but still majority share of total source items. In each case, the second language of publication is the native language. Added together, English-language and native-language items amount to 99 percent of the total. Thus these nations are bilingual in the sense that they are proficient in two written scientific languages, English and their own.

WHO CITES WHAT LANGUAGES

Another indicator of language use is the frequency of citation of foreign language literature. Table 4 presents the nations that most often cited source items written in English, German, French, Russian, Spanish, and Japanese, in order of citations.

Again, within each language the lead citing nations are native speakers. Over 60 percent of all citations received by English-language source items were from U.S., U.K., Canadian, and Australian citing papers. The two

TABLE 4

WHO CITES WHAT LANGUAGES, LISTING NATIONS IN ORDER OF CITATIONS TO LITERATURE PUBLISHED IN THE TOP SIX LANGUAGES OF THE 1984 ISI DATA BASE

Source Language Citing Nation	Items	Citations, 1984-88	% of Total Citations	% of a Nation's Citations of Items Written in a Given Language	Total Impact	Cited Impact
English	759,753	2,841,591	100.0		3.74	7.84
United States		1,294,461	45.6	99.6	1.70	5.25
United Kingdom		258,466	9.1	99.2	0.34	2.24
Japan		171,761	6.0	98.3	0.23	2.62
Federal Republic of Germany		162,586	5.7	91.9	0.21	2.39
Canada		136,204	4.8	99.3	0.18	2.03
France		135,084	4.8	93.2	0.18	2.24
Italy		64,927	2.3	98.8	0.09	1.92
Australia		61,755	2.2	99.5	0.08	1.84
Netherlands		60,965	2.1	99.0	0.08	1.93
Sweden		54,002	1.9	99.1	0.07	2.01
USSR		44,351	1.6	66.5	0.06	9.68
Switzerland		43,624	1.5	96.4	0.06	1.91
Israel		27,525	1.0	99.5	0.04	1.65
152 other nations		325,880	11.5			
German	43,533	27,745	100.0		0.64	2.78
Federal Republic of Germany		13,757	49.6	7.8	0.32	2.38
German Democratic Republic		2,979	10.7	17.9	0.07	1.87
United States		2,102	7.6	0.2	0.05	1.52
Switzerland		1,216	4.4	2.7	0.03	1.62
Austria		1,077	3.9	7.7	0.02	1.48
United Kingdom		1,049	3.8	0.4	0.02	1.20
USSR		454	1.6	0.7	0.01	1.22
Japan		448	1.6	0.3	0.01	1.67
France		402	1.4	0.3	0.01	1.25
Netherlands		379	1.4	0.6	0.01	1.34
Canada		297	1.1	0.2	0.01	1.37
58 other nations		3,585	12.9			
French	35,050	17,081	100.0		0.49	2.55
France		9,263	54.2	6.4	0.26	2.11
United States		1,774	10.4	0.1	0.05	1.43
United Kingdom		642	3.8	0.3	0.02	1.23
Canada		566	3.3	0.4	0.02	1.43
Belgium		539	3.2	2.0	0.02	1.45
Federal Republic of Germany		458	2.7	0.3	0.01	1.27
Italy		394	2.3	0.6	0.01	1.32
Switzerland		390	2.3	0.9	0.01	1.30

(continued)

TABLE 4 Continued

Source Language Citing Nation	Items	Citations, 1984-88	% of Total Citations	% of a Nation's Citations of Items Written in a Given Language	Total Impact	Cited Impact
Japan		323	1.9	0.2	0.01	1.44
USSR		257	1.5	0.4	0.01	1.19
Spain		235	1.4	0.9	0.01	1.32
Netherlands		178	1.0	0.3	0.01	1.16
87 other nations		2,062	12.1			
Russian	30,578	26,284	100.0		0.86	2.34
USSR		21,414	81.5	32.1	0.70	2.21
United States		564	2.1	—	0.02	1.19
United Kingdom		244	0.9	0.1	0.01	1.04
44 other nations		4,062	15.5			
Spanish	7,161	945	100.0		0.13	1.72
Spain		388	41.1	1.5	0.05	1.78
Chile		123	13.0	4.4	0.02	1.64
United States		91	9.6	—	0.01	1.17
Argentina		85	9.0	1.4	0.01	1.49
28 other nations		258	27.3			
Japanese	5,743	2,809	100.0		0.49	2.07
Japan		2,139	76.1	1.2	0.37	1.84
United States		256	9.1	—	0.04	1.21
United Kingdom		77	2.7	—	0.01	1.60
Canada		53	1.9	—	0.01	1.15
Federal Republic of Germany		33	1.2	—	0.01	1.18
USSR		29	1.0	—	0.01	1.04
France		28	1.0	—	0.01	1.12
29 other nations		194	6.9			

Germanies account for 60 percent of all citations to German-language source items, and France for 54 percent of French citations. Source items in Russian and Japanese are cited primarily by the native-language producers, the USSR (82 percent) and Japan (76 percent), respectively.

The fourth column of data in Table 4 shows that, except for the USSR, English-language source items received over 90 percent of every listed nation's total citations. This is to be ex-pected, given that English-language source items amount to 85 percent of the 1984 ISI data base. The data simply reinforce the axiom that English is the internationally accepted language for research communication.

UNIVERSAL UNILINGUALISM?

The data in Table 4 indicate that most nations are essentially unilingual in the sense that they almost exclusively cite source items written in English. But it is important to stress that, while the percentage of citations to non-English-language items may seem insignificantly small, the absolute number amounts to an important share of each language's total citations. For example, just 0.2 percent of U.S. citations were to German-language source items, but these 2100 citations are 7.6 percent of the total for German. West Germany cited English-language source items 92 percent of the time, but the 7.8 percent of West German items that cited German-language source items constitute half of the language's total.

The United States and the United Kingdom usually are among the top three nations citing the literatures in German, French, Russian, and Japanese, trailing only the respective native-language nations. Together they account on average for about 10 percent of all citations received by these languages. The exception is Russian, where U.S. and U.K. citations are just 3 percent of its total citations.

WHO CITES WHAT NATIONS

The language-use data presented here raise an interesting question: How international is science? The data on Japanese-language and Russian-language source items show that they are solely produced and cited by Japan and the USSR. But these interlingual links only indirectly touch on the question of science's internationality. An answer requires knowing which nations have most frequently cited the literature of other nations. Table 5 presents this information, listing countries in order of their citations to source items authored in the United States, the United Kingdom, the Federal Republic of Germany, Japan, the USSR, Canada, and France.

Not surprisingly, each nation is its own most frequent citer. For example, of the 1.5 million citations received by U.S. source items, 63 percent were from other U.S. source items —the self-cited rate. These amounted to 72 percent of all citations from U.S. source items—the self-citing rate. The United Kingdom cited itself about 38 percent of the time, and this represents 41 percent of all citations from U.K. source items. West Germany's self-cited rate is 39 percent, and its self-citing rate is 35 percent. For Japan, the rates are 47 percent and 43 percent, and for the USSR, 67 percent and 44 percent.

At first glance, these data seem to indicate that U.S. source items are perhaps less aware of the international literature compared to other leading nations, in the sense that a smaller proportion of its citations— 28 percent—refers to non-U.S. literature. A different perspective is obtained, however, when self-citing rates in Table 5 are compared to each nation's proportionate share of all 1984-88 ISI citations, shown in Table 2.

The 1.5 million citations received by U.S. source items represent 51.6 percent of all ISI citations to addressed source items. All things being equal, U.S. source items would be expected to receive an equivalent percentage of the United States' total citations. Instead, they received 72.4

TABLE 5

**WHO CITES WHAT NATIONS, LISTING CITING NATIONS IN ORDER OF
CITATIONS TO VARIOUS NATIONS' LITERATURES, 1984-88 ISI DATA BASE**

Cited Nation Citing Nation	Items	Citations, 1984-88	% Cited	% Citing	Total Impact	Cited Impact
United States	303,613	1,495,949	100.0		4.93	9.28
United States		940,976	62.9	72.4	3.10	6.48
United Kingdom		84,278	5.6	32.4	0.28	1.96
Federal Republic of Germany		59,965	4.0	33.9	0.20	2.13
Canada		57,576	3.8	42.0	0.19	1.84
Japan		56,408	3.8	32.3	0.19	2.30
France		52,210	3.5	36.0	0.17	2.04
Italy		23,710	1.6	36.1	0.08	1.76
Australia		21,456	1.4	34.6	0.07	1.57
Netherlands		21,300	1.4	34.6	0.07	1.64
Sweden		17,546	1.2	32.2	0.06	1.66
Switzerland		17,386	1.2	38.4	0.06	1.72
USSR		16,026	1.1	24.0	0.05	1.57
134 other nations		127,112	8.5			
United Kingdom	67,439	279,260	100.0		4.14	7.69
United Kingdom		105,747	37.9	40.6	1.57	3.17
United States		73,624	26.4	5.7	0.95	3.98
France		10,498	3.8	7.2	0.19	2.72
Federal Republic of Germany		12,271	4.4	6.9	0.16	2.04
Canada		9,969	3.6	7.3	0.13	1.69
Japan		8,820	3.2	5.1	0.11	2.10
Australia		6,462	2.3	10.4	0.08	1.61
Italy		5,233	1.9	8.0	0.08	1.72
Netherlands		5,072	1.8	8.2	0.08	1.60
Sweden		4,696	1.7	8.6	0.07	1.72
Switzerland		3,616	1.3	8.0	0.05	1.71
USSR		3,203	1.1	4.8	0.05	1.55
107 other nations		30,049	10.8			
Federal Republic of Germany	41,147	160,682	100.0		3.91	7.22
Federal Republic of Germany		62,077	38.6	35.1	1.51	3.60
United States		39,539	24.6	3.0	0.96	3.98
United Kingdom		9,433	5.9	3.6	0.19	1.80
Japan		6,584	4.1	3.8	0.16	2.06
France		6,576	4.1	4.5	0.16	1.94
Canada		4,180	2.6	3.1	0.10	1.71
USSR		3,015	1.9	4.5	0.06	1.55
Switzerland		2,888	1.8	6.4	0.07	1.66
Italy		2,785	1.7	4.2	0.07	1.64
Netherlands		2,765	1.7	4.5	0.07	1.63
Sweden		1,995	1.2	3.7	0.05	1.65
Australia		1,971	1.2	3.2	0.05	1.58
98 other nations		16,874	10.5			

(continued)

TABLE 5 Continued

Cited Nation Citing Nation	Items	Citations, 1984-88	% Cited	% Citing	Total Impact	Cited Impact
Japan	39,840	162,842	100.0		4.09	6.43
Japan		75,681	46.5	43.3	1.90	3.72
United States		37,909	23.3	2.9	0.95	3.25
United Kingdom		7,602	4.7	2.9	0.17	1.64
Federal Republic of Germany		6,384	3.9	3.6	0.16	1.81
France		5,656	3.5	3.9	0.14	1.73
Canada		4,004	2.5	2.9	0.10	1.58
USSR		2,732	1.7	4.1	0.06	1.40
Italy		2,398	1.5	3.7	0.06	1.57
Netherlands		2,010	1.2	3.3	0.05	1.47
Sweden		1,567	1.0	2.9	0.04	1.54
81 other nations		16,899	10.4			
USSR	40,295	43,325	100.0		1.07	3.02
USSR		29,067	67.1	43.6	0.72	2.36
United States		3,978	9.2	0.3	0.10	2.26
Japan		1,060	2.4	0.6	0.03	1.71
Federal Republic of Germany		1,029	2.4	0.6	0.03	1.76
United Kingdom		931	2.1	0.4	0.02	1.36
France		919	2.1	0.6	0.02	2.12
57 other nations		6,341	14.6			
Canada	32,181	120,950	100.0		3.76	6.80
Canada		40,604	33.6	26.6	1.26	3.22
United States		39,183	32.4	3.0	1.22	3.66
United Kingdom		7,823	6.5	3.0	0.24	1.74
Federal Republic of Germany		4,144	3.4	2.3	0.13	1.77
France		4,086	3.4	2.8	0.13	1.74
Japan		4,040	3.3	2.8	0.13	1.93
Australia		2,147	1.8	3.5	0.07	1.48
Netherlands		1,721	1.4	2.8	0.05	1.48
Italy		1,653	1.4	2.5	0.05	1.52
Sweden		1,609	1.3	3.0	0.05	1.48
Switzerland		1,181	1.0	2.6	0.04	1.54
USSR		1,173	1.0	1.8	0.04	1.38
93 other nations		11,586	9.6			
France	31,621	119,516	100.0		3.78	6.96
France		44,655	37.4	30.8	1.41	3.40
United States		29,794	24.9	2.3	0.94	3.87
United Kingdom		7,360	6.2	2.8	0.23	1.87
Federal Republic of Germany		5,760	4.8	3.3	0.18	1.98
Japan		4,736	4.0	2.7	0.15	1.97
Canada		3,495	2.9	2.6	0.11	1.66

TABLE 5 Continued

Cited Nation Citing Nation	Items	Citations, 1984-88	% Cited	% Citing	Total Impact	Cited Impact
Italy		2,699	2.3	4.1	0.09	1.68
USSR		2,084	1.7	3.1	0.07	1.48
Netherlands		1,950	1.6	3.2	0.06	1.68
Switzerland		1,754	1.5	3.9	0.06	1.56
Australia		1,504	1.3	2.4	0.05	1.55
Sweden		1,456	1.2	2.7	0.05	1.53
Belgium		1,253	1.0	4.7	0.04	1.42
Spain		1,155	1.0	4.6	0.04	1.46
100 other nations		9,861	8.3			

percent of all citations from U.S. source items. Dividing actual by expected citations received gives a value of 1.4—that is, the United States cites itself 1.4 times more than the ISI mean of citations to the United States. In comparison, the United Kingdom's self-citing rate of 40.6 percent is 4.2 times greater than the 9.6 percent share of all ISI citations it received. The ratio for West Germany is 6.3; for Japan, 7.7; and 29.1 for the USSR. The higher the ratio, the greater the disparity between a nation's citation of its literature and the world's citation of that nation's literature.

In this light, the USSR again stands out as a country whose literature has a restricted circulation. Of all citations to ISI-covered USSR source items, 67 percent are from other USSR-produced source items. As usual, the United States is the second citing nation. But the United States accounts for only about 10 percent of all citations to the USSR, compared to its average of about 25 percent of all citations to the United Kingdom, the Federal Republic of

Germany, Japan, and France. The reason is that the United States and all other citing nations are citing the 39 percent of the ISI-covered Soviet literature published in English. No Western nations show meaningful awareness of Russian-language Soviet research.

To a lesser extent, the same is true of Japan. From a citation perspective, Japan is more like the Western nations than the USSR. As we have seen, no Western nations cite Japan's Japanese-language source items to a significant extent. But these items amount to only 8 percent of Japan's ISI-covered literature. Its predominant English-language output is what the world cites. The data in Table 5 show high international awareness of Japan's source items: they are cited about as often as those from West Germany, France, Canada, and other leading nations.

SUMMARY AND CONCLUSION

The data presented here document the predominance of English as the primary language of international research. More source items are published in English by both native and nonnative speakers than any other language, and they have the highest impact. Also, most major scientific nations, regardless of their native language or languages, cite the English-language literature almost exclusively.

In most non-English languages represented in the ISI data base, especially Japanese and Russian, the majority-share producers and consumers are the native-speaking nations. Thus barriers of varying permeability exist around all non-English languages to some extent. These barriers, however, do not prevent or diminish a balanced awareness of research from a given country. As was shown, there is good intranational citation of the world literature, and it is primarily through a nation's English-language publications that the rest of the world learns of its research.

It should be kept in mind that this analysis reflects only one portion of the spectrum of research communi-cation—formal publication. It might be argued that research publications are the most linguistically transparent form of communication: they are high in numeric and graphic content, and their structured narrative uses a high proportion of technical terms having universal meaning. Thus unilingualism might not be a hard barrier against comprehending the gist of published research.

Unilingualism is a limitation in other, perhaps more professionally important, forms of communication, however. For example, leading-edge research is discussed in personal conversations, departmental meetings, professional conferences, and other verbal exchanges between colleagues well before it appears in print. Thus conversational fluency in more than one language remains a valuable professional asset for researchers. It is also personally enriching, enabling researchers to appreciate more deeply the expression of other nations and cultures—their art as well as their science.

ANNALS, *AAPSS,* 511, September 1990

The Foreign Language Needs of U.S.-Based Corporations

By CAROL S. FIXMAN

ABSTRACT: This article summarizes the results of 32 interviews conducted in nine companies of varying type and size. The purpose was to help identify the foreign language needs of U.S.-based corporations. These needs seem to depend in part on a company's type of product or service, its corporate culture, its geographical areas of involvement, and its size. Different types of positions will require different types and levels of foreign language skills. In general, while cross-cultural understanding was frequently viewed as important for doing business in a global economy, foreign language skills rarely were considered an essential part of this. Language problems were largely viewed as mechanical and manageable problems that could be solved individually—primarily by hiring foreign nationals or interpreters or translators. Smaller companies trying to enter the global market often seemed more sensitive to the value of foreign languages than larger companies did. They do not have access to the same resources as their larger counterparts, and they are dealing in a worldwide community of smaller companies, where English is less likely to be the lingua franca.

Carol S. Fixman is director of International Programs at Temple University. Prior to that she developed and directed international education programs at the American Assembly of Collegiate Schools of Business as well as in West Germany at the Carl Duisberg Gesellschaft and Konrad Adenauer Stiftung. She received her Ph.D. in German literature from Brown University and has taught at the University of Bonn in West Germany.

NOTE: This article is drawn from a study commissioned by the National Foreign Language Center and published in May 1989 in its series of occasional papers.

THIS study is aimed at identifying how and when foreign language competence makes a difference in the international operations of U.S.-based corporations. What kinds of skills are required, and how do companies gain access to them?

The role of foreign languages in U.S. businesses has been examined in the past. In particular, a RAND Corporation report from 1979 and studies by Marianne E. Inman from 1979, 1985, and 1989 are noteworthy.[1] Each of these surveyed large companies only and received information mainly from one representative of each firm, usually in the area of human resources.

I did not seek to replicate these past surveys. Instead, I asked multiple representatives of a variety of companies to help identify what the main issues are for them today in foreign language competence and what future trends they see developing in their areas.

I conducted a total of 32 interviews in nine companies selected to provide examples of different types and sizes.[2] Four of the companies are *Fortune* 500 industrial firms, including the areas of computers and telecommu-

nications; chemicals; and foods and beverages. One is a major accounting and consulting firm, and one a major money-center bank. Two companies register annual revenues between $50 and $150 million: an import-export firm and an office-supplies manufacturer. One company, with revenues under $10 million, manufactures auto-repair supplies.

The 32 individuals whom I interviewed represent a variety of perspectives not only due to the differences in type and size of company but also as a result of their various positions and backgrounds. All deal with some aspect of international operations. Their functions are as follows: 8 are in human resources, 7 in training and development, and 5 in line international management; 3 are technical managers, and another 3 are in client service; 2 are in strategic planning, 2 more are in public affairs, and 2 are top managers in smaller companies. There was some overlap. For instance, one of the technical managers also had responsibilities in line international management, and one of the top managers of a smaller company also fulfilled technical functions.

Most of my interview partners had served abroad for their firm either in short assignments—one to three weeks—or longer assignments of one to three years. Four are bilingual or multilingual, speaking Portuguese, Japanese, French, Greek, Italian, German, and Spanish; six are of non-U.S. origin—Japanese, Greek, Mexican-German, and British.

In each case, I asked questions pertinent to their positions. The questions mainly centered around foreign language needs within their firms as

1. Sue E. Berryman et al., *Foreign Language and International Studies Specialists: The Marketplace and National Policy* (Santa Monica, CA: RAND Corporation, 1979); Marianne E. Inman, *Foreign Languages, English as a Second / Foreign Language, and the U.S. Multinational Corporation* (Arlington, VA: Center for Applied Linguistics, 1979); idem, "Language and Cultural Training in American Multinational Corporations," *Modern Language Journal,* 69(4):247-55 (1985); idem, "Corporate Language Strategies for Global Markets" (Paper, May 1989).

2. This sample is not statistically representative. Generalizations should therefore be drawn with care.

well as in relations with outside parties such as joint-venture partners, customers, distributors, suppliers, and foreign governments.

CORPORATE RATIONALE FOR
FOREIGN LANGUAGE NEED

In general, businesspeople whom I interviewed tended to view a foreign language as divorced from its cultural context. Most had experienced firsthand the difficulties arising from different management styles in various parts of the world. They saw cross-cultural understanding as important for doing business in a global economy. Few considered knowledge of a foreign language a key element in this understanding, however.

Not surprisingly, the less foreign language knowledge my interview partners had, the more they tended to view foreign language use as a mechanical skill, of only secondary value to cross-cultural understanding. Corroborating this, one multilingual manager added that international businesspeople who can deal only in their own language are blinded by their narrow perspective. As he put it, from their limited vantage point they can manage without foreign language skills; however, they do not know how effective they could be with these skills.

An international human resource manager at a large computer and telecommunications firm provided a case in point. He explained that in some countries, such as Korea, where U.S. expatriates of his company do not speak the native language, "they just have a hard time." For him, learning the language would not make a significant difference, since in the larger worldwide scheme of things, his company was experiencing success.

A few of my interview partners who had had extensive international experience observed that businesspeople with little or no exposure to foreign languages felt threatened by those with more. Thus, in self-defense, they relegated language skills to a position of secondary importance and preferred to deal with colleagues more like themselves.

A strategic planner at a large chemical company commented that most U.S. businesses are not dealing well with the rest of the world largely because Americans basically do not value cultural diversity. In his eyes, businesses deal with foreign languages on an ad hoc basis. When they perceive a specific need, they locate someone to fill it, but they do no more than that. They do not see the longer-range importance of foreign language skills in developing a global mind-set.

This short-term, mechanical value attributed to foreign languages predominated in the comments of most of my interview partners. Many pointed out that foreign languages did not actually present a problem since they could be managed. In other words, when needs arose, appropriate skills would be located. As one individual explained, "You can manage foreign languages. It's the culture that trips you up." Even the most intransigent adversary of corporate foreign language training at one firm that I visited readily admitted to the importance of international experience for his company's executives.

Like many corporate representatives, he considers foreign language skills something that can be purchased on an ad hoc basis—distinct from international experience, which must be acquired.

TYPE OF CORPORATE PRODUCT OR SERVICE AS A DETERMINING FACTOR

In general, companies in the service sector appeared to recognize more of a primary need for foreign language skills than those in the industrial sector. The basis of the service sector is not a physical product but rather expertise that has to be conveyed from person to person, such as tax and management consulting, auditing, or banking. The medium of conveyance—and therefore language skills—in these fields assumes special importance, as was affirmed by a number of my interview partners. The industrial sector, on the other hand, is selling its expertise in the form of a physical product. Though the product must be marketed, it seems somewhat less dependent on interpersonal communication for success.

One issue that deserves further examination is whether, within the industrial sector, certain types of products cause companies to come into more contact with local populations abroad than others. Increased contact with local populations would generate foreign language needs for a U.S.-based company. For example, high-technology companies would generally seem to be less responsive to local needs in each country. They are more likely to rationalize their production globally in order to cover the high cost of research and development. In other words, operations in one geographic area will not necessarily serve that area alone.[3] In comparison, the food industry has to respond to health regulations in individual countries. Also, packaging may need to be rendered more appropriate to each particular area. It is not possible to draw meaningful conclusions about this issue based on the small number of companies that I interviewed; however, it may be worthwhile to pursue it in future, more definitive studies of factors determining foreign language needs of corporations.

GEOGRAPHIC AREA OF INVOLVEMENT AS A DETERMINING FACTOR

There are several reasons why the geographic area of a company's overseas involvement may have a bearing on its foreign language needs. In some countries, companies must be more responsive to local political imperatives than in others. As several of my interview partners indicated, if a firm operates in a country with restrictions on foreign ownership, local content of products, and numbers of foreign employees, it probably will have more to do with the local population. More host-country nationals will be involved in company

3. For further comment, see Yves L. Doz, "Strategic Management in International Companies," *Sloan Management Review*, 21(2):27-46 (1980); idem, "Managing Manufacturing Rationalization within Multinational Companies," *Columbia Journal of World Business*, 13(3):82-94 (Fall 1978).

operations, either on a primary level—for example, as company employees —or on a secondary one, as, for instance, government and trade union officials.

Another plausible meaning of geographic location for foreign language needs was suggested by a strategic planner in the food and beverage company that I visited. He suggested that as a firm increases its business in developing countries, it will find that knowledge of English is less widespread in the local populations. Thus it will become more important for company employees to know the local languages.

In particular, Latin America was named by several companies as an area where it is difficult to find individuals who speak English. Many of my interview partners also indicated that businesspeople and government officials there are more likely to insist on speaking their native language even if they do know English. This is a matter of pride for them. One executive from a chemical company reported that he had participated in negotiations with a Latin American head of state who, though a Harvard graduate, insisted on conducting negotiations in Spanish with an interpreter. My interview partner showed understanding for this attitude. How many American businesspeople or government officials would negotiate in a foreign language in the United States, if they could?

Other countries that were named as particularly difficult for conducting business in English include Japan, Korea, China, and the Soviet Union. This seems to have less to do with local pride and more with the fact that English skills simply are not very common there. In all of these areas, U.S. companies appear to have a greater need to have access to skills in the local languages.

THE SIGNIFICANCE OF CORPORATE CULTURE

A corporate culture generally is understood as the particular management style of a company.[4] In all of the large companies that I examined, emphasis was placed on employees' feeling part of a larger family. Great importance was attached to loyalty and lengthy service to the company, especially in the upper echelons of management. For example, the 34 senior management officials at the money-center bank that I visited had accumulated an average of 20 years of service each.

Corporate culture becomes significant in international operations for several reasons. The language and culture of the parent company constitute the carrier of the corporate cul-

4. For further comment, see B. R. Baliga and Alfred M. Jaeger, "Multinational Corporations: Control Systems and Delegation Issues," *Journal of International Business Studies*, 15(2):25-40 (Fall 1984); C. Paul Dredge, "Corporate Culture: The Challenge to Expatriate Managers and Multinational Corporations," in *Strategic Management of Multinational Corporations: The Essentials,* ed. Heidi Vernon Wortzel and Lawrence H. Wortzel (New York: John Wiley, 1985), pp. 410-24; Susan C. Schneider, "National vs. Corporate Culture: Implications for Human Resource Management," *Human Resource Management,* 27(2):231-46 (Summer 1988).

ture. Thus a firm that establishes subsidiaries abroad—or, in the banking industry, branches—transfers its culture to these operations. Most firms that I studied admitted that their corporate cultures could not simply be transplanted to other countries but had to be adapted. Foreign language needs usually arise in the adaptation process.

For example, the bank that I studied sometimes acquires banks abroad. These are banks that frequently have their own corporate identity and need to be integrated into the corporate mount of the new parent company. This is accomplished by sending teams to the new location from the U.S. headquarters for a transition period of approximately three years. The team needs to be skilled in the local language of the new site. During the transition period, they train a second tier of managers—host-country nationals —and gradually turn the operation over to them.

A line manager of the food and beverage firm that I visited reported that his company transmitted its corporate culture through training, example setting, and leadership. Last year it established a new plant in the south of France. The individuals selected for leadership roles at this new site were French or third-country nationals. They were brought to the United States for training and to assimilate the culture of the company. If their English proved insufficient, they were sent to remedial English classes. Subsequently, the management group attended a team-building exercise for one week. This was conducted in English. The most telling point for me, however, was my interviewee's comment that English was used "because no one was capable of doing it in French." Thus two foreign language needs arose here. One was English as a second language and could be filled. The other was helping the management team from France assimilate and adapt to the company culture in their own language. This remained an unfilled, though recognized, need.

A company's attitude toward adapting its corporate culture seems related to whether it identifies itself as a global company or as a U.S. company operating internationally. Two of the firms that I visited conveyed this distinction to me. One has a relatively large number of non-Americans in its senior management team and appears less interested in superimposing a U.S.-based corporate culture on subsidiaries abroad. The other is implementing plans to transform itself into a global company. Interview partners there were concerned about developing a global mind-set among employees. Companies of this type seem more likely to have foreign language needs that arise from adapting their corporate cultures abroad.

COMPANY SIZE

Small and medium-sized companies do not have access to the resources of their larger counterparts to help them function effectively in the global marketplace. The interviews that I conducted at three small and medium-sized businesses suggest that it is precisely this sector that needs the most assistance in dealing with a multicultural and multilingual business world.

One significant problem in encouraging smaller firms to export their goods and services was pointed out to me by a representative of the import-export company that I visited. He observed that smaller U.S. companies seek to export their products mainly when their domestic sales are down. Their interest in exporting then wanes when domestic sales increase. This prevents a company from developing a long-range international strategy and has a negative influence on the company's long-term success abroad. It also has ramifications for the firm's foreign language needs. A company seeking short-term, quick success is less likely to invest in foreign language training for its employees, much less hire an individual largely for language skills that may not be useful in one year's time.

The smaller companies that I examined are currently attempting to export their products abroad. It is interesting that their representatives showed more sensitivity to foreign language and culture needs than many of my interview partners from large multinational companies. A line manager from one large company suggested that her firm had had international operations for so long that the management's international sensitivity was taken for granted—incorrectly so, in her opinion. If a company's awareness of foreign language needs is any measure of international sensitivity, this manager's observation could be applied to most of the larger companies whose representatives I interviewed.

In examining multinational firms, it is worthwhile to keep in mind that they deal largely in a world of other multinationals whose main business language has been English worldwide at least since the end of World War II. As English has become more pervasive in international business, U.S.-based companies perhaps have seen less reason to place a premium on foreign language skills.

Smaller companies, however, enter the global marketplace without the English-speaking networks to which their larger counterparts have access. Also, they are dealing with a community of smaller companies, where English-language proficiency may not be as prevalent. For example, an executive of one small company that I visited explained that he would like to sell his product to mom-and-pop companies abroad, as he does in the United States. His lack of foreign language competency makes this extremely difficult, however, since smaller operations abroad usually cannot deal with him proficiently in English. In addition, he cannot demonstrate his product in the foreign company's cultural context. This individual is so sensitive to the importance of foreign languages that he opens his standard response letter to foreign inquiries with the sentence: "Please excuse my inability to reply in [German]."

The differences between smaller and larger companies' foreign language needs become especially clear in examining their reactions to the planned unification of the European Economic Community in 1992. The larger companies that I visited anticipated no change in their foreign language needs as a result of 1992. One computer and telecommunications firm has established a major project in its Paris office dealing with the market unification. They are concerned with reconciling national differences in issues such as pensions, insurance, and so forth. "Foreign languages are the last thing they are worrying about," explained one manager. In fact, several individuals at large companies speculated that after 1992, their foreign language needs would decrease because the European Community would have a greater need for a common denominator in communication. This would be English. In contrast, the representatives of smaller companies whom I interviewed estimated that their foreign language needs would increase in 1992. While the larger companies already operate in European countries, the smaller ones see a clear and sometimes urgent need to enter the European market before it closes to them. This means more than using distributors to sell their products abroad. They feel compelled to establish an actual presence in Europe in order not to be excluded from that market.

Both of the smaller manufacturing companies that I studied are seeking to open a branch in a European Community country. One even intends to manufacture products there. Both of my interview partners were keenly aware of the foreign language needs

that they will incur in this process. These needs will not differ significantly from those of larger firms, though the smaller companies will have to fill them differently.

WHO NEEDS FOREIGN LANGUAGE SKILLS?

In general, my interview partners expressed the view that the farther down the hierarchy an American's business associates are, the more important it is for him or her to know their language. Lower-level employees abroad are less likely to be proficient in English. Thus, for instance, someone dealing with wage earners would have a greater need for foreign language skills. This does not necessarily mean that Americans of lower rank need more foreign language proficiency. The type of position is important here. For example, engineers who supervise local blue-collar workers in constructing a new plant abroad are unlikely to be able to communicate with them in English. They will either have to speak the workers' language or employ a go-between.

Similarly, although country heads in large firms usually occupy relatively powerful positions, they may deal directly with employees in much lower ranks. One former country head was responsible for 13 plants in a Latin American country. He undertook on-site reviews of these plants every month. At first he conducted the reviews in English; however, he found that outside the capital city, the employees could not communicate well in English. Many individuals who should have spoken up did not. Thereafter he held his reviews in

Spanish. It was more important to him that the employees interacted than that he understood every detail. This country head spoke Spanish but took bilingual Latin American employees with him to the plant reviews as a safety net.

An executive of one multinational company mainly dealt with individuals of his own rank when he served as head of European operations. The codetermination laws in Germany, however, called for representatives of company wage earners to serve on the Board of Directors. He had to communicate with them. As it was, he used an interpreter. The same was true of another U.S. executive, in Holland, who had to deal with Dutch wage earners on the company's Works Council.

Only one interview partner contradicted the view that American businesspeople mainly need foreign language skills in dealing with lower-level employees. This was a multilingual public affairs officer at a large company. In his view, individuals in upper-level positions have a greater need for foreign languages, since they are managing international activities of great complexity. If they rely on interpreters, they will view situations only through others' eyes. Furthermore, he pointed out that foreign languages have the longer-term benefit of enabling the speakers to view the world in many ways—from a variety of perspectives. Very few of the individuals whom I interviewed agreed with this.

Most senior managers with whom I spoke asserted that English worked as the main vehicle of business communication. If necessary, an inter-

preter would be used. One executive of a multinational company insisted that even if he were fluent in another language, he would not negotiate in it, since this would put him at a disadvantage.

The real value of foreign languages for senior management was usually placed on a secondary level, as a tool that would help a manager understand nuances and social conversation with foreign nationals. One executive explained that he would like to understand the conversations that take place on the side of official meetings. Also, he admitted that a lack of foreign language knowledge limits the business contacts whom he can get to know. He avoids individuals who are uncomfortable using English. Furthermore, he views foreign languages as important stepping stones to understanding other cultures. But he perceives all of these advantages as ancillary and concluded that he really can "get by almost anywhere in the world without foreign language ability."

For another executive, knowledge of foreign languages has a social, a "comfort" value, but he, too, considered this to be of secondary value. A senior planning official in a multinational company asserted that he can do his job without knowledge of other languages. It just takes longer. In his mind, foreign languages serve more of a goodwill purpose for executives. Elementary skills help businesspeople socially, as it helps them show that they have an interest in their conversation partner's country.

Most individuals whom I interviewed perceived foreign languages to be of only secondary value for executives. Nonetheless, a few did insist that establishing rapport with a foreigner by speaking his or her language on social occasions was of primary importance for business. One cited the proverbial decisions that are made on the golf course. He and others pointed to the role that languages play in developing a relationship of trust and confidence with a business partner. Most of my interview partners, however, relegated this role to a position of lesser importance.

An executive in a small company asserted that if he could speak another language, he would gain greater credibility abroad. It would not matter which language this was; he merely wished to demonstrate to foreigners that he did not expect the world to revolve around the United States. Thus, for him, a foreign language would help convey an attitude, not just business facts.

In looking at the importance of foreign language skills for senior management, my interview partners in general placed more emphasis on outcome than on process. They usually agreed that speaking a business partner's language could help build confidence and good rapport; however, most concluded that this would not be of bottom-line value to them. The process of building a long-term working relationship was not of primary significance for them.

It is interesting that even the most ethnocentric company that I visited considered it important for their executives of tomorrow to have international experience in order for them to be able to function in a global economy. A manager in one multinational firm pointed out that, unfortunately,

only one member of his company's senior management currently had served abroad on a lengthier assignment. It was this one person's contacts abroad, however, that had brought about the largest and most significant business transaction in the company's history. In spite of that achievement, even this interview partner joined the general consensus that foreign languages are not a key component of the much desired international experience in U.S.-based businesses today.

WORK CALLING FOR FOREIGN LANGUAGE SKILLS

In speaking with corporate representatives, I distinguished between cross-cultural communication within the company and that with the external environment. Communication within the firm would, for instance, be between headquarters and subsidiaries abroad, between subsidiaries, as well as within individual subsidiaries. The external environment includes business contacts such as joint-venture partners, distributors, and suppliers as well as foreign government officials, trade unions, and the like.

Communications with the external environment

Businesspeople usually find dealings with the external environment abroad more difficult because they do not have the same leverage over their communication partner that they might have within their own company. An American cannot insist that English be spoken. In contrast, when a businessperson is communicating with an employee of lesser rank within the company, the employee will usually make every effort to render communication easier for him or her. In negotiating with an outside business partner or government official, it will usually be to the American's advantage to facilitate communication. Working through an interpreter might be an option, but nuances may be missed and difficulties can be encountered in getting points across in just the right way. Furthermore, it will be hard to understand what the others are saying among themselves, as many of my interview partners asserted. A public affairs manager described her discomfort at "going into negotiations in a foreign language when others are whispering among themselves in their languages. They're discussing strategy. It would be very important to understand these conversations."

One human resource manager whom I interviewed pointed out that making a cultural or linguistic mistake in cross-cultural communication within one's own company is not as damaging as it might be in dealing with the external environment. Within one's own company everyone is "all one family," the corporate culture being a strong connecting link. Thus one who errs is more likely to be given the benefit of the doubt. This is not the case in dealing with individuals outside the company.

Smaller companies seem to have more difficulty in negotiating with foreign partners. The executive vice-president of a small auto-repair manufacturer pinpointed two sales that he had lost because he could not speak the language of his partner, although he did use an interpreter: one in francophone Africa and one in Austria. He admitted that he did not know how much additional business he was missing by not knowing foreign languages.

Companies that I studied in the service sector insisted that employees who deal with clients must know the clients' language. Thus, for instance, a condition for employment in line positions of the Latin American division of the money-center bank that I visited is knowledge of Spanish. In the accounting firm that I visited, tax accountants and auditors who deal with subsidiaries of Japanese and Korean companies in the United States must know Japanese and Korean, respectively. In neither case are many Americans hired for these positions, since they rarely have the necessary combination of business and language skills.

Human resource managers abroad often deal with local governmental authorities regarding visa issues for overseas employees who are Americans and third-country nationals. One of my interview partners had served in his company's European headquarters in Switzerland and found that his lack of French proficiency was an obstacle in meetings with the Swiss cantonal authorities regarding work permits. He explained that he could always understand the basics through an interpreter, but the nuances, which frequently were quite important, were difficult.

One aspect of dealing with the external environment that does not necessarily involve person-to-person communication is strategic planning. Companies gather information on foreign countries in order to facilitate their planning for that area and worldwide. Almost all of the planners whom I interviewed receive material from their foreign subsidiaries in English. Employees at the subsidiaries abroad both select and translate documents considered important for the planning process. In the event that material is located at headquarters, it usually is faxed to a subsidiary abroad for translation. Smaller companies with no overseas subsidiaries have to contract out translations.

Telecommunications companies need to understand the laws, regulatory schemes, and trade policies of foreign countries, since telecommunications are government controlled in many areas. A manager in one computer and telecommunications company where I conducted interviews regularly sends documents to outside translators; however, the telecommunications language often presents a problem. Delays occur that have direct repercussions for business. For example, the latest West German telecommunications law evidently was not translated into English for five or six months. Unless one understood German, one could not have access to it. The English translation of regulatory schemes from Spain lagged behind the original text one year. This manager found solace in the fact that the European Community now is having more of its official documents printed in English, and the Japanese "are doing better in getting things trans-

lated into English . . . because they want to get into the U.S. market." In Latin America, however, Argentina evidently is the only country whose government distributes telecommunications materials in English.

If companies receive materials in advance of their need, they usually can have them translated. But this manager reported attending a meeting of the Organization for Economic Cooperation and Development in Paris at which documents were distributed ad hoc. She could not understand them, nor could the interpreter accompanying her deal with them quickly enough to be of use to her.

Companies that enter into joint ventures with foreign companies have foreign language needs deriving from ongoing relations with their business partners. For example, the food and beverage company that I visited is a joint-venture partner with local bottlers throughout the world. Company personnel frequently must deal in the language of the bottler.

I asked the chemical and the computer and telecommunications companies about security problems with joint-venture partners. It would seem that the less one understands of a partner's language, the less likely one is to detect theft of technology. Representatives of one firm showed surprise at the question and dismissed it with the explanation that secrecy agreements solved any problems. When I asked about China, however, one of the managers admitted that the company shared with that country only technology that the firm had already surpassed. A representative of another firm admitted that despite legal agreements to avoid security problems, intellectual-property issues did arise on occasion. My limited interviews cannot provide evidence that these problems would cease if foreign language proficiency were more widespread; however, this does seem to be an area that would benefit from more extensive foreign language skills.

There are many forms of international business partnerships besides joint ventures, such as franchise contracts, licensing agreements, and joint research and development projects. In any of these cases, U.S.-based firms need foreign languages in negotiating and maintaining relationships with outside partners. Companies also have contract relationships with outside affiliates that serve specific needs, such as importers and distributors.

The import-export company I studied does 99 percent of its business overseas, with local distributors as its partners. If a distributor does not have a good command of English, they work through an interpreter. Although this company handles exports to 70 countries, it has only several employees—of a total of 36—with foreign language skills. They were not hired primarily because of these language skills.

A medium-sized manufacturing company that I studied saw a greater need for foreign language knowledge in dealing with distributors and importers. The company hired a managerial employee with proficiency in Spanish to handle business with Latin America. Knowledge of Spanish was a prerequisite for this posi-

tion. The company also employs a secretary from El Salvador who can provide support services in Spanish. The president of the International Division speaks French and German and uses these languages with business contacts. Transactions with Japan currently are handled in English; however, this evidently is not satisfactory, and the company is considering hiring someone with skills in Japanese in the future. Following the initial phase of business with distributors and importers, foreign language is important if there are problems or if a change in or expansion of relations is desired. My interview partner at this firm consciously tries to maintain good rapport with foreign contacts. For example, sometimes when he receives telexes from French or German companies in English, he responds in their language as a matter of courtesy. For administrative follow-up, English is used because most of the staff at headquarters do not have foreign language skills.

Internal company communication

One important aspect of internal company cross-cultural communication is personnel evaluation. It makes sense that in order to be able to assess employees appropriately, it is best to view them in their cultural context. Not many human resource managers pointed to the importance of language in this process, although one senior manager at a multinational company was very sensitive to the complications of this issue. Perhaps his own foreign nationality—he is British—extensive experience abroad, and knowledge of three foreign languages rendered him especially aware of these problems. He observed that Americans often experience difficulty in dealing with foreigners, even if they are conversing in English. For him, the issue was not so much the ability to speak the other person's language as the ability to understand the reasons for their different behavior.

He explained that a foreigner may find it difficult to communicate in English and therefore may not appear especially intelligent to a native English speaker. An American who has never tried to speak a foreign language is less likely to empathize with the foreigners' situation and will tend to judge them without taking this difficulty into account. He recounted his experience with a quality-insurance director in an overseas plant for which he was responsible. Although this person was performing well, the U.S. vice-president for quality insurance did not recognize this. To him, the local quality-insurance person appeared slow, lacking energy and initiative. The main problem was that the foreign national's English was poor.

An internationally experienced and multilingual manager in another large firm experienced similar incidents. His company's Italian subsidiary hired an Italian salesman according to U.S. standards: he was cool and collected and showed little emotion. Ultimately, however, the company found that he could not communicate well with other Italians, who found him too detached. This same manager recounted another telling incident in cross-cultural personnel evaluation. In conducting a performance review with a Swiss national, a U.S. manager of his company in Switzerland began in the usual American fashion by praising the employee's positive attributes. He complimented the Swiss employee for being loyal and punctual and then continued on to more negative points. In the end, the Swiss was certain that his review had gone well. When the company subsequently decreased his salary, he filed suit against them. In both cases, American managers were not familiar enough with their host country's culture. My interview partner considered knowledge of the foreign language an integral part of that culture.

Many of the companies that I visited named marketing as an area with foreign language needs. Individuals involved in promoting a product or service abroad will find it important to know the language of the relevant countries. A manager dealing with Latin America in a computer and telecommunications company explained that brochures in Spanish from their partners sometimes have to be translated for internal use in the United States. This company also developed promotional brochures aimed at Hispanic households in the United States. A U.S. advertising agency was used for this purpose. My interview partner furnished the agency with the main thrust of what the company envisioned. The advertising agency then developed it and translated it into Spanish. My interview partner explained that it was important for him to understand the Hispanic mentality for this project.

He worked closely with the Hispanic group of his company's domestic operations.

In the lore and literature on international business, examples abound of advertising that was misguided due to linguistic or cultural blunders. For instance, "Body by Fisher" was translated into Flemish as "Corpse by Fisher." Schweppes Tonic Water was promoted in Italy as "bathroom water." The Chevrolet Nova did not sell well in Latin America, perhaps because "no va" in Spanish means "it does not go."

Technical employees in international operations of U.S.-based companies demonstrated foreign language needs to me in four main areas: plant construction, technology transfer, installation and maintenance of equipment, and troubleshooting.

In constructing new plants, American engineers frequently must supervise local nationals. One large company reported that in building a new site in France, a U.S. team has worked through a French management group. This group has subcontracted to an engineering firm, and so forth. Thus Americans have not dealt with the North African construction workers and others who do not have knowledge of English. Once the plant is completed, the senior managers, who are not Americans, will be trained in English. They in turn will train others in French. Most companies that I interviewed conduct training sessions in English and use interpreters if necessary.

Another company, which is building a plant in China, sent U.S. expatriates to start up the plant and conduct training for three to six months. Bilingual Hong Kong Chinese are understudying them, while serving as interpreters, and will become the leading managers when the Americans leave. This seems to be a widespread practice among U.S. companies.

An engineer in a firm installing equipment in Latin America found it difficult to monitor the project with his elementary knowledge of Spanish. Maintenance on equipment abroad seems to be conducted mainly by local nationals.

Companies often dispatch troubleshooters to solve short-term technical problems. One interview partner pointed out that they travel to many different countries and thus cannot possibly speak all of the languages involved. They do deal with local nationals; however, the senior-level employees abroad supposedly speak English and act as interpreters.

In general, the companies that I visited considered it rare to find engineers and technical employees with foreign language knowledge in any country. One individual estimated that one in five engineers with whom he works in Latin America understands English, and some who know English are afraid to speak it. Another interview partner explained that U.S. technical employees have access to only a limited circle of people abroad, since few of their foreign counterparts know English. He estimated that in each of the subsidiaries only one engineer is proficient in English.

Research and development is an area that seems to have relatively unfilled foreign language needs. The individuals who mentioned this area to me had observed that few American researchers had foreign language skills. An article in the *New York Times* reported on a Japanese initiative to form research consortia aimed at developing new superconductors. The Japanese were openly recruiting foreign companies to cooperate in this effort; however, U.S. companies shied away from this project. One of the reasons cited was the lack of knowledge of Japanese on the part of U.S. researchers.[5]

WHERE ARE FOREIGN LANGUAGES NEEDED?

English is the business language of all of the companies that I visited. It is not surprising that most foreign language needs occur in U.S. companies' operations abroad, for it is there that they are dealing with foreign nationals both within and outside the firm.

Several interview partners expressed surprise at my suggestion that foreign languages might also be needed at their U.S. headquarters. This would not be to deal with foreign employees in the United States, for as managers assured me repeatedly, English is an absolute prerequisite for employment in their American offices. Indeed, companies seem poorly equipped to communicate in any language but English from headquarters.

One multilingual technical manager illustrated a case in point. When he first began communicating abroad

5. David E. Sanger, "Japanese Busy Seeking Superconductive Products," *New York Times,* 29 Jan. 1989.

in Spanish and German, he was told that the Hewlett-Packard computer used for electronic communication had no provision for foreign language symbols such as accents and the German umlaut. With a great deal of effort he discovered that the computer did have these capabilities. Evidently no one in the company had ever used these symbols, for no one knew how to produce them on the computer. My interview partner found it indicative that both Hewlett-Packard and IBM produce these foreign symbols through a combination of several keys, rather than through separate individual keys, which would be more user friendly. This suggests that the many U.S. business offices relying on Hewlett-Packard and IBM have little use for foreign languages in their written communications.

An engineer at a computer and telecommunications firm speaks with Latin American partners or affiliates weekly by telephone. Since his Spanish is elementary, a bilingual employee usually helps on the speaker phone. His greatest difficulties occur in communicating with Colombia, as his partners there do not have speaker phones.

Telephone conversations present problems in several companies that I visited. Not only is this type of communication among the most difficult since body language and facial gestures are missing, but calls sometimes come unexpectedly. This is so much of a problem for one large company that it has compiled a list of stand-by interpreters to assist with telephone calls in foreign languages. The interpreters are company employees—at headquarters—who happen to have foreign language skills.

An executive in a small company explained to me that he has to request a conversation partner who speaks English when he calls abroad. Often he has to wait five minutes or longer until someone can be located. If he has the name of an English speaker, he sometimes chooses to place a person-to-person call, in order to avoid initial difficulties.

A large accounting firm has Japanese and Korean practices in several of its offices in the United States. There are 100 bilingual English-Japanese staff located in 15 offices throughout the country; the number of Korean employees is, evidently, smaller. These practices service subsidiaries of Japanese and Korean companies located in the United States. There are also several English-German bilinguals dealing with subsidiaries of German companies in the United States. Thus, although foreign language needs may arise more frequently abroad, companies also require language skills in their U.S. offices.

WHAT TYPES OF FOREIGN LANGUAGE
SKILLS ARE NECESSARY?

All of my interview partners agreed that where foreign languages are called for, fluency is necessary for substantive business matters. One manager in a large company cautioned that aiming for anything less than fluency awakes false expectations in business transactions. This is not to say, however, that U.S.-based companies demand foreign language fluency of their employees. Someone has to be able to negotiate, maintain working relations, assure technology transfer, construct new plants, install and maintain equipment, and engage in other activities with foreign affiliates and partners. As businesspeople at headquarters usually cannot do this because of language problems, a solution for each situation is sought—through interpreters and translators, outside contractors, or foreign-national employees in subsidiaries abroad.

In general, basic survival skills in a foreign language were cited by most of my interview partners as their main goal and that of their colleagues, if they sought to learn another language at all. This is not to say that they could not have used fluency for their business. Rather, they merely did not expect to achieve a high level of proficiency and thus would seek assistance when this was necessary.

I asked representatives of each company what type of foreign language skills they deemed necessary for U.S. executives. Almost all agreed that in-depth knowledge was not essential. Many added that an executive deals with numerous parts of the world and cannot learn all of these languages proficiently. Most agreed that superficial knowledge of a number of languages is a more realistic goal for someone in senior management, in order that he or she can carry on a social conversation with peers abroad.

Upper-level businesspeople seem to consider oral skills more important than written ones. Perhaps this is because they intend to use the skills in a social context, which would mainly involve speech.

Those who are proficient in foreign languages use reading and writing skills as well as speaking and understanding. One bilingual manager pointed out, however, that he did not write in another language frequently because his monolingual American colleagues needed access to these documents as well.

One senior technical manager whom I interviewed at a large company suggested that technical employees do not need to write much in foreign languages, but they should be able to read newspapers and technical manuals. For these materials, an elementary reading ability would suffice. He indicated that a technical vocabulary is limited, even in English. Oral skills help those technicians who interact with foreign nationals.

HIRING AND
CAREER ADVANCEMENT

In general, foreign language skills do not seem to play an important role in either hiring or career advancement. Most companies concurred that, all things being equal, foreign language knowledge would give a candidate an edge; however, rarely would a company hire an individual primarily for these skills. Technical expertise was seen as more important. An executive at a medium-sized company provided an exception to this. If his firm opens an office in Europe, foreign language knowledge will be of primary importance for the director there. The U.S. executive

would even be willing to train an individual in the business end, if the latter brought the necessary language proficiency. This executive, however, remained an anomaly among my interview partners.

The larger companies that I visited rarely hire individuals from outside the company for assignments abroad. The Americans whom firms transfer abroad are usually selected from the ranks of their domestic operations. Since these U.S. employees were originally brought in for domestic operations, it is not surprising that foreign languages were not important in the hiring phase. I could find few companies that requested information on foreign language skills on their application forms. One large computer and telecommunications firm had included this information on its application form in the past but has now removed it.

My interview partners in large companies were confident that when foreign language skills were needed, they could be found in their company. An executive of a large accounting firm explained that they had a data base with information on 20,000 employees, including the status of their foreign language skills. This company does request a self-evaluation of foreign language skills at the time of hiring, though this information evidently is not updated subsequently. The executive explained that if personnel officers received a request to send someone abroad, they could usually find someone with the necessary language background. A disproportionate number of these are Mormons who have acquired foreign language skills through their earlier missionary work. Others are individuals who studied a language in high school and then take refresher courses before departing for abroad. Nonetheless, my interview partner admitted that this was not sufficient to fill the needs of the company.

One reason for this is that the firm mainly hires individuals directly from their undergraduate studies. The nature of their work requires them to have studied accounting, and undergraduate business programs usually do not have a foreign language requirement. If the company hired graduates of master's programs in business administration, it might have more employees with undergraduate liberal arts degrees including a foreign language component.

I could find no companies that directly included information on foreign language skills in performance reviews of their employees. One internationally experienced executive pointed out that companies look at whether the employee is getting the job done. If the employee fails to do so because of poor communication, he or she will receive a poor evaluation. Thus foreign language is not assessed as a separate skill, but if it is necessary for the job, it will make a difference in a performance review.

In general, my interview partners did not deem foreign language skills important in career advancement, but international experience in general was viewed as meaningful. Here, as in businesspersons' perceptions of what is key for senior management, foreign languages do not play into their considerations, while the more general category of international ex-perience does. Again, foreign language proficiency seems to be viewed as a skill separate from and less important than its cultural context.

U.S. EXPATRIATES

One bank executive with 15 years of service abroad for his company recounted to me how international staffing had changed over this period of time. When he first went overseas, almost all key functions in the company's branches were performed by Americans. U.S. expatriates typically remained in one country for longer periods of time, compared to current practice, and did not move from post to post, as is more common today. Since they lived in one country longer, most of them learned to speak the language. Further incentive for learning the language was provided by the fact that each branch abroad was managed almost as a separate entity. This executive explained that today expatriates are more mobile. As a result, they do not have as great a stimulus for learning the language of their host country as they did before.

Most U.S. expatriates assume upper-level managerial or technical positions abroad. Country-head positions, however, usually are occupied by host-country or third-country nationals in the firms that I visited. Several individuals explained that in newer regions of involvement, the top positions tend to be filled by Americans because host-country nationals there have not had time to rise through the company ranks yet. Representatives of a company that still employs a large number of Americans as country heads estimated that their firm gradually would begin replacing these expatriates with foreign nationals. This may be partly a financial consideration, since on the average it costs a company triple an employee's U.S. salary to assign him or her abroad. Americans are one of the few people to be taxed universally, and the company usually pays relocation costs and other perks abroad as well.

But one executive at a large company contended that few Americans were country heads because so many did not have the necessary foreign language skills. A personnel director of another large company explained that her firm had an international network of professionals who could transfer to most places in the world, but these usually were not Americans because of the foreign language component.[6]

THE ROLE OF
FOREIGN NATIONALS

As has been indicated, foreign nationals are playing an increasingly important role in the overseas opera-

6. For further comment, see Anders Edstrom and Jay R. Galbraith, "Transfer of Managers as a Coordination and Control Strategy in Multinational Organizations," *Administrative Science Quarterly*, 22:248-63 (June 1977); Stephen J. Kobrin, "Expatriate Reduction and Strategic Control in American Multinational Corporations," *Human Resource Management*, 27(1):63-75 (Spring 1988); idem, *International Expertise in American Business*, IIE Research Report no. 6 (New York: Institute of International Education, 1984); Rosalie L. Tung, *The New Expatriates: Managing Human Resources Abroad* (Cambridge, MA: Ballinger, 1988).

tion of U.S.-based companies. This is true of smaller companies as well as larger ones. Smaller firms often contract the services of local distributors or representatives to sell their products abroad. These host-country and third-country nationals are usually bilingual and compensate for the lack of foreign language skills in the U.S. firm.

Both smaller and larger companies employ foreign nationals at their U.S. headquarters. They do not seem to be employed in large numbers; however, more important is the fact that their cultural and linguistic background rarely is a primary reason for their having been hired. Although I have cited examples of companies using the language skills of this group, not all foreigners feel that their background is taken advantage of. A senior-level manager in a large company claimed that his foreign origin had not been important in his being hired. In fact, he finds that people in the company have difficulty relating to him. As a result, he downplays his international background rather than encouraging others to take advantage of it.

U.S.-based companies also hire foreign nationals as independent contractors to provide specific services abroad. An example was cited earlier of a company that hired a management group in France to provide for the construction of a new plant. The bank that I visited hires local management consulting firms with bilingual staff to assist it with negotiations in regions where it employs no local nationals. This is typically the case in new areas of involvement.

FUTURE TRENDS IN
FOREIGN LANGUAGE NEEDS

The U.S.-based companies that I studied indicated that they probably will be hiring an increasing number of foreign nationals for positions overseas. At the same time, most predicted that they would need more foreign language skills among all of their employees. Companies that are changing their identity and organizational forms to become more global envision a particular need for foreign languages, so that employees can serve on global business teams.

Certainly firms demonstrate a growing need for individuals with Japanese-language skills and business expertise. Other geographic areas where companies require an increasing combination of language and business skills are Latin America, China, and gradually, the USSR. It is of growing importance for technicians and researchers to know foreign languages, as these areas become less and less a domain of the domestic sphere in the United States. As U.S. companies become more global, the service industries filling their banking, accounting, and consulting needs will have to be more internationally oriented. Employees serving corporate clients will need more international exposure, as one interview partner observed. Foreign languages would seem to play a role here. Or will Americans simply speak more loudly, as one disillusioned manager suggested and a recent study indicated?[7]

An executive with many years of international experience with his bank reflected on the changes in overseas communication in the past twenty years. In the 1960s, communication via telex was expensive, and telephone calls were rare. Overseas branches sent their accounting information to U.S. headquarters at the end of the year—the Christmas surprise, as it was termed. This was ultimately changed to monthly reports sent by mail, and only in 1970 did the bank begin sending the reports by cable. Today, the bank has its own electronic mail system. The phone is used extensively, and people fly more. Therefore, the intensity and volume of communication is greater and more immediate. Businesspeople are more mobile, and in general there is a greater mixing of cultures.

This trend undoubtedly will increase in the future, but what does it mean for foreign language needs? Many of my interview partners concurred that this will render English more important as the lingua franca of business. At the same time, they admitted that different cultures must develop a better understanding of each other, which includes being familiar with other languages. One manager described this as a catch-22 situation. While the world is getting smaller and requires Americans to be more adaptable to other countries, other countries see a greater need to

7. Korn/Ferry International and Columbia University Graduate School of Business, *Rein-* *venting the CEO* (New York: Korn/Ferry International, 1989). In this survey of 1500 executives in 20 countries, foreign language skills were ranked lowest by Americans. In contrast, Japanese, Western European, and Latin American executives considered these skills significantly more important.

learn English as a common denominator in the business world.

Indicative of this observation is the reaction that many of my interview partners had to the planned unification of the European markets in 1992. Though many saw that both U.S. and European businesspeople would have to become more multicultural and multilingual, instead of bicultural and bilingual, most predicted that English would become even more necessary in Europe as a common denominator.

There was a clear tendency among my interview partners to view international experience as crucial for the leaders of U.S.-based companies. This seems to be a relatively new recognition, as the current senior management of many of the firms that I visited had no significant international experience. Managers in a variety of areas agreed that this must and would change in the future. Foreign language skills do not play a role here for many of these individuals; however, as U.S. businesspeople gain insight into what the new demand for international experience means, perhaps this will change. For the moment, too many would agree with one manager who found that his greatest difficulty in cross-cultural communication was understanding the various forms of English that his business partners spoke—Japanese English, Chinese English, Spanish English, and so on.

ANNALS, *AAPSS,* 511, September 1990

Foreign Language Use Among International Business Graduates

By RICHARD D. LAMBERT

ABSTRACT: American business is constantly being urged to employ more executives who can operate successfully abroad in one or another foreign language. Nonetheless, the employment prospects for Americans with foreign language competences remain relatively low. To both meet and stimulate that limited demand, several business schools have instituted programs that combine general business courses with foreign language training and international studies. This article reports on a survey of 600 graduates of three of the best-known international business programs of this type. The purpose of the survey was to determine the importance of a foreign language competence in the careers of these specially trained business school graduates.

Richard D. Lambert is the founder and director of the National Foreign Language Center at the Johns Hopkins University. He is professor of sociology emeritus at the University of Pennsylvania, where he taught for forty years. Before his retirement he taught at Pennsylvania's Lauder Institute of International Management. He has served as an editor of The Annals *of the American Academy of Political and Social Science for thirty years. His recent publications include* Beyond Growth: The Next Stage in Language and Area Studies; Points of Leverage; *and* International Studies and the Undergraduate.

THE greatest barrier to the expansion of foreign language competences in the United States is the low value placed on such competence by American society as a whole. For instance, a recent Gallup survey commissioned by the National Geographic Society[1] ranked foreign language at the bottom of a list of school subjects ranked in order of importance to adults. This low estimation of the value of foreign language skills in the society at large is evident even in sections of the society where expanding international contacts might have been expected to create a greater need for foreign language skills. As the articles in this volume indicate, however, the occupational demand for foreign language skills remains spotty at best. In particular, American business seems to be devoutly monolingual, in spite of overwhelming evidence that almost every American business concern is increasingly involved in international markets or international competition. Survey after survey,[2] including Carol Fixman's investigation commissioned by the National Foreign Language Center[3] and reported in this issue of The Annals, informs us that American companies, even those with numerous foreign transactions, place foreign language competence close to the bottom in their list of desiderata in hiring new employees. The feeling that chief executive officers sometimes express that business in general should do something to cosmopolitanize its executive corps and increase its foreign language competences does not seem to translate into individual corporate policy. In particular, the message does not seem to penetrate to the personnel officers, who believe that foreign language skill is an abundant commodity that can be bought if and when it is needed. Even then, the tendency is to employ native speakers rather than English-speaking Americans who have learned a foreign language in school.

The generally low evaluation of foreign language skills and the limited occupational demand for them are accompanied by a generally low level of competence among adults in our society. While we have no relevant survey data, one would suspect that, aside from ethnic or immigrant communities, only a very small proportion of American adults have genuinely usable competences in one or another foreign language. Certainly, relatively few of them leave the formal educational system with a high level of foreign language skill,[4] and much of the language competence Americans do acquire in school lies unused and largely forgotten by the

1. "Americans Get Low Grades in Gallup Geography Test" (Washington, DC: News Service of the National Geographic Society, 27 July 1988).

2. This literature is reviewed in Richard D. Lambert, Points of Leverage: An Agenda for a National Foundation for International Studies (New York: Social Science Research Council, 1986), pp. 31-38.

3. Carol S. Fixman, The Foreign Language Needs of U.S.-Based Corporations, National Foreign Language Center Occasional Paper Series (Washington, DC: National Foreign Language Center, 1989).

4. See Thomas S. Barrows et al., College Students' Knowledge and Beliefs: A Survey of Global Understanding (New Rochelle, NY: Change Magazine Press, 1981), p. 128; Richard D. Lambert, International Studies and the Undergraduate (Washington, DC: American Council on Education, 1989), pp. 65-69.

time they become adults. Relatively few Americans take foreign language training after they leave school or college, and when they do, except for some of the occupational uses discussed in this volume, the skill levels they attain are quite low.

It is this situation of low demand for, and low supply of, foreign language competences among American corporate executives that some of our business schools have attempted to combat. Many business schools have introduced courses or concentrations in international business.[5] A few of them provide their students with an unusual combination of a usable foreign language competence, a set of general business skills, and a familiarity with the special demands of international business. We are here concerned with three such programs: the program combining the master of business administration and master of arts at the Wharton School's Joseph H. Lauder Institute of Management and International Studies, the Monterey Institute of International Studies, and the University of South Carolina's master of international business studies. Each has a heavy foreign language component and provides instruction in a variety of languages. In reading the findings reported in this article, it should be remembered that the survey used to collect the data covered only foreign language use. There are many valuable aspects of international studies training other than language that are not discussed in this report.

5. See John Thanapoulos, ed., *International Business Curricula: A Global Survey* (Waco, TX: Academy of International Business, 1986).

Implicit in these and similar programs are two premises. The first argues that, in spite of the generalized evidence that there is a low corporate demand for foreign language skills, there is an important specialized job market for graduates who possess those skills. The second premise takes as given the current low corporate demand for foreign language skills but holds either that these programs will meet such demand as there is or that the best way to change that situation is to place the specially trained graduates of these programs in corporate executive suites. Sponsors of international business programs believe that, in the long run, their graduates will demonstrate the worth of special international and foreign language training and will begin to deparochialize the American corporate world. In short, the supply will create the demand.

SURVEY SAMPLES

To explore these premises, a questionnaire was mailed to all of the graduates of the three programs. Table 1 indicates the total number of graduates to whom questionnaires were mailed in each program and the number of questionnaires returned.

Contrary to my expectations, the graduates of the programs are very similar on all but a very few, relatively unimportant aspects of their postgraduation careers, so for this article I have combined them into a single sample. Nor does there seem to be much selectivity bias in the sample. Each of the three programs pro-

TABLE 1

QUESTIONNAIRES MAILED AND RETURNED, BY PROGRAM

Program	Number Mailed	Number Returned	Percentage Returned
Lauder	137	83	60.6
University of South Carolina	1,002	404	40.3
Monterey	373	133	35.7
Total	1,512	620	41.0

TABLE 2

ALL RESPONDENTS, FOREIGN STUDENTS, AND
AMERICANS NOT STUDYING A FOREIGN LANGUAGE

	Lauder	University of South Carolina	Monterey	Total
All respondents	83	404	133	620
Foreign students	17	79	18	114
Americans without foreign language	1	7	2	10
Americans with foreign language	65	318	113	496

vided me with data on all of their graduates that enabled me to compare those who returned their questionnaires with all graduates on a number of key variables—nationality, domestic versus overseas current address, year of graduation, and language studied. On each of these variables the samples were close approximations of the universes from which they were drawn.

Americans who studied a foreign language

Since my primary interest here is in what happens to Americans who have a foreign language competence, for the first steps in the analysis I have excluded two groups of respondents from the sample: students who are nationals of other countries and the few American students who were not required to take a foreign language while enrolled in the international business program.

Table 2 indicates the total number of graduates who returned questionnaires, the number of respondents who were foreign students, and the number of American nationals who reported English as the language they studied in the program. The last line indicates the primary sample on which most of the analysis will be based: American alumni who studied a foreign language in an internationally oriented business program.

IMPORTANCE OF LANGUAGE COMPETENCE IN THE JOB MARKET

First, how much competence in what languages did the American alumni take out of the program into

TABLE 3

LANGUAGE STUDIED AND SELF-RATED SPEAKING COMPETENCE

Language	Number of American Alumni with Specified Competence Level					
	Survival	Beyond survival	Use for communication	Near native	Equal to native	Total
Russian		2	2	2	1	7
French	2	10	57	53	7	129
Spanish	1	3	35	49	12	100
Portuguese		2	30	28	7	67
German		6	58	56	10	130
Arabic	3	3	4	1		11
Chinese	1	4	14	2	2	23
Japanese	1	3	9	7		20
No information					9	9
Total	8	33	209	198	48	496

the job market? Table 3 indicates the languages they studied while in the program and the degree of speaking proficiency they reported having at the end of their training.

The continued emphasis on Western European languages in our formal education system is also characteristic of the training of American international business majors; 86 percent of the American alumni in our sample had studied French, Spanish, German, or Portuguese. The relative popularity of the European languages studied by American international business students differs somewhat from the normal ranking of enrollments of students in general, however. Among college students, Spanish, French, and German normally have the highest enrollments, in that order, followed by Russian at a considerable distance and Portuguese a quantum step lower. The relatively strong showing of German and Portuguese among the international business majors reflects the economic importance of Germany and Brazil. The predominance of French over Spanish is a little more difficult to explain.

The non-Western European languages—Arabic, Chinese, Japanese, and Russian—are much less well represented. In view of the likely composition of our trading partners in the decades to come, the low percentage of international business graduates who studied a non-Western European language and the relatively low level of competence they had in it when they graduated are disturbing omens for the future. Particularly notable is the almost total lack of attention paid to Russian or any of the Eastern European languages. It seems that the catalytic role envisioned for these alumni does not yet include a major broadening of our nation's capacity to deal with many of the countries outside Western Europe and Latin America.

The level of competence in foreign languages claimed by these students is surprisingly high. While self-ratings in language skill always tend to be slightly inflated, the confidence these students expressed in their ability to speak the European languages is striking. About half of those who rated themselves in one or another of the European languages believed that their competence was near or equivalent to that of a native speaker. Listening and reading competences were reported to be even higher, while writing competence was, as usual, somewhat lower. Given this level of fluency, it is unlikely that the level of competence reported was gained entirely in language courses in the programs, tucked in, as they must be, at the edges of an overfull business curriculum. More than half of the students indicated that they were relatively fluent in the language before admission to the program. Indeed, the Lauder program demands a high level of language competence for admission.

Self-rated competence in the non-Western European languages is uniformly lower both at admission and at graduation. This reflects in part the greater difficulty in mastering what are referred to as truly foreign languages as well as the fact that many students are just beginning their training in those languages when they enter the program, whereas almost all the students have had prior college-level instruction in one or another of the Western European languages. The difference in competence levels is another aspect of the difficulty of shifting our national pool of foreign language competences to meet the demands of a changed economic and political international environment. To provide a cadre of American international business majors with a high level of competence in non-Western languages will require either the upgrading of instruction in these languages at the college level or lengthening the training period at the graduate level.

Subsequent language training

One sign of the low value that corporations put on foreign language competence is the relatively few companies that make arrangements for new or reinforcing language training. Only about a third (36.3 percent) of the corporations into which the alumni were hired provide for language training. When they do, it is largely through contracting with proprietary language schools (22.8 percent) or paying for private instruction in the United States (16.3 percent) or overseas (6.7 percent). Relatively few (9.1 percent) provide foreign language within the company itself. The multi-billion-dollar training industry that provides a wider variety of technical skills within the corporation devotes very little time to foreign language training.

Accordingly, only a minority of students—30.8 percent—had taken more language training after graduation, and most of that on-the-job language study was of relatively brief duration: 69.8 percent of it lasted less than six months, and only 16.4 percent was for a year or more.

It is not surprising, therefore, that, as Table 4 indicates, most alumni reported that their language skills declined after leaving their international business program, and only

TABLE 4
CHANGES IN FOREIGN LANGUAGE COMPETENCE

	Number of Alumni	Percentage
Decreased greatly	58	11.7
Decreased somewhat	201	40.5
Stayed the same	109	22.0
Increased somewhat	75	15.1
Increased greatly	47	9.5
No response	6	1.2
Total	496	100.0

about a quarter of them reported any growth in their foreign language competence.

FOREIGN LANGUAGE IN SECURING A JOB

How useful is foreign language competence in the job market? We asked the alumni how important they thought their language competence had been in securing their first job, and, for the subset who had changed jobs, how important foreign language competence had been in finding their current job. Table 5 indicates their responses to these two questions.

Whether these figures are gratifying or not depends upon whether one concentrates on the half-full or half-empty glass. It would be helpful if we could compare the experience of those alumni with other international business majors from the same institutions, but unfortunately no such surveys exist. Nonetheless, the data are interesting in their own right. For about a third of the workers, a foreign language competence was of no help in securing an entry job. Of the American alumni, how-

ever, 41 percent reported that it was an important or very important factor; within that group, 26 percent indicated that it was very important. As we will note later, these figures are surprisingly high given the low levels of utilization of those language skills on the job.

Does the importance of a foreign language competence increase as the alumnus changes jobs? The right-hand columns in Table 5 give the responses of alumni who had changed employers since graduation. The distribution of responses relating to the current job is roughly similar to that of the first job, with, if anything, a drift down the scale in importance. A foreign language competence was even less important in finding the second job.

Foreign language use on the job

Even if a foreign language competence was an asset for American alumni in finding a job, was it an important career asset once the worker was on the job? Table 6 presents the percentages of alumni who report varying degrees of relevance of their for-

TABLE 5

IMPORTANCE OF FOREIGN LANGUAGE IN SECURING FIRST AND CURRENT JOBS

Importance	First Job		Current Job*	
	Number	Percentage	Number	Percentage
Handicap	4	0.8	4	1.3
Irrelevant	148	31.4	114	37.3
Helped some	126	26.8	74	24.2
Important	70	14.9	56	18.3
Very important	123	26.1	58	19.0
Total	471	100.0	306	100.0

*Only those whose current job is different from the first job after graduation.

TABLE 6

RELEVANCE OF FOREIGN LANGUAGE COMPETENCE TO
PERSONNEL STATUS (Percentage of alumni)

	Percentage yes
Employer knows of competence	99.1
Competence entered in personnel file	83.3
Formal certification of competence	4.0
Extra pay for competence	8.0

	Degree of Relevance				
	Handicap	Irrelevant	Helps some	Important	Very important
Employer considers valuable	0.2	30.6	21.0	22.5	25.6
Employer rewards	1.1	45.6	22.6	17.7	13.0
Factor in promotion	0.4	53.5	25.3	12.6	8.1
Factor in assignment	0.4	31.0	25.5	24.0	19.1

eign language competence to their personnel status within the company.

These data give some indication of corporate awareness of their employees' foreign language competences, but rewards for the possession of those skills are problematic. In most cases, the company knows about the worker's competence and even enters it in the personnel file, although it is not sufficiently important to be formally certified by any kind of rating or testing procedure. Indeed, almost half of the alumni report that their employer finds such a competence valuable in a general way. Two-thirds of the alumni say that a foreign language competence is important to assignment in their company, although, as we will note later, this does not normally mean overseas assignment.

Translating this general awareness and positive evaluation of a foreign language competence into a tangible benefit in a company's reward structure is another thing, however. Almost half the alumni say that it is totally irrelevant to the reward system in general, more than half say it

TABLE 7
IMPORTANCE OF USE OF FOREIGN LANGUAGE IN VARIOUS BUSINESS ACTIVITIES

| Activity | Level of Importance (percentage of respondents) | | | | |
	Handicap	Irrelevant	Helps some	Important	Very important
Accounting	1.3	62.8	15.5	10.5	10.0
Negotiations	0.5	47.4	18.2	15.1	18.8
Financial planning	0.8	65.7	15.9	8.4	9.2
Labor management	0.7	59.0	10.1	15.8	14.4
Marketing	—	41.5	21.7	19.1	17.6
Sales	—	40.1	20.7	15.7	23.5
Social interaction	—	25.7	24.5	17.5	32.5
Meetings	0.3	46.2	17.3	14.3	22.0
Telephone	0.3	32.3	21.5	13.8	32.1

has no bearing on promotion, and only 8 percent say that a foreign language competence brings extra pay. Foreign language competence in the business world seems to be like good teaching in research universities: everyone is in favor of it, but detecting its influence on promotion, pay, or other dividends of the reward structure is difficult.

For a better look at the job relevance of foreign language competence, we asked the alumni to do two things. First, we asked them to rate the importance of their foreign language competence to various aspects of their job. Second, we asked them to indicate the frequency with which they were called upon to use that competence in various situations. Table 7 indicates the American alumni's responses.

In none of the activities do half or more of the alumni consider a knowledge of a foreign language important or very important. Most striking are the more than 50 percent who believe a foreign language competence is irrelevant in labor management and the 40 percent who so rate it for marketing and for participation in business meetings. Accounting and financial planning are believed to be the least affected by a foreign language competence, two areas that attract a substantial number of the graduates of international business programs.

Table 8 indicates the importance of a foreign language in another way: the frequency with which it is used by the respondent in a variety of settings.

Given the low value of foreign language instruction in the reward system, the relatively low importance attached to competence for many business activities, and the low frequency of use in commonly occurring situations, alumni must wonder whether the time and energy invested in studying a foreign language in the international business program were well spent.

Corporate foreign language environment

This picture of the limited use of the foreign language competences of

TABLE 8

FREQUENCY OF USE OF FOREIGN LANGUAGE (Percentage of respondents)

	Never	Occasionally	Frequently	All the Time
In the office	17.5	37.5	31.3	13.8
During travel	9.1	59.1	24.1	7.7
At home	9.5	52.3	27.7	10.5

the American international business majors can be understood by looking a little more closely at the corporate environment in which they operate. First of all, these alumni tend to work for U.S.-based companies: 90.7 percent of their employers have their headquarters in the United States. More generally, the international business majors are not likely to encounter a foreign language on the job. Two-thirds of the alumni report that virtually all communication in the corporation is in English; 91.0 percent say English is the language most frequently used at headquarters; and 90.0 percent say that almost all communications overseas are in English as well.

Most telling, however, is the fact that the American international business majors tend to be posted not abroad, where their foreign language skills might have greater immediate relevance, but in the United States. Table 9 indicates the current place of work of the American alumni.

It will be noted that only 11 percent of the American business majors were stationed abroad. About a quarter of all graduates of the three programs were posted abroad at the time of the survey, but most of them were foreign students returning to their homeland with an American business degree. Clearly, the American international business majors are currently not being used where their language competences would have greater value, in overseas positions. Nor is this situation likely to improve in the near future. There is currently a downward trend in the placement of all American executives overseas. One of the reasons for the lack of the utilization of American international business majors in overseas assignments is that corporations are sending fewer and fewer of their personnel abroad in any event.[6] There are a number of reasons for this trend, but one is very persuasive. The cost to an employer of sending an executive to Great Britain for the first year averages $300,000, and in other countries, such as Japan, and for more senior executives, the figure could easily approach $1 million. It is not surprising that the number of executives of American companies stationed abroad is steadily declining, and it is unlikely that this trend will be reversed in the near future.

Aside from the small proportion of American international business graduates who were posted abroad, the distribution of those graduates among the various countries is inter-

6. Joann S. Lublin, "Grappling with the Expatriate Issue," *Wall Street Journal*, 11 Dec. 1989.

TABLE 9
CURRENT ADDRESS OF ALUMNI

Continent	Number	Percentage
North America	442	89.1
United States	441	88.9
Canada	1	0.2
Latin America	10	2.0
Brazil	4	0.8
Colombia	1	0.2
Costa Rica	1	0.2
Ecuador	1	0.2
Mexico	1	0.2
Puerto Rico	2	0.4
Europe	27	5.4
Austria	1	0.2
Belgium	3	0.6
Denmark	1	0.2
France	5	1.0
Germany	11	2.2
Great Britain	4	0.8
Netherlands	1	0.2
Switzerland	1	0.2
Middle East	1	0.2
Saudi Arabia	1	0.2
South Asia	1	0.2
Pakistan	1	0.2
Southeast Asia	1	0.2
Philippines	1	0.2
East Asia	13	2.6
China	2	0.4
Taiwan	2	0.4
Hong Kong	3	0.6
Japan	6	1.2
Oceania, miscellaneous	1	0.2
New Zealand	1	0.2
Total	496	100.0

esting. First, it should be noted how wide the dispersal is: they are assigned to 23 different countries. But 50.0 percent are stationed in Europe and another 18.5 percent in Latin America. Other areas are only very lightly touched, and Africa and Eastern Europe not at all.

Overseas assignments and language utilization

The lack of overseas assignments has a particularly negative effect on foreign language utilization. The American international business graduates who were assigned abroad

TABLE 10

**IMPORTANCE AND USE OF FOREIGN LANGUAGE BY
ALUMNI IN THE UNITED STATES AND ABROAD** (Percentage of respondents)

	Assignment	
	U.S.	Abroad
Importance in finding first job		
Handicap	1.0	0.0
Irrelevant	34.0	9.8
Helps some	27.9	17.6
Important	15.2	11.8
Very important	21.9	60.8
How valuable an employer considers foreign language to be		
Handicap	0.2	0.0
Irrelevant	34.0	3.8
Helps some	22.7	7.5
Important	21.8	28.3
Very important	21.3	60.4
Relevance of foreign language to reward system		
Handicap	1.2	0.0
Irrelevant	49.4	14.0
Helps some	22.9	20.0
Important	16.2	30.0
Very important	10.3	36.0
Factor in promotions		
Handicap	0.5	0.0
Irrelevant	56.6	28.0
Helps some	25.4	24.0
Important	11.8	20.0
Very important	5.8	28.0
Does foreign language competence attract extra pay?		
Yes	7.2	14.3
Change in competence level		
Decreased greatly	12.4	7.5
Decreased somewhat	43.5	20.8
Stayed same	24.0	7.5
Increased somewhat	14.0	26.4
Increased greatly	6.2	37.7

NOTE: All of the differences shown in the table are statistically significant at the $p < .01$ level.

gave a higher value to foreign language competence and reported using it more than those resident in the United States. Table 10 compares domestically posted alumni and those posted overseas with respect to the importance and degree of use of a foreign language in various job-related aspects.

In examining these comparisons, several things are clear. First, it should be noted that the contrast is by no means discrete. There were alumni who remained in the United

States but still gave a high importance to and reported great use of foreign language skills, and there were alumni working abroad who did not. Second, even allowing for this overlap, however, it is clear that foreign assignment greatly increases the value and the use of foreign language skills. While there was still a sharp differential between statements of the general importance of foreign language skills and receiving payoffs for them in the official reward system, in every category those stationed abroad reported a higher value for and use of foreign language skills. Those on foreign assignment also had a better chance of retaining or increasing the language skill they left graduate school with.

CONCLUSION

The implications of these data are clear. Even when a deliberate effort is made on the part of individuals and universities to train specialists with combined business, international studies, and foreign language skills, the utilization of the foreign languages in the corporate workplace is limited. To a considerable extent, this situation is a function of the English-language-bound culture of the corporations that hire them and of the limited and declining practice of post-ing Americans abroad, where foreign language skills are more likely to be used.

This situation does not seem likely to change in the near future. Even when far-seeing corporate leaders express regret about the lack of cosmopolitanism in American business in general, individual corporations, even those from which the chief executive officer who voices such regrets comes, tend to preserve the old corporate culture. That culture is not likely to create the kind of environment that will effectively use the special skills, particularly foreign language skills, that international business majors bring to the job market.

It may be that in the long run the demands of the international environment and the availability of executive trainees with first-rate education in all three of the skill areas —foreign language, business, and international studies—will create an increased demand for and utilization of foreign language skills. To do so, they must alter the corporate culture in a way that both encourages overseas posting of executives and adapts company practice to a more multilingual operating style. In the short run, these data suggest that the current English-oriented, domestic-assignment tradition of American corporations is winning out.

ANNALS, *AAPSS*, 511, September 1990

The Foreign Language Needs of U.K.-Based Corporations

By NIGEL B. R. REEVES

ABSTRACT: With Europe as its principal export market today, the United Kingdom is beginning to understand the importance of foreign languages for success. The advent of the single European market will massively reinforce the integration of the United Kingdom as a trading nation into the European Community, while there is a clearly defined trend toward the creation of transnational companies alongside multinationals and U.K.-based exporters. Europe will remain a culturally and linguistically diverse market in both consumer taste and management style, requiring linguistic and intercultural skills for successful marketing and for internal company communication in the new transnationals. Summarizing the functions of foreign language competency in exporting and in multi- and transnational corporations, the article concludes with a look at Europe's broader future developments. The opening up of Eastern Europe, which will be dominated economically by Germany, will see the emergence of German as the European lingua franca alongside English but will not remove the need in the United Kingdom for French, Spanish, or the principal languages of the Middle and Far East, Arabic and Japanese, for global trading.

Nigel B. R. Reeves obtained his B.A. in German and French at Oxford in 1963, receiving a doctorate from the same university in 1970. He has lectured at the Universities of Lund, Sweden, and Reading, becoming full professor of German at the University of Surrey in 1975. He is now professor of German and head of modern languages at Aston University. He has published widely on language education for overseas trade, was made an officer of the Order of the British Empire for services to export education in 1987, and received the Goethe Medaille of the Goethe Institute, West Germany, in 1989.

I T seems to be a general rule that those who argue most vehemently that there is little need to learn foreign languages are almost without exception the ones who have not done so themselves and who remain unaware of the advantages."[1]

CHANGING PERCEPTIONS FROM THE 1970s TO THE LATE 1980s

The educational needs of industry largely depend on commercial perceptions and judgments. Perceptions, in their turn, are colored by historical experience. This observation is clearly illustrated by the attitude of business in Britain toward foreign language competency. Until the 1950s and even early 1960s the United Kingdom's principal trading partners were English speaking. They were the former dominions and colonies of the once mighty British Empire together with the United States. Particularly in the former British possessions, even twenty years ago modern methods of marketing and selling did not seem to be required; they were still captive markets and English was the language of trade.

The gradual end of the Empire in the postwar years, the phenomenal growth of Western Europe, especially among the original six members of the European Economic Community, and the eventual entry of the United Kingdom into that Community in 1973 led, however, to a substantial and rapid change in U.K. trading patterns. By 1978 more than half of U.K. exports were sold in European countries, and only a quarter in English-speaking markets. At the same time, Britain's share of world exports of manufactured goods had slipped from nearly 25 percent in 1950 to less than 10 percent in the late 1970s. It is evident that British industry had failed to make the necessary adjustments to its new trading circumstances. This failure was to be starkly revealed in 1983, when, for the first time since the Industrial Revolution of the late eighteenth century, the British trading balance in manufactured goods went into deficit.

In the late 1970s there was still only modest recognition in British industry of the connection between successful marketing and selling in foreign language countries and knowledge among the exporting team of those languages. In a report entitled *Foreign Languages for Overseas Trade*,[2] produced by a study group of the British Overseas Trade Board chaired by the Duke of Kent and of which I was a member, a significant discrepancy was observed between the views toward foreign language competency of British exporting industry and of the commercial counselors of British embassies, whose task was to explore business opportunities for U.K. companies. The counselors, even in countries like West Germany, where English was widely spoken by industrial execu-

1. Stephen Hagen, *Language in British Business: An Analysis of Current Needs* (Newcastle upon Tyne: Newcastle upon Tyne Products in association with the Centre for Information on Language Teaching and Research, 1988), p. xxx.

2. British Overseas Trade Board, Study Group on Foreign Languages, *Foreign Languages for Overseas Trade* (London: British Overseas Trade Board, 1979).

tives, believed that vital chances were being missed through a lack of expertise in the foreign language, extending even to the apparent inability of U.K. companies to offer product brochures and correspondence in German.

A survey of some 200 companies commissioned in the same year, 1978, by the Royal Society of Arts, London, confirmed the low standing of languages in companies' recruitment policies and the professional qualifications of executives. But it also showed a positive correlation between companies that had won the Queen's Award for Export and their employment of people with foreign language skills.[3] In short, successful exporting companies were beginning to change from the traditional British trading stance of providing customers with what the company thought best to listening to what customers wanted and expected. They realized that if one wants to listen, one needs to listen in the customers' own language.

In the most extensive series of language-need surveys yet carried out, Stephen Hagen and a group of university and polytechnic professors across the United Kingdom have recently revealed a continuing trend toward a new perception of foreign language needs.[4] The surveys targeted most of the mainland British regions, received positive responses from a total of some 1150 firms, and

3. *Languages and Export Performance: A Study Prepared for the BETRO Trust Committee of the Royal Society of Arts by the P. E. Consulting Group* (London: Royal Society of Arts, 1979).

4. Hagen, *Language in British Business.*

were carried out between 1984 and 1987, the majority being completed in 1986. In northern England, where matching samples for 1977 and 1984 were available, a 10.5 percent increase in foreign language use was recorded. Of all firms, 75 percent surveyed stated that they had used one or more foreign languages in recent years, but, most telling of all, an average of 44 percent of companies across Britain admitted that they could have significantly improved their trade performance had they had access to appropriate foreign language competencies and facilities. This is a remarkable turnaround in perception, especially when we note that the majority of those companies reporting deficiencies in foreign language capacity either produced largely for the U.K. domestic market or exported principally to English-speaking markets.

THE ADVENT OF THE SINGLE EUROPEAN MARKET

These surveys referred, however, to past performance and were conducted prior to any widespread awareness in the United Kingdom of the advent by the end of 1992 of the single European market. Today the United Kingdom finds itself in an economic and political situation without historical precedent. Within two years it will be part of a unified, highly industrialized capitalist market of some 320 million consumers, the vast majority of whom—some 260 million—do not speak English as their mother tongue. In addition, the historical development of most of the consumers in that market has been divergent from Britain's—except in wartime—since England lost its last continental possessions in the Hundred Years War and turned its aspirations and ambitions toward overseas territories and deep-sea trading destinations.

The concept of the single European market rests on three principles: the free movement of goods and services, the free movement of capital, and the free movement of people. Some 279 measures have been introduced by the European Commission in order to remove the still-existing barriers, and the vast majority have now been satisfied by the European Parliament and the Councils of Ministers. Most popular attention has focused on the movement of goods and the concomitant removal of customs barriers, but it is the free cross-border sale of services that is the most radical element in this first principle. Banking, insurance, financial services, and transport will be most fundamentally affected, all areas in which the United Kingdom stands to gain substantially, as I and my coauthor David Liston have argued in a recent comprehensive study of Britain's international service industries.[5] But such opportunities could still belong to a simple free trade zone. The creation of such a zone is not the intention behind the single European market, as the European

Commission's white book of 1985, largely written by Britain's commissioner to the European Community (EC), Lord Cockfield, makes clear.[6] The intention is ultimately a form of political union, driven by economic integration.

Economic integration is to be achieved by the free movement of capital and of people. Mobility of capital is changing the nature of business in Europe. In the first half of 1989, for example, some 600 European mergers and acquisitions took place, worth 15.4 billion European currency units (ECUs).[7] By the end of the third quarter transactions worth a further 18.0 billion ECUs had been concluded. In the first half of the year France was the top acquiring nation, with the United States in second place and the United Kingdom a close third. In the third quarter, the United States surged to first place with acquisitions of 6.5 billion ECUs.[8] The major target countries were the United Kingdom, France, and Italy, followed by West Germany and Spain. Add to this the third principle, the right of EC citizens to work anywhere within the Community and of EC professionals to practice freely in any member state by virtue of the mutual recognition of qualifications soon to be enshrined in an EC directive, and we have the makings of a truly unified European economy with or without the early adoption of a single currency or a single European central bank.

5. David Liston and Nigel Reeves, *The Invisible Economy: A Profile of Britain's Invisible Exports* (London: Institute of Export; Pitman, 1988).

6. European Communities, Commission, *Completing the Internal Market*, Com. (85) 310 final, 1985.

7. *European Deal Review*, 22 Nov. 1989, no. 1.

8. Nikki Tait, "Mergers and Acquisitions: France and the US Set the Pace," *Financial Times*, 19 Dec. 1989.

The most authoritative analysis of the consequences of these measures, the Cecchini report,[9] predicts three outcomes: growth, integration, and concentration. Growth could be on the order of 7 percent of the gross domestic product in the medium term, with savings through the elimination of trade inefficiencies of some £130 billion per annum. Integration will continue through the process of merger and acquisition, and concentration will result from the same process. Indeed, it is foreseen that concentration will be so drastic that eventually the number of companies in the EC will reduce by 50 percent from today's numbers.

Until the recent past we could broadly distinguish between four types of company operating in and for Europe. One comprised small local and regional firms absorbed with their own immediate domestic markets. They could range from retail outlets, through a variety of service and maintenance activities, to distribution networks, to small-scale manufacturing and engineering plants. Beyond these were the small to medium-sized companies serving national markets and, in the manufacturing sector, usually with a proportion of exporting activity. This second category appears to be the one identified by Hagen as that most urgently revising its view of the need for foreign language competency, and the category that stands to gain and lose the most through liberalization of European trade.

9. Paolo Cecchini with Michel Catinat and Alexis Jacquemin, *1992, the European Challenge: The Benefits of a Single Market* (Aldershot: Gower, 1988), esp. pp. 91-102.

The third category was typically composed of manufacturers or service industries, such as banks, whose principal plant or headquarters remains firmly in the home state but that possess a sophisticated distribution and marketing network throughout the Community. Examples are a number of the major European car manufacturers, including Rover and Jaguar, and the British clearing banks. The fourth category is the multinational company that has a multicentered manufacturing strategy, usually to serve national and regional markets, and that is often in single European national or U.S. ownership. To this four-layered structure we must now add the transnational European company, the consequence of the surge in mergers and acquisitions. This type of company is usually in international ownership with a trans-European board. Its plants and outlets are distinguished less by their serving national European markets than by dedication to a particular product in the total range.

This is, of course, a simplification, and many companies are hybrids of these categories. Nevertheless, the scheme serves to highlight a new management issue that is emerging with the single European market: how to manage a multi- or, better, a transcultural concern that is now not only selling across borders but owned and directed across borders.

Whereas the surveys to which I referred in the first section of this article were all concerned literally with foreign languages for overseas trade, the new challenge, which is only now being recognized, is the mastery of foreign languages for selling in the multilinguistic domestic market that the European market constitutes and for controlling companies that have to be both directed and managed across cultural and linguistic boundaries.

We have to ask whether, in the face of such a challenge, the line of least resistance will and should be taken, namely, to use English as the common international language. Indeed, will the integration of a continent whose mother tongues are predominantly other than English ironically result in the hegemony of English?

EUROPEAN CULTURAL DIVERSITY AND INTERCULTURALITY

The constitutions of democratic countries, including the most recent, all reveal their eighteenth-century origins in the American and French revolutions and the thought of the Enlightenment. Today we need to add to the bills of rights a further human right that could hardly have been foreseen before the Industrial Revolution, the right to be a consumer, to consume in such a way that quality of life is ensured, to know precisely what one is consuming, and to have a say in the products one is offered. Market research and consumer and environmental lobbies are the industrial response, on one hand, and the popular response, on the other, to this manifestation of humanity in the affluent society. Indeed, it could be argued that it is recognition of this right to be a consumer as a basic element in humanity that has been the twin engine of the 1989 revolution in Eastern Eu-

rope, alongside the historically more familiar call for freedom of expression and for political emancipation.

This call for consumer self-determination helps to explain one of the major causes of stagnation in the progress toward a truly common EC market in the 1970s and 1980s. The official EC policy of harmonization of standards and specifications came up against enormous national resistance. Some of the causes célèbres verged on the tragicomic. The British fought to preserve their concept of the sausage, which contained so little meat and so much fat and bread that Britain's European partners could not consider it to be a sausage at all. The Italians struggled to preserve their definition of pasta, which could only be made with a special variety of flour. The Germans battled still more bitterly to conserve their monopoly on pure beer, which for centuries in Germany could be brewed only from barley malt, hops, water, and yeast.

These conflicts have now been resolved by confirmation of the freedom to trade in goods that have satisfied standards recognized in any one of the individual member states. This principle of mutual recognition is evidence of the fundamental importance still adhering to cultural tradition and cultural diversity in Europe. For arguably what we have in Europe is not a common market at all but a diverse market operating within broad, legally determined margins. In a world where the consumer is increasingly powerful, no wise company will choose to ignore that diversity.

Indeed, it is a matter of contention whether there can be more than a limited deployment of global marketing concepts in Europe and beyond. ICI (Imperial Chemical Industries), for example, had a very successful advertisement for fibers for stockings and which featured a picture of women's legs. In France it won an award. In the United States it had to be withdrawn.[10] Showing how regional tastes may be, we can even quote the example of a British brewer based in Yorkshire that sells its beer in the south of England through a series of advertisements based on the drinking habits of an archetypal tweed-capped Yorkshireman. In its own area it does not show those advertisements.

The tactic of making an international product seem indigenous and local can also be highly successful. Humor is an important ingredient in U.K. advertising. The advertising consultant Tim Delaney recommended that Sanyo use John Cleese, the celebrated comic actor and writer, for their campaign and "over several years it turned a remote technologically-oriented Japanese hi-fi company into a firm that seemed almost British, building a warm relationship with the public."[11] Still more telling was the campaign of the Dutch multinational company Philips, which employed two other renowned television parodists, Mel Smith and Griff Rhys-Jones. "The great success of the campaign, like so much British television comedy, was that it was totally in tune with the British audience." But, it is noted significantly, "much of the best British advertising doesn't translate."[12]

This is precisely the point. Much successful advertising is culture specific. That is why it appeals, but by the same token it cannot be transferred across cultural boundaries. Indeed, among the few successful non-nationally conceived advertising campaigns in Europe have been those selling products that seem equally exotic yet equally familiar to all Europeans: U.S. products such as Levi jeans, Coca-Cola, and Marlboro cigarettes. The limit to the range of such universally marketable products is illustrated by the great commercial difficulties being encountered by the European satellite television stations, which depend for their income on pan-European advertising.

The clash of management styles in transnational European companies reflects the same phenomenon of cultural diversity. One may contrast the old confrontation model adopted in Britain, now being modified into the leadership model, with the consensus model of the Federal Republic of Germany, characterized by a mixture of hierarchical distance and legally established codetermination of company policy between management and the employed. Managerial authority expresses itself differently in almost every one of the member states, ranging from the community-based approach of Danish companies to the strict hierarchy that character-

10. "The 1989 UK Marketing Award," *Financial Times*, 2 Nov. 1989.

11. Torin Douglas, "Make 'em laugh," *Business Life*, 22:84-87 (Aug.-Sept. 1989).

12. Ibid.

izes many large Italian firms. But the boards and the top management of the new transnational European companies have to operate as cross-cultural teams yet at the same time must evolve corporate cultures that neither submerge national differences nor themselves disappear beneath the shifting sands of cultural diversity.

This challenge has led to the search for the Euro-executive, the manager who, in a neat definition by the personnel consultancy company Saxton Bampfylde, "is able to operate with equal confidence anywhere in Europe." Their study published in 1989[13] shows that there are too few such people and that when they are found they mostly come from the Netherlands, Belgium, or Scandinavia. In our present context, this observation is of importance for it suggests that successful Euro-executives are people who, as the result of possessing as their mother tongue a minority language such as Danish, Swedish, or Flemish/Dutch and/or through growing up in a multicultural and multilinguistic society, have easily developed linguistic competence in several languages and have evolved a natural sensitivity toward cultural distinctions and others' values and perceptions. For the manager of the transnational company no less than for the traditional export executive, then, linguistic proficiency forms the basis for that other essential quality, interculturality.

In her recent investigation of the foreign language needs of U.S.-based corporations for the National Foreign

Language Center at Johns Hopkins University, Carol Fixman showed that in the perception of many U.S. companies cultural awareness is not only separable from foreign language competency but actually of more importance.[14] But while it may be regarded as essential for overseas executives involved in international and transnational business to gain insights into the different customs and values of the societies and business cultures with which they deal, it is difficult to see how they could penetrate the mind-sets of their business partners—or opponents—without even being able to read a local newspaper let alone a trade journal or engage in an off-the-record conversation with customers, distributors, agents, or workers on the shop floor.

This returns us to the question of English as the language of international trade and as the house language of multi- and transnational corporations.

LANGUAGE AND CULTURE IN
THE MULTI- AND TRANSNATIONAL
CORPORATION

In a small interview-based survey of 23 companies using college foreign language training facilities that I carried out in 1984-85,[15] I ascertained eight main categories of motivation for language learning. The

14. Carol S. Fixman, *The Foreign Language Needs of US-Based Corporations,* National Foreign Language Center Occasional Papers Series (Washington, DC: National Foreign Language Center, 1989), pp. 2, 8.

15. See David Liston and Nigel Reeves, *Business Studies, Languages and Overseas Trade: A Study of Education and Training* (London: Pitman; Institute of Export, 1985, 1986), pp. 118 ff.

13. *The Search for the Euro-Executive* (London: Saxton Bampfylde International, 1989).

companies ranged in size from one self-employed person to one of the world's largest companies, British Petroleum, the latter representing several independent subsidiary companies with widely differing products. Thirteen of the companies were manufacturers, with products ranging from automobiles and automobile components to costume jewelry and chocolate confectionery. One was a manufacturers' agent, one a management consultant, a third an engineering consultant. Two major British banks were also represented.

The eight motives were

— for staff at the headquarters and office to translate and/or check company literature, to handle and translate correspondence, to send telexes—now faxes, of course—and to deal with telephone calls;
— for sales and marketing forces to obtain current market intelligence; to make direct contact with customers, thereby circumventing agents; to revive an ailing market; to open up new markets previously inaccessible because of the language barriers; to sell through trade fairs; to improve and deepen existing business relationships;
— to establish more satisfactory purchasing arrangements;
— to carry out more effective negotiations, even where English was the official medium, ensuring that clear and accurate company policy statements are made and allowing insight to be gained into the other party's approach through, among other

things, understanding their exchanges between themselves;
— to improve customer service through better knowledge of customers' needs and through the training of indigenous or foreign-language-proficient British service engineers;
— to communicate with a parent or subsidiary company;
— to oversee and conclude the licensing of an overseas merger; and
— to control the on-site construction of a plant.

Of these it is particularly the office function, negotiations, and communications with other branches of the company that become highlighted in the new breeds of multi- and transnational European companies, though marketing and market research remain of vital importance. In a recent article, Michael Pearson, an executive with a multinational company based in the United Kingdom, has stressed the following functions for foreign language proficiency, reflecting the evolution of needs as we move from the exporting company to the multicentered company with manufacturing activities across Europe and overseas.

He stresses the importance of languages

— for marketing and selling;
— for company communication, despite the official use of English as the company language and in particular for product development; computer projects; planning and budgeting, including that which occurs at

board meetings; and participating in senior appointments;

— for communication with associated companies, knowledge of the company being especially important;

— for transactions with new acquisitions; and

— for legal agreements such as licensing.

Pearson concludes succinctly, "It is just not possible to run any worldwide organisation effectively from a monolingual headquarters."[16]

These observations are borne out by the testimony of a number of other multi- and transnational companies. Lord Rayner, chairman of Marks and Spencer, the clothes and food retailer, recently spoke of the delicate process of preserving the corporate philosophy while adapting to the differing tastes and expectations of customers across Europe, to be achieved by a two-way familiarization process by British, French, and German executives with their varying "social, cultural and business climates."[17]

Peter Blackburn, head of the European Division of Rowntree-Mackintosh, the chocolate manufacturer, stressed in a paper presented prior to the company's takeover by the Swiss giant, Nestlé, the importance of languages for personnel management and control: "In a situation where you are dealing with foreign daughter companies, you need to know what is going on to maintain control, to assess and develop people,

to manage the business and deal with people at all levels."[18] A few months later, after the takeover, another leading executive in the company confided to me that knowledge of French was now essential in order to participate effectively in meetings at the Swiss headquarters despite formal use of English.

The inadequacy of English for all levels of communication that are necessary in an efficient transnational corporation, even where English is the company language as in the previous examples, has also been stressed by Mike Smith, former joint managing director of the SEMA Group, the pan-European computing services company: "A commitment to language learning is essential; even though the official language of the group is English, on important matters people have to communicate in their native language."

The mirror image of this view is found in the Peugeot-Talbot company based in Coventry and in full French ownership. Here it is regarded as essential that the maximum number of employees learn French in order to communicate successfully with their counterparts in France. But the language-learning program is not directed toward a set group of mechanical language forms; it is an instrument for introducing the learners to French culture, way of life, and management style.[19]

For the multinational British-based pharmaceutical corporation

16. Michael Pearson, "Languages in a Multi-National Company," *Linguist*, 28(5):146-47 (1989).

17. Lord Rayner, "Strategies for the 1990s," *Debates: The Journal of the European Business School, London,* 1989, vol. 4.

18. Peter Blackburn, "Languages in a Multinational Business," in *Language in British Business,* ed. Hagen, p. 151.

19. Marion Smart, "Language Training at Peugeot Talbot," in *Language in British Business,* ed. Hagen, pp. 178-85.

Beecham, language learning is especially important for the development of appropriate products, adapted to the special needs of individual markets:

The need to develop and extend so-called core brands internationally means that commercial executives, in particular, must be familiar with all the facts which impinge on the likelihood of the successful launch of a given product in a given country. These factors include culture and attitudes, taste, both physical and conceptual—activities and products of competitors, positioning, pricing, patterns of usage and distribution, business methods in general.[20]

These examples underline the fact that in the single European market, in all its cultural and linguistic diversity, English alone will not suffice if a European company, whether U.K.-based or not, is to be efficient with rapid internal communication and effective, sensitive personnel management. We shall see English confirmed as the house language of many transnational companies and as a common language between many speakers of English as a second language. But English will be supplemented as a management tool with other major European languages, and recent events suggest that English will not be without its rival as the lingua franca of Europe.

THE REVOLUTIONS OF 1989 AND
THE RETURN TO AN UNDIVIDED
EUROPE: THEIR SIGNIFICANCE FOR
THE LANGUAGES OF TRADING

The Revolution of 1989, in success or even in failure, will shape the character of the

20. John A. S. Watson, "How and Why Beecham Products Want to Recruit Linguists," in *Higher Education for International Careers*

twenty-first century; in historic terms it marks the beginning of the new century and the end of the old one. . . .

What will this new age be? Certain themes are apparent already. There will be a lot of Goethe in it. It will be a German age, perhaps to the degree that the age of Louis XIV was French, that the age of Queen Victoria was British and that the twentieth century has been American. The reason will be the same. The nation which has the strongest economy in the world has a cultural influence disproportionate to its economic lead.[21]

Even as we West Europeans were focusing our attention on the single European market as the new Europe, events in Eastern Europe changed the face of the continent; indeed, restored Europe to being a complete continent of independent states without imperial domination such as was only briefly witnessed in the few years between the Treaty of Versailles and the emergence of the Third Reich.

Observers on both sides of the Atlantic have raised the central issue of the reunification of Germany with varying degrees of apprehension and calm. With events moving so rapidly, it would be bold to argue when or how German reunification will occur; but political crystal-ball gazing diverts us from the reality that the Federal Republic will very soon be the dominant economic force not only in East Germany but in Poland and Czechoslovakia also. In 1988 the Federal

(Birmingham: Aston University Modern Languages Club; Centre for Information on Language Teaching and Research, 1988), p. 59.

21. William Rees-Mogg, "Year of Change That Heralds a German Age," *Independent*, 4 Dec. 1989. Rees-Mogg is the former editor of the London *Times*.

Republic already exported nearly three times as much in value to the Eastern bloc—$11,181 million—as the next greatest exporters, Japan, at $3905 million, and the United States, at $3637 million. Britain, with $2128 million, was behind Austria, which, with a population of only 7 million, was exporting $2644 million.[22] Shortly before his assassination, Alfred Herrhausen, president of the mighty Deutsche Bank, declared his bank's interest in making credits to Eastern Europe and financing joint ventures provided they made commercial sense.[23] Volkswagen has already started to set up a factory at Chemnitz (Karl-Marx-Stadt) to produce Golf engines for Wartburg cars. Plans are being laid to extend high-speed road and rail links on an east-west line to supplement the postwar north-south network. Deutsche Mobilfunk hopes to extend its system of digital mobile telephones to East Germany. Talks between East and West German economic ministers have already focused on cooperation in a number of high-technology areas, including medical and environmental technology. Czechoslovakia's Prime Minister Marian Calfa has stated that German and Austrian firms seemed "to be best placed to understand the needs and problems of Czech industry and [to be] ready to meet them halfway."[24] Lech Walesa, speaking in London, almost complained that U.K. companies had

shown so little interest in investing in Poland compared with German companies.

What we are witnessing, in short, is a return to the old cultural and economic linkages of the pre-1930s era, with the restoration of Germany, with its ports like Bremen and especially Hamburg on the Elbe, to its natural hinterland and likewise of Austria to its sphere of influence in Hungary, Czechoslovakia, Yugoslavia, and probably Bulgaria and Romania.

One of the reasons given by opponents to foreign language learning in corporations is that we do not know in which of many languages to invest, whereas our foreign competitors can safely concentrate on English. Repeated surveys in the United Kingdom through the 1970s and 1980s, however, bear out the result of Hagen's surveys, that French and German dominate, with German in rather more demand in the north of Britain and French in the south, followed at some distance by Spanish, Arabic, Japanese, Russian, and Chinese.[25]

In this article I have concentrated on the European dimension in the United Kingdom's trade as its current largest component and prospectively as still more significant. This should not be seen to exclude the vital importance of language teaching and learning in Britain of oriental languages such as Arabic, Japanese, and Chinese or even Korean and Thai or of some African languages. The reasons are strategic and diplomatic as well as commercial and scientific, as

22. United Nations commodity trade data quoted in *Financial Times*, 8 Dec. 1989.

23. David Lascelles, "Slow to Strike But Sure of Aim," *Financial Times*, 28 Nov. 1989.

24. Interview by A. H. Hermann, *Financial Times*, 15 Dec. 1989.

25. Hagen, ed., *Language in British Business*, p. xxii.

demonstrated in a major report on the status of these and many other non-European languages presented by Sir Peter Parker to the University Grants Committee in 1986.[26] This report, "Speaking for the Future,"[27] showed a perilous lack of provision in the United Kingdom both in the major commercial languages of the East and in less commonly used but strategically important languages like Turkish, Farsi, and Tamil. As a consequence new posts, particularly in Japanese and Arabic, were created in U.K. universities. The supply, for example, of Japanese graduates with accompanying training in economics was found to be far too small for the potential demand of the City of London, let alone of manufacturing companies.

Nevertheless, in the coming decades the United Kingdom is bound to find itself even more integrated into a European economy spanning Eastern and Western Europe, in which the engine of growth is based in German-speaking countries. In 1986 the Federal Republic already possessed 33.6 percent of total EC manufacturing output and was 78 percent greater in production than France, 100 percent more than Italy, and 140 percent more than the United Kingdom.[28] Germany's strength lies above all in machine

26. The present author was a member of the University Grants Committee's investigatory team.

27. "Speaking for the Future: A Review of the Requirements of Diplomacy and Commerce for Asian and African Language and Area Studies" submitted by Peter Parker (Report, University Grants Committee, Feb. 1986).

28. Quoted by Martin Wolf, *Financial Times*, 30 Nov. 1989.

tools, electronically steered manufacturing systems, and vehicles. These are precisely the type of goods that the Eastern countries will need to restore their decayed infrastructures.

It is difficult to imagine under these circumstances how German as the language of engineering—and, indeed, of the concomitant management and craft training schemes that will be required—can fail to be restored to its prewar status—or strengthened in its de facto postwar status—as the lingua franca of Eastern Europe. We are, then, very likely to see German emerge as a second international language of industry, assuming immense importance in Europe, though not ousting English as the supreme international language. But even with that said, we may not forget that we can expect by early next century a closely linked European market of some 450,000 million inhabitants, excluding Russia. This, barring political catastrophe, will grow to be the driving force of the world economy, competing vigorously with the more scattered economies of the Pacific Rim and the mature economy of the United States.

The United Kingdom's role could well be determined by its advantageous possession of the English language, making it as at present a favored center for investment by the United States and Japan without the European Market. If this is the case, and the present evidence points in that direction—three quarters of all companies taken over in 1988 were British, while nearly 50 percent of all EC acquisitions in the first nine months of 1989 were in the United

Kingdom[29]—Britain's traditional trading role will be reinforced. But it will be trading in a paradoxically diverse yet integrated market. Because Britain is massively outnumbered by its partner and neighbor states, directly British-based or transnational British-European corporations will depend

29. *European Deal Review,* press release, Oct. 1989.

more
and in
cal tra
an Eng
to comm
in a nei
English-s
complete.
guages and
will be the

ANNALS, *AAPSS*, 511, September 1990

Foreign Language Acquisition in European Management Education

By ROBERT CRANE

ABSTRACT: This article deals with trends in language use in European management education, both current and long-term. Beginning with a survey of the history of management education in Europe, the article traces the explosive growth of the management education field in Europe in the last few years. The relative importance of language acquisition in European—as opposed to American—management studies is also noted. The differences in the type and degree of integration of language learning in business education between various countries and institutions were brought out through a 1985 conference held on the topic in Lyons, France. Through a survey of 14 European countries carried out in November 1989, the author ascertained that the integration of the two fields had progressed dramatically since 1985. The business and language faculties in many European business schools are melding as the former retrain to teach in foreign languages and the latter to teach business-related subjects. One language—English—has assumed continentwide dominance in management education. Thanks to faculty retraining, a new diversity can now be found in European business curricula.

Robert Crane holds a Ph.D. in French language and literature from the University of North Carolina, Chapel Hill. He has published widely in Europe and North America on integrating language studies into the business curriculum and on internationalizing business studies. He conceived and organized a series of international seminars for business and language faculty and for executives on curricular and economic issues in France and the United States. He is currently dean of the Centre d'études franco-américain de management in Lyons, France.

T HE novel, observed Stendhal in the early nineteenth century, is really a broad mirror held up to the past. Despite the political upheaval of his day, Stendhal found common threads in human nature, which he traced through his novels. His vision spanned Europe, its history, and its social classes.

Similarly, any study of the role of foreign language acquisition in management education in Europe today must adopt the broadest of scopes. Basic questions must be asked: What is foreign language? What is management education? In view of events in Eastern bloc nations, what is Europe?

One thread that binds these questions together is history. This article will begin with a brief history of the origins of management education in Europe to its present, rather chaotic, state. A first snapshot of the place of language learning in European management education will be given through the July 1985 colloquium "Languages and Internationalizing Business Studies," held in Lyons, France. The findings of this colloquium will be used as a benchmark to trace the evolution of certain trends—in particular, the melding of language and management elements in education. A comparison will be made of the results of the 1985 colloquium and two events in 1989: the conference "Language Learning in Business Education," organized by the Escuela superior de administración y dirección de empresas and held in Barcelona, Spain, in February 1989, and a survey, "The Place of Language in Management Education in Europe," carried out by me in November 1989. Finally, projections will be made

based on current trends concerning language learning in European management education as 1992 approaches. Completely outside this diachronic framework, a few observations will be made on the corporate world and the place of languages within companies. Certainly, there is a need for a thoroughgoing study of this important and as yet unexplored field.

HISTORICAL BACKGROUND

Business schools appeared in Europe in the nineteenth century in response to some of the forces Stendhal described in his novels: developing industrialization, demographic movements toward the larger cities, and the rise in position and wealth of the bourgeoisie. In France, for example, the first business schools were created around the middle of the last century in the larger provincial cities—Rouen, Marseilles, Lyons—and the idea spread rather quickly. Even in such a northerly country as Estonia, degrees in commercial studies were being awarded prior to World War I. But the thrust of such studies was largely local—training sons to assume their father's businesses—and dealt mostly with the bookkeeping side of business. The role of foreign languages was virtually nil in this system.

As in many other fields, the close of World War II also marked the end of this comfortable situation. Confronted by national economies in ruins in the postwar period, business people and management educators began casting about for inspiration to develop the managers needed to rebuild their nations. After some hesitation the model most widely adopted was that of the United States.

The choice of the American model was a logical one since the United States appeared triumphant to European eyes in all areas at the time and since, thanks to the patient efforts of the American Assembly of Collegiate Schools of Business, which is the national association of business schools in the United States, the field of American management education had attained a degree of sophistication unknown at that time in Europe.

Thus, during the 1960s, planeloads of European management students and professors were flown to the United States to study U.S. management techniques. When they returned to their respective countries, these leaders in management education often incorporated American methods and courses into their curricula. As a result, for example, organizational behavior—*en anglais dans le texte*[1]—became a standard in the core curriculum in France. More generally, American English became de facto the second language in European management schools. This phenomenon was to be of considerable significance when the schools began communicating with each other. At the same time, new schools in Europe were being opened with the direct or indirect participation of American institutions. Thus the Cranfield School of Management in Great Britain opened its doors thanks to a recent British graduate of Harvard who had returned to Bedfordshire. Harvard also played an institutional role in founding and developing Institut euro-

1. Translation: In English in the text.

péen d'administration des affaires (INSEAD) in Fontainebleau, France. Again, the participation of an American institution in its creation lent strength to the position of the English language at INSEAD, an institution that at the time was trilingual—French, English, and German.

Following this wave of input from the United States, the European schools continued to develop while maintaining ties to the United States. Gradually, the American background was recast in a European mold. Thus organizational behavior became organizational behavior within French firms. Nevertheless, the U.S. influence remained through the case studies and texts available. From the beginning, one major difference between European and American management education was the insistence in Europe on languages, one or two foreign languages being required in many cases.

RECENT RAPID GROWTH IN
EUROPEAN MANAGEMENT EDUCATION

Once firmly launched in the 1960s, the field of management education in Europe grew apace over the next two decades. In the mid-1970s, a European business school association was founded in Brussels, the European Foundation for Management Development (EFMD). The emergence of the EFMD marked the coming of age of management studies in Europe and provided a forum for the exchange of ideas among European schools. Despite the enormous disparities in systems between France, West Germany, and the United Kingdom, for example, cooperation was facilitated through the EFMD.

In each of the countries, there was a certain stability in the system. France had its *grandes écoles* and its universities, West Germany its *Fachochschulën* and universities, and Britain had limited management education based on a system much like that of the United States. This diversity and relative stability began rapidly unraveling under the pressure of pent-up demand for business studies.

Britain is a clear example of this explosive development. As early as the late 1960s, British colleges of advanced technology, which were then becoming universities, as well as many polytechnics were looking for fields with high demand in which they could meet a need. A substantial number of these institutions found international business education, with both business and language components, to be that field. This phase in the evolution of British management studies was only a harbinger of the future, dynamic growth of the sector, however. Rapid growth followed the 1987 publication of two national reports on the state of management education in the United Kingdom and abroad. The Handy Report, on business studies abroad, and the Constable Report, on business studies in Britain, revealed a shortage of professional training among British managers and led to a nationwide call for more management education. This call has resulted in an increased number of spaces in existing institutions; in more distance learning, using television, videocassettes, and so on; and also in the creation of new, mostly private business schools. Pent-up demand was and is driving a major increase in British management studies.

Britain, however, is only one case in the current explosive growth in European business education. Similar forces in France, Spain, and Italy —to cite only three countries—have brought about similar results. Thus the neat national patterns of management education with national rankings of institutions—clear, although largely incompatible from one nation to the next—have now been infinitely complicated. Not only have the past suppliers of such education been retained, but many new players have also appeared, particularly in the private sector.

A FIRST BENCHMARK:
THE BUSINESS-LANGUAGE
MIX IN 1985

In Lyons, France, in 1985, "Language and Internationalizing Business Studies," the first international colloquium on its topic, brought together 125 delegates from 12 nations in Western Europe and North America. Two-thirds of the delegates came from the language field, one-third from the business field. The official languages of communication were English and French, which were used in roughly equal proportions.

The result of the colloquium, in addition to bringing together for the first time business and language professors from two continents, was to reveal the different approaches to and levels of advancement in international management education—institution by institution and country by country. To return to the earlier example of Britain, it was found that the United Kingdom had by far the largest number of integrated language and business programs—more than fifty at that time. The British experience in joint honours was also the longest, since it began with the experiment with the polytechnics and colleges of advanced technology in the late 1960s. Furthermore, the British alone had also developed a scale to measure the degree of integration between the business and the language components.

The five steps in the British definition of integration ranged from (1) completely separate teaching of the business and language courses with a literary emphasis in the latter, through (2) a business-language approach to language, to (3) interaction between professors in the two disciplines, the language curriculum being developed entirely by the language department. In a fourth step toward integration, the curriculum was generated jointly by the business and language faculties, with business-content courses being taught directly in the foreign languages. At the fifth and highest level of integration, consortia of universities taught business subjects in the foreign languages, had mandatory stays on campuses and in companies in target-language countries, and awarded joint diplomas. It should be noted that the original impetus behind these developments in the United Kingdom was market forces, that is, company demand for internationally trained employees, which translated into student demand for the appropriate courses of study.

The case of Denmark was rather different from that of Britain since the initial push in the direction of combined language and business studies came from a 1981 decision by the Danish government to promote such studies. Interestingly, the prestigious Copenhagen School of Economics and Business Administration continued to develop its two excellent faculties: one in business with a strong language component and the other in applied language. Elsewhere in Denmark, courses of study combining language and business were created on different university campuses.

Among the other European nations represented at the 1985 colloquium, some—France, for example—had undertaken serious efforts to combine language and business, the usual approach being to teach an ever increasing number of business courses in English. In still other European countries—Spain, for instance—there had been no perceptible attempt to internationalize business studies through the integration of language and business. In short, the 1985 colloquium gave an overview of which schools and nations were most active and advanced in merging language and business to internationalize their curricula.

BUSINESS-LANGUAGE OVERLAP

One interesting conclusion drawn from the 1985 colloquium was that the line separating business from language instruction was becoming ever more indistinct. In the case of the more advanced schools, business professors were giving some of their courses directly in the foreign languages—mostly in French and German in Britain, and in English elsewhere. This trend has continued and has become more marked since 1985, particularly as concerns instruction in English.

There are several aspects of this last observation that merit examination. First, the movement toward English as a teaching language on the Continent might be seen as in contradiction with maintaining a balance between and a certain quantity of business languages. If English is the language of instruction at elite graduate-level institutions such as France's INSEAD or Switzerland's International Management Development Institute or of undergraduate institutions such as France's Center for Franco-American Management Studies, it is also used for varying proportions of the teaching in other Continental business schools. English, of course, is the world language of business and increasingly the European language of general communication. Furthermore, the goal of such European Community programs as the European Community Action Scheme for the Mobility of University Students (ERASMUS) is to move European students and faculty between Community university-level institutions. As a consequence, English has emerged as the common vehicle for communication on a multilateral basis among business schools in Europe. Thus, to participate fully in the movement of people and ideas in Europe for the moment, European business schools must use English.

The importance of English does not contradict the principle of linguistic balance, however. Obviously, a Dutchman studying business in English in France will retain his mother tongue and perfect his French through contacts outside of class. Nonetheless, since 1985 there has been a clear movement toward teaching wholly or partially in English among Continental business schools.

A second phenomenon observable since 1985 is the ever accelerating cross-training of teachers. If business professors are increasingly giving their courses in marketing, management, and other topics in foreign languages, it is also true that language teachers are retooling to teach non-language-content courses. For example, at the École supérieure de commerce de Lyon, in France, a course dealing with the functioning of the European Community is team-taught by a professor of English and a professor of German. The class is given half in one language and half in the other. Similarly, a course at the Eindhoven University of Technology, in the Netherlands, focuses on difficulties Dutch have in negotiating in French-speaking cultures. Specialized courses such as these, which require a considerable investment by the teachers, have been opened in addition to the now standard courses on the economic environment in the English-, German-, and Spanish-speaking worlds offered by many business schools.

The end result of cross-training among the schools pursuing this approach seems likely to be a unified faculty capable of offering a variety of courses from a wide range of perspectives in different languages. Already on certain campuses retrained language faculty are accepting posts within departments of human resource management, marketing, and so on.

Interestingly also, the broad international overview of former language teachers retrained in business has allowed a small number of them to assume key posts in management education around Europe. Two striking examples of this phenomenon are the director of the master's program in international business at the Cranfield School of Management in Great Britain, who is also professor of French, and the director of the master's program in business administration at the École supérieure de commerce de Lyon, France, who is a professor of English. In view of the increased importance of an international perspective and of language skills within the European Community, academics possessing a dual background will undoubtedly continue to come to the fore.

Perhaps the Danish model from the 1985 Lyons colloquium contained the seeds of current trends in language development in European management education. The difference between an economics graduate with a strong background in languages and a language graduate with a firm grounding in economics, business law, or other business-related field, is really one of degree, so to speak. Indeed, the Copenhagen School of Economics and Business Administration has drawn on the strengths of both faculties to create its integrated Modern Languages and Economics Center. This approach seems to be the nub of recent developments in Europe: business and language forces are being combined, faculty from both sides are retraining and recasting their knowledge to form new course patterns, and men and women of international vision—whatever their initial field—are rising to positions of responsibility in European management education.

FINDINGS FROM THE SURVEY ON LANGUAGE IN EUROPEAN MANAGEMENT EDUCATION (NOVEMBER 1989)

There were 85 responses to a survey addressed to the attendees of the February 1989 conference of the Escuela superior de administración y dirección de empresas, "Language Learning in Business Education," in Barcelona, Spain, and to the institutional members of the European Foundation for Management Development. The responses from 14 European nations could be broken down into five general categories: (1) university-level business schools, (2) national or international management organizations, (3) companies, (4) private management centers, briefing centers, or consultants, and (5) language schools.

Several general conclusions are readily apparent from the geographical distribution and typology of the respondents. Most strikingly, Spain, which had scarcely undertaken any business-language cooperation in 1985, is now heavily involved in both fields, whether taken separately or together. Both the number of Spanish business schools and the number of language schools responding were high—6 and 5, respectively—an indicator of increased interest in Spain in international business and contacts. This development corresponds to Spain's integration into the European Community. The second national observation is that Britain continues to lead the field. Again, the numbers of respondents from British business schools and language schools were high—20 and 4, respectively. Furthermore, the level of sophistication in course offerings in both fields can only be matched by Holland and Belgium.

Third, most business schools responding offer a part of their curriculum in English. As mentioned earlier, a small number of schools offer their entire curriculum only in English. This phenomenon is natural in Britain but also is found in Switzerland and in France. On the contrary, few schools offered no courses whatsoever in English.

Among the languages offered, English easily was the most prevalent. French and German formed a second group, with Spanish following. Other languages cited with some frequency were Portuguese, Italian, Russian, Japanese, and, in the Scandinavian countries, Swedish. Dutch for foreigners was mentioned in Holland and Belgium. Chinese and Hebrew were mentioned by a small number of institutions.

As concerns the level of integration of language and business study, a sea change has apparently occurred since the 1985 colloquium, at which a rough balance between the traditional—that is, literary—and business-language approaches to

language learning was found. In answer to the question, Which of the following schemes best describes the place of language study at your institution? the business-language approach to language teaching was indicated by 30 respondent business schools as opposed to only two schools indicating the traditional, literary approach. It should be noted that many respondents indicated several types of business-language integration according to the level, course of study, or language involved. Thus a clear evolution toward business-oriented language teaching has taken place over the last few years.

Furthermore, for 19 institutions, coordination takes place between business and language teachers concerning course organization and content. Such interdisciplinarity has been taken a step further by 3 institutions—Aston University, Great Britain; École supérieure de Lyon, France; and European Business School, West Germany—which team-teach certain courses using business and language faculty. Finally, beyond those non-British and non-Irish institutions offering their entire curriculum in English—such as the International Management Development Institute and the Center for Franco-American Management Studies—12 also give business courses by business professors in foreign languages. Among those institutions indicating no foreign language courses, all but 2 either were in Britain or were all-English-language institutions on the Continent.

The final question in the survey dealt with the probable evolution over the next five years of language education within the institutions polled. If we are to believe the respondents, language learning still has halcyon days ahead of it in management studies. Twenty-two respondents felt that a greater variety of languages would be offered at their institutions in the future, while only 2 foresaw the disappearance of the language department. Similarly, 16 predicted a higher general linguistic level among incoming students, while only 1 perceived a decline in level and that in only one language, French, and this in a Flemish-language institution in Belgium. Here we skirt a key issue not treated in our survey: the general excellence of language preparation in European secondary schools. Obviously, this preparation is fundamental to all further language acquisition at the university level.

The need for retraining by both language and business faculty is widely perceived. Eighteen respondents indicated that their institution's language teachers were or would be retraining in business subjects, while 17 respondents said their business teachers were or would be learning foreign languages. The languages being acquired by the business faculty included German (seven responses), French (six), English (five), Japanese and Chinese (one each), and "all European languages" (one). It is undoubtedly significant that retraining is being undertaken by both business and language teachers, thus reinforcing the theory of convergence between the two fields.

Finally, 19 respondents believed their institutions would receive "more non-local business faculty mem-

bers" in the future. The formulation leaves open whether the foreign faculty will be European, taking advantage of such European Community programs as ERASMUS or the Community Programme for Education and Training in Technologies whose purpose is to move people and ideas around the European Community.

A SUBSET OF THE NOVEMBER 1989 SURVEY: CORPORATE LANGUAGE EDUCATION IN EUROPE

While the number of corporate responses—six—cannot be considered representative in any sense, it is nonetheless worthwhile to note the comments of these five multinational firms and one industry school in the absence of a thoroughgoing study of European corporate language policies and practices.

Undoubtedly the most striking comment on corporate language policy was that of a senior executive of Nestlé S.A., of Vevey, Switzerland. The spokesman said that Nestlé, a major multinational, has no language policy since most company executives speak one or two foreign languages as a matter of course. Nestlé does, however, give language training on a case-by-case basis to managers or spouses who express a need for such training. Outside instructors are used for this training.

The spokesman remarked that the different world markets of Nestlé are autonomous, and in certain cases— the Spanish market, for example— language training is offered for executives. On the other hand, within company headquarters in Vevey, language use literally varies from floor to floor. English, Spanish, French, German, and Swiss German are all used for communication, with English being at present the most widely used language. Significantly, the senior executive himself speaks or understands six languages.

Kodak offers training in English, French, and German at both its international office in London and its French headquarters in Paris. Language training is also offered in the other British offices and the German offices. The language courses are adapted to the specific professional needs of the Kodak personnel involved.

As English is the international language of IBM, the courses given at the company's International Education Centre in La Hulpe, Belgium, are conducted in that language. On the other hand, within IBM generally, education is primarily delivered in each national company and thus in the national language. There are some small programs in English-language instruction within the national companies.

At 3M Spain, however, a separate language department focuses on English-language training. The goal of 3M Spain's English-language program is to achieve a linguistic level high enough to allow the staff to give substantive business courses directly in English.

These unexpected corporate replies to the survey on language in management education in Europe raise more questions than they answer. Is the language ability of Nestlé executives a unique case? If so, why? Why do U.S.-based multinationals like Kodak and 3M offer their European employees language training? Hence an unexpected result of the survey is the perception of the need for an in-depth study of language use in European companies.

CONCLUSION: WHITHER EUROPE?

Through this brief examination of European management education and the place of language in it, several trends and a general picture have emerged. The trends include (1) the generalization of a combined business-language approach to language instruction in countries previously untouched by the phenomenon, (2) the accelerating integration of the business and language curriculum and of the two faculties, (3) an enrichment of course offerings through the recasting of the skills and knowledge of business and language faculty into new molds, (4) the concurrent increased use of English as the vehicle for European communication and thus of instruction to European audiences, and (5) the advancement of language professors to positions of influence within management education. The larger picture that is emerging is that of a Europe in which, as Charles Quint put it, a man is worth the number of languages he speaks. A benchmark for Western Europe, as one participant in the 1989 Barcelona conference pointed out, may well be a knowledge of one Latin language, one Germanic language, and one's mother tongue. The opening of Eastern Europe, with its embryonic business schools, brings even that broad definition of minimum linguistic skills into question. Indeed, the decade of the 1990s will be an exciting one for Europe, its management education, and its languages. Even a modern-day Stendhal would be hard put to encompass the scope of new European developments.

ANNALS, *AAPSS*, **511**, September 1990

Developing Competitive Skill:
How American Businesspeople Learn Japanese

By BERNICE A. CRAMER

ABSTRACT: Despite a crying need for more Japanese competence in the American business community, bilingual businesspeople are still surprisingly rare. Members of a specially convened focus group—American businessmen in Japan—discuss the reasons why this is so. They include the difficulty of learning the language while employed full-time, suspicion of bilinguals on the grounds that they have gone native, and the negative influence of an international stint on many American corporate career paths. In fact, American bilinguals find their best job prospects with Japanese companies at home or abroad or with American companies in Japan. There are few opportunities waiting for them in American company headquarters. In the future, we need to prepare our young Asian studies majors more realistically for the job market, to demonstrate to corporations the potential rewards of long-range commitment to the Japanese market, and to become more aware of our changing place in the international order.

Bernice Cramer earned her B.A. at Cornell University, followed by graduate training in the FALCON Japanese program. She spent 13 years in Japan, first in a Japanese multinational and later as principal of a corporate communications consulting firm. She founded the Forum for Corporate Communications in Tokyo (1979) and served as chair of the Marketing Committee of the American Chamber of Commerce in Japan (1988). She is currently president of PAOS Boston Inc., a management and marketing consultancy.

THE United States is not well prepared for international trade,'" said former Governor Gerald L. Baliles of Virginia, chairman of the National Governors' Association, as quoted in the *New York Times* in 1989. "'We do not know the languages, the cultures, or the geographic characteristics of our competitors.'" The article continues, "It is not surprising if this sounds familiar. In 1979, President Jimmy Carter's Commission of Foreign Languages and International Studies concluded, 'America's scandalous incompetence in foreign languages also explains our dangerously inadequate understanding of world affairs.'"

The *New York Times* continues, "The 1979 commission practically wrote the script for the 1989 statement by the governors. It noted that the Japanese have hundreds of sales representatives familiar with American speech and ways. Only a handful of Americans trying to sell United States merchandise in Japan were similarly prepared."[1] In fact, despite the overwhelming importance of the U.S.-Japanese relationship—termed "the most important bi-lateral relationship in the world" by former U.S. Ambassador to Japan Mike Mansfield —there are still more Americans studying Latin than Japanese.[2]

Despite what looks like a crying need for more Japanese competence

1. Fred M. Hechinger, "About Education: Seeking to Shore Up America's Future by Understanding Foreign Languages and Cultures," *New York Times*, 15 Mar. 1989.
2. Stephen Karel, "Going International: On Language," *American Demographics*, May 1989, p. 54.

in the American business community, the numbers of people who combine responsible business positions with Japanese fluency are still surprisingly small. The purpose of this article is to uncover the reasons why this is so, with a particular focus on the American business community in Japan.

MOTIVATION FOR ACQUIRING
JAPANESE FLUENCY:
A HISTORICAL PERSPECTIVE

Japanese-language proficiency is still enough of a specialized skill that it is possible to categorize neatly motivation for acquiring it. An empirical survey of present-day American businesspeople in Japan reveals three generations of language-acquisition types, plus a special category.

First generation:
The military

The first generation of Japanese-proficient Americans was created during World War II, through the good offices of the U.S. military. Many of these people became intensely fluent in the language and familiar with the culture and chose to remain in Japan after the Occupation, either in military positions, in private business, or in an educational or consulting capacity. These people are now in their late sixties or seventies; thus many are retired or close to it.

One of the best known of this generation is Jack Seward, author of *Japanese in Action* and many other books on the Japanese people, culture, and language. The author's biography in

Japanese in Action describes his career:

Jack Seward . . . began his Japanese studies in 1942 and was later graduated second in his class from the longest and most comprehensive course in Japanese ever offered in the United States. He lived in Japan for over twenty years as an Army officer, government civilian employee, and businessman.[3]

This is perhaps a typical career path for Japanese specialists of Mr. Seward's generation. As he says in *Japanese in Action,* "For years after the close of World War II, jobs with the U.S. government, including the military establishment, were the best—indeed the only—way to live in Japan."[4]

Second generation:
The romantics

A second generation of Japan specialists was created in the 1960s and early 1970s. These were people who were seduced by the romance and mystery of Japan, whether in Zen Buddhism or aikido.

One Tokyo-based American, marketing manager for an American packaged-goods company, puts it this way: "I first came to Japan in 1972, after graduating from a midwestern university where I was a Japanese history major. Particularly back in the 60s, the more esoteric and unusual your major was, the more comfortable you felt on campus. So I looked for the courses that had the fewest people in them."[5]

Many university students in the late 1960s and 1970s soaked up the antibusiness sentiments prevalent at the time; this is one reason why they tended to get into business later in their careers, often almost coincidentally. Our marketing manager's career path led him to business indirectly. He continues, "My purpose in coming to Japan was to learn Japanese. I had planned to return to the U.S. and go into a graduate studies program. After three years, I decided that academia was not for me, and I've been working in business ever since."

This generation tends to be in their late thirties and forties, therefore they are among the prime candidates for managerial positions at American companies operating in Japan.

Third generation:
The businesspeople

The current generation of Japanese-speaking businesspeople centers on those who studied the language specifically for business advantage. At least since the late 1970s, it has been apparent that Japan would play a major role in the world economy. This situation has enticed an increasingly large number of young Americans to study Japanese language, come live in Japan, and become steeped in the culture.

3. Jack Seward, *Japanese in Action* (Tokyo: John Weatherhill, 1968), author's note on inside back cover.
4. Ibid., p. 201.

5. Participant A in a Briefing Breakfast organized by the American Chamber of Commerce in Japan for the purpose of this article, 5 Dec. 1989.

Among the resources available to these students are linguistically sound courses rooted in a cultural context, such as the Full-Year Asian Language Concentration (FALCON) program at Cornell University. FALCON prepares the student to actually use the language in its proper cultural context; it is not limited to teaching just grammar and vocabulary.

Another businessman, a consultant with nearly forty years in Japan, says it this way: "It is becoming self-understood that you cannot work in Japan without speaking Japanese anymore. This whole flood of you younger people coming in here speak it. And nobody would hire anybody anymore who doesn't speak Japanese."[6]

The younger American business generation in Japan today does indeed tend to be more fluent than any generation that preceded it. One rule of thumb is the "*o-jozu desu ne*" ("How well you [speak]!") measure. When I first moved to Japan in 1975, and for ten years afterward, Tokyo cabdrivers tended to praise lavishly any effort to speak Japanese on the part of a foreign passenger. "How long have you lived in Japan?" "The language is hard, isn't it?" "Japan is a difficult country to live in, don't you think?" and other similar questions were inevitable. These days, a central Tokyo cabbie does not bat an eye at a young, Japanese-speaking foreigner. When asked, they say that nowadays most of their foreign passengers speak at least a little Japanese.

There are a few exceptions to this increased fluency: foreign exchange traders, foreign lawyers, and others

in specialized occupations who may have been transferred to Japan for their particular knowledge.

Special category: The
missionaries and their families

Throughout the postwar period, one prolific source of Japanese speakers has been the missionary community and, in particular, the Mormon Church. It is surprising how many American businesspeople with good Japanese got their start as 18- or 19-year-olds in the two-year-long missionary program sponsored by the Mormons in Japan.

One man, now a high-level banker representing an international institution in Japan, explains it this way:

I first came to Japan in 1965. I came as a Mormon missionary for two and a half years. Took a leave of absence from college to do so. . . . I knew nothing when I came here. I lived in the countryside and just had to speak it to eat. At that time, there was not very much spoken English available, particularly in places like Kofu and Kanazawa, where I lived. So it was very much a practical method to begin with. I listened to NHK radio every morning, to try to get correct pronunciation. I studied [by] myself through textbooks, through experience.[7]

WHICH CAME FIRST,
THE JAPANESE OR THE JOB?

In a focus group of five American businessmen stationed in Japan, held 5 December 1989 in Tokyo, it was clear that those with fluent Japanese learned it for their own reasons

6. Participant B, ibid.

7. Participant C in a Briefing Breakfast organized by the American Chamber of Commerce in Japan.

first and only later looked for a business use for their language skill. None of the participants could recall a case of a businessperson who was transferred to Japan without language skill and then picked it up on the job or through tutoring.

Moderator: In listening to this group of people, the three of you who rate your Japanese as pretty good all learned it in informal programs of self-study. Is that typical?

Participant C: For people of a certain age, including myself, most of us did get into Japanese almost accidentally.

Participant D: I think one thing we all have in common was that we had the opportunity to be here [in Japan] in a student, or nonbusiness, role, where we had the time to devote to learning Japanese. I don't know how people can have a full-time job and try and learn Japanese at the same time.

Participant C: I have never met a businessman here who has come to Japan without the language and who has been able to learn it here. Never met one.

Participant A: Neither have I.

Participant D: The only exception might be those people in business who must use Japanese to survive within their company. There's professional reinforcement. No one will learn Japanese working a ten- or twelve-hour workday and then trying to go study on their own. . . . People tend not to realize how difficult a language Japanese is when they're over in the U.S. planning to come over here. They know they're going to be sent to Japan, and they go through a three-month or a three-week course or something in preparation for it, with the best intentions, but they don't realize what they're getting into.

Another conclusion that can be drawn from the focus group is that the good Japanese speakers start learning the language early: at age 19, 20, and 21, respectively, in this sample group.

The participant with nearly forty years in Japan was one who did not speak Japanese. He explained,

I'm beginning to feel very badly [in this conversation]. I've been here for a long time and I don't speak the language. But I was 32 when I came, and I had a very much full-time job ever since I came here, with the exception of six weeks between jobs when I took a total immersion course because I thought I could break the "sound barrier." It didn't work.

IS JAPANESE-LANGUAGE FLUENCY REALLY NECESSARY TO DO BUSINESS IN JAPAN?

Many Americans who meet senior Japanese businesspeople in the United States are pleasantly surprised at their generally high level of English fluency. Is it really necessary to know Japanese in order to do business in Japan? they may wonder. And if so, why would a good interpreter not suffice?

The key answer is that Japanese is more than a language—it is a window into a way of thought and action that is very different from our own. The Tokyo focus group put it this way:

Participant C: It's what you don't say that's sometimes more important than what you do say. It's how you say it.

For example, you can use the Japanese expressions *kentoo shimasu* or *kangaete okimashoo*. Literally translated, the statements mean "I'll study it" and "I'll think about it"—meanings that seem close in English. In practice, one means "I *will* study it" while the other means "You haven't got a chance." Telling the difference takes time and experience.

Participant A: A lot of people may claim that the use of the language is really crucial in a business environment, and you have to tease apart whether they're talking about the vocabulary itself or whether they mean the process of bootstrapping yourself into cultural familiarity with the language ability. I think in Japan that's especially true. The advantage I see among businesspeople here who speak Japanese is often more cultural than it is simply communicative. . . . Even using interpreters—say, in a multiparty negotiation including some people who have no Japanese—those participants who do speak have some cultural fluency that allows them to measure the flow of the negotiations with a great deal more sensitivity.

This view of the unusual intertwining of Japanese lingual and cultural fluency is supported in an article in the *Japan Society Newsletter* by Jay Rubin, professor of Japanese literature at the University of Washington in Seattle. "Japanese, we are told, is unique. It is not merely another language with a structure that is different from English, but it actually says things that are never said in English and cannot be translated into English—or into any other language. . . . [This] is wrong. The Japanese language can express anything it needs to, but Japanese *social norms* often require people to express themselves indirectly or incompletely."[8]

8. Jay Rubin, "Teaching the Language of the Infinite," *Japan Society Newsletter,* Nov. 1989, pp. 2-4.

Clearly, the ability to understand and use these social norms to one's advantage is a key business skill. That would appear to necessitate understanding the language as a window into the culture.

GOING NATIVE AND OTHER SPURIOUS OBJECTIONS TO JAPANESE FLUENCY

American businesspeople in Japan —and the stateside executives who hire them—have traditionally put forth a number of reasons why it is not necessary or even desirable to speak Japanese in order to do business in that country.

Chief among these is the concept of going native, or losing an American perspective. Members of the Tokyo focus group commented on the phenomenon.

Participant B: Japanese really is a state of mind as much as it is a language, and that's where the danger starts. The question is, how well can you handle that [state of mind] without becoming over-Japanized, and forgetting what you're really here for, which in most instances is to represent foreign interests.

Participant D: I think that's something we all get criticized for, especially in a U.S. company—the having "gone native" kind of thing. People want you on the one hand because you speak Japanese; on the other hand, if you speak Japanese well and you're culturally identifying with the whole structure of Japanese society, Americans get confused as to whose side you're on. I think that happens quite a lot.

A second, often-cited objection to speaking Japanese in business situations is that it "puts you in their territory." This theory is cited by Jack

Seward in *Japanese in Action:*

Seward's Third Law: The more fluent a foreigner becomes in the Japanese language, 1) the more he will tend to be avoided by many Westernized Japanese and 2) the more ordinary Japanese will expect him to abide by their customs and conduct himself, in general, as a Japanese would.[9]

The idea is that speaking Japanese essentially allows the Japanese to set the ground rules. The focus group tended to discount this notion.

Participant C: I have heard that argument and I have never quite bought off on it. First of all, I don't believe that you can ever get good enough that you are accepted [as a Japanese]. I think you are always a *gaijin* [foreigner].

Sometimes Japanese people do try to use [language fluency] to their advantage. A Japanese person will say, "You speak Japanese, you ought to know that this is the way we do it." Well, it isn't necessarily the way all Japanese do it, it's just the way that person wants to do it, and he's taking advantage of the fact that you know something about the language and the culture.

So I don't buy the general argument that [speaking the language forces cultural submission]. I think it's very much a self-serving argument.

Another common argument is that the Japanese themselves are uncomfortable with foreigners who speak their language well. Again, focus-group members tended to discount this theory.

Participant C: I can count hundreds of times when the other party knows that I know enough Japanese to be fluent in it, and they've been greatly and visibly re-

9. Seward, *Japanese in Action*, p. 206.

lieved. In fact, they've trotted out people that they would not have [otherwise introduced us to] if we had not been able to handle their language. I think it's when they see it as a business disadvantage that they get uncomfortable, rather than simply the fact that you speak Japanese and you might be getting too much like a Japanese yourself.

Participant D: When I was working with Japanese food companies, the Japanese wholesalers, if I didn't speak Japanese there was no way we could get anywhere. . . . There was just no English-language capacity on their side.

ARE THERE JUSTIFIABLE OBJECTIONS TO JAPANESE FLUENCY IN BUSINESS?

One of the most common mistakes made by American businesses in Japan is hiring Japanese nationals with good English skills, assuming that they have business acumen on a par with their language ability. Often the two skills have no point of intersection.

The same is often true of Americans with Japanese fluency. Here is what the focus-group participants had to say:

Participant A: I think there's still a major problem with Japanese speakers. Most of them learn Japanese for some reason other than business, and [most] are not that interested in business. . . . Somehow, those people who can learn Japanese well and can also fit into a business role are a rarity. There are lots of people who can learn how to speak Japanese, and there are lots who are good at business, but putting them together, they intersect at a very small point. Because many of the things I think are common to those people who learn Japanese are not so common in the business world.

Participant D: Language is just a tool. And the most important part of that tool is being able to communicate. . . . [Even with fluency], you still have to have the basic business skills to succeed in this country. Those are the primary issues, and language becomes a kind of secondary function.

"Is the job applicant interested in Japanese or in my business?"

In fact, multinationals are often concerned about a job applicant's real interest, wanting to know whether the person really cares about business or is just looking for a way to stay in Japan. Participant E, an attorney who did not speak Japanese, echoed this sentiment:

Participant E: There's a very well-known foreign attorney here who hires a sizable number of American and other foreign attorneys to come and work for him. And he makes it a prerequisite that they don't speak Japanese. . . . He's found that the point of intersection between Japanese-language skills and business skills is very small, and he's tried to focus his hiring on a group of people who he senses are the best attorneys. He really doesn't want people coming over here who are interested in developing Japanese skills, if that's the real reason they're coming.

Participant C: I can confirm that from a hiring point of view. For a long time, if somebody came to us who had a Ph.D. in Japanese and had taught for a while and then all of a sudden found business, they were looked on as being suspect. What were their real motives? Were they looking for just an avenue to be able to live in Japan, or were they really interested in business? The emphasis up through today is that you have to be a good banker

first. And then if you have the language skills, that's a big plus. But if you didn't cross the first hurdle, there just wasn't any interest on our part.

In other words, the Japanese facility may be a useful adjunct to a solid business skill or interest; however, Japanese language and experience by themselves do not make a compelling candidate for most business positions.

"I want to do anything that uses my Japanese."

Job applicants often bring hardship upon themselves by tying their entire career path to their Japanese ability. This naturally makes the hiring company look at them as a resource with relatively narrow application—an easy resource to pass by in the hiring process or, if hired, even to divest itself of if times get tough.

Participant C: On the part of the interviewer or the employer, it's a question of motivation. If someone comes in and says, "I want to do anything where I can use my Japanese," then what I'm thinking is, "Is this person really interested in my business or is he interested in his Japanese?" It's very important the way the applicant positions himself to his potential employer.

Participant A: But to the young person who has learned Japanese and feels that he is capable in the language, quite often the only thing he feels that he has to sell is his Japanese ability.

ARE BILINGUAL AMERICAN EXECUTIVES REWARDED FOR THEIR SKILL?

We have seen that American business in general looks for business acumen and interest before Japanese-language ability in recruiting. Now let us turn to the incentive for putting in the long hours and exceptional effort that developing the two sets of skills requires. Are the rare gems with both adequately rewarded?

The combination of business skills and language fluency does seem to be a winner, once both have been demonstrated.

Participant D: Once you make it into a company, [Japanese ability] does make a big difference. Then you're known as a businessman who speaks Japanese. That tag is always put on you.

Participant C: And that's a highly desirable commodity. In my case, I've worked with about four different institutions. I've always been approached with something that was clearly more desirable, and I don't kid myself—I think it's because I've had business skills but it's also because I've had language skills.

The great lie: Why American bilinguals cannot find jobs in the United States

Many American businesses are sadly behind in their determination to build a cadre of Americans with both Japanese and business skills. Experience with young job seekers tells me that they are much more likely to find employment with a Japanese company, either in Japan or in the United States, or possibly with an American company in Japan. The job opportunities with American companies in America are notably absent for Japanese speakers.

Participant A: It's not a one-sided issue; it's not a situation where young college students should decide that learning Jap-

anese is important. American business also has to decide that having this skill is an important part of doing business; they have to actively recruit these people. If they aren't [recruiting], then probably the ones who are identifying the need [for Japanese] are the Japanese companies themselves.

Participant D: I think [language specialists] are a national resource that American businesses have to make an effort to develop for their own individual uses.

In an occasional paper for the National Foreign Language Center, Carol S. Fixman, director of International Programs at Temple University, writes,

Since companies can find few Americans fluent in Japanese, and since companies do not seem to be training employees for fluency in Japanese, they usually rely on Japanese nationals to satisfy their language needs. A training director whom I interviewed commented that Japanese-English bilinguals can ". . . write their own ticket today." This is borne out by my interviews in all companies. . . .

Japanese-American bilinguals are in such great demand that one New York-based information management service has been successfully publishing a recruiting magazine for three years now. Issued four times a year, this magazine consists of advertisements placed by U.S., Japanese, and other international companies seeking bilingual Japanese-English employees.[10]

In fact, the job situation for young bilingual Americans is not as rosy as it seems in this citation. If the job seeker is happy to work for a Japa-

10. Carol S. Fixman, *The Foreign Language Needs of U.S.-Based Corporations,* National Foreign Language Center Occasional Paper Series (Washington, DC: National Foreign Language Center, 1989), p. 16.

nese company—either in Japan or in the United States—there will be many opportunities. Japanese companies rightly recognize that they need American employees who can communicate with their Japanese counterparts.

The reputation of Japanese companies for isolating nonnative Japanese in dead-end jobs is often a deterrent to a job seeker with talent, however. As one Harvard MBA put it, "If you take a job with a Japanese company, your section-mates will wonder why you couldn't get a job with a 'real' [that is, an American] company."

There are also considerable opportunities for bilinguals with American companies in Japan, and many young people take advantage of these. Most, however, eventually want to return to the United States after some period of time in Japan, whether three, five, or more years. After all, America is their homeland and the place where many eventually expect to raise a family.

The problem is that there are almost no opportunities for Japanese speakers in the U.S. headquarters of American companies. This situation is confirmed by a partner at one of the world's largest executive search firms, a partner whose practice centers on placement of Japanese-speaking Americans.

When I get a candidate who has returned to America from a stay in Japan, I worry that they're just looking for a way to get back to Asia. First I have to make sure that they really are here to stay. If they are, the Japanese firms in the States can use them; if they're looking to get back to Japan, I could place

them with an American firm there. But there's nothing else. I can't in good conscience place them with American companies at home.

Many Japanese speakers with newly minted college degrees feel that they have, in effect, been lied to by the placement officers of their universities. A business degree and Japanese fluency should lead to a good position in corporate planning or international marketing, they reason. Unfortunately, this is rarely the case.

Does American corporate strategy target Japan?

The disinterest of many American companies in Japanese speakers is largely the result of corporate strategy that does not realistically provide for expansion in the Japanese market.

Participant C: It's really more a reflection of each company's goals and priorities than anything else. Maybe some companies perceive Japan as not being very important to them. I would find that hard to believe in today's world, given Japan's economic position, but I think that's it. That's a more fundamental problem, not a language problem.

But I don't think it's unusual, either. I think that many American businesses underestimate their potential in this market. They take a look at it and say, "This is very difficult, the distribution system is awful, and so forth, we can't do business here. We're just going to do the minimum amount necessary to keep our toes wet, but that's about all we're going to do." And I think many of them give up too soon. [Corporate strategy vis-à-vis Japan therefore] is just as much a problem as recognition of the importance of ability to speak Japanese.

Participant A: Quite often you get heads of international departments who think that "international" is only Europe.

This attitude is all the more evident in the face of 1992's European Community unification and 1989's free-trade pact with Canada. Many American companies echo the attitude of one advertising agency chief financial officer, who told me in a private conversation, "Why should our clients put their dollars into an assault on the Japanese market? There's already a long line of dead bodies ahead of them—people who tried Japan and failed. Europe is easier—at least they speak our language."

Widespread reporting of Japanese nontariff trade barriers and generalized fear of unfair business practices keep many American businesses from putting as much effort into developing the Japanese market as they might otherwise.

And traditionally, American companies have treated their Asian offices as virtual dumping grounds for people they wanted to keep away from headquarters—the corporate equivalent of being sent to Siberia. For example, Robert Sam Anson writes in *Manhattan inc.*, "Asia, to the post-Luce Time Inc., was, says a former Time executive, 'a place you sent problem guys you didn't know what to do with.' "[11]

American companies are less than international

The problem is not limited to experience with Japan. American companies tend to underreward executives with international experience in general. According to a *Wall Street Journal* article,

In a survey of 406 North American executives who had just completed foreign assignments, nearly all said they had expected foreign postings to benefit their careers. But more than half said the experience turned out to be a detriment, according to Nancy Adler, a management professor at McGill University in Montreal, who conducted the survey. Significantly, Ms. Adler found that responses didn't vary by industry or site of foreign assignment. . . .

Most senior managers at Ford Motor Co., for instance, once worked at its Ford of Europe subsidiary. Nevertheless, "for the vast majority of people [in middle and senior middle management] at Ford, foreign assignments are a career negative," says one company vice president with wide overseas experience, who asks not to be named. "No one judges the experiences [to be] as valuable as you think they are."[12]

The general parochialism of American companies is echoed in a survey of 1500 managers worldwide, conducted by Columbia University and Korn/Ferry International and reported in the *Wall Street Journal*.

Ranking skills important to CEOs [chief executive officers] in the 21st century, 35% of Americans thought "experience outside the headquarters country" was very important, compared with 73% to 74% of foreign counterparts. Some 62% ranked "an international outlook" very

11. Robert Sam Anson, "The Pacific Press Wars," *Manhattan inc.*, Nov. 1989, p. 55.

12. Thomas F. O'Boyle, "Grappling with the Expatriate Issue: Little Benefit to Careers Seen in Foreign Stints," *Wall Street Journal*, 11 Dec. 1989. Reprinted by permission of The Wall Street Journal, © Dow Jones & Company, Inc. 1989. All Rights Reserved.

important, compared with 81% of Europeans, 87% of Latin Americans and 100% of Japanese.[13]

Clearly, we have a ways to go

In summary, it seems to me that there are several key points to be made with reference to the use of Japanese by American businesspeople in Japan today.

1. There is a very small pool of Americans with both business and Japanese ability.

2. Most of these people learned the language before starting their business careers and believe that it would be difficult for an American executive to pick up the language on assignment to Tokyo.

3. Japanese ability—along with the related ability to penetrate the culture—is seen as a key to business success in the country.

4. American bilinguals find their best job prospects with Japanese companies, or with American companies in Japan, but not with American companies at home.

5. The basic reasons for the lack of opportunities at home are the shallow commitment of many American companies to expansion in Japan and the generally insular attitude of many U.S.-based corporations.

What is needed? Clearly, we need to prepare our young Asian studies majors more realistically for the job market they will find outside the academic world. To U.S. corporations we need to demonstrate the potential rewards of long-range commitment to the Japanese market. Finally, we, as a society, need to become more aware of our changing place in the international order as well as the associated obligation to become more cosmopolitan in our outlook.

13. "U.S. Managers Still Focus on Home Front," *Wall Street Journal*, 12 July 1989. Reprinted by permission of The Wall Street Journal, © Dow Jones & Company, Inc. 1989. All Rights Reserved.

ANNALS, *AAPSS,* 511, September 1990

Language Training and Beyond:
The Case of Japanese Multinationals

By ROSALIE L. TUNG

ABSTRACT: This article seeks to unravel some of the reasons for the success of the Japanese in the global economic arena. One factor is hypothesized to be the significant amount of effort that Japanese multinationals devote to human resource management, especially as it pertains to preparing their people for living and working overseas. The article reviews the cross-cultural programs found in 18 Japanese multinationals. In general, such a program includes language training, field experience, graduate programs abroad, in-house training programs, and outside agencies. The implications for U.S. multinationals are discussed.

Rosalie L. Tung is Wisconsin Distinguished Professor, Business Administration, at the University of Wisconsin, Milwaukee. She has served on the faculties of the Wharton School and the University of Oregon and has taught at Harvard University and the University of California, Los Angeles. She is the author of seven books and many journal articles on the subject of international management. She has lectured widely at leading universities and is actively involved in management development and consulting activities around the world.

IN the past decade, the United States has been conceding its economic leadership to the Japanese in one industry after another—first it was automobiles, then it was the banks. In 1986, the per capita income in Japan exceeded that of the United States for the first time. More recently, the Japanese, who traditionally were averse to mergers and acquisitions, have become avid dis- ciples in the game of corporate takeovers. In short, the erosion of U.S. economic leadership in the world appears to have reached crisis proportions. In fact, "international competitiveness" has become the latest buzzword in Washington.

While the reasons for the growth in Japan's economic might are manifold, a pivotal factor, in my opinion, is how that country has harnessed its human resources to pursue organizational and national goals. After all, Japan is virtually devoid of raw materials; its primary resource is its people. In my book *Key to Japan's Economic Strength: Human Power,* I hypothesized that much of Japan's success in the world economic arena can be attributed to the attention the country devotes to developing its people for operating in a global context.[1] This is all the more remarkable considering that the Japanese, by culture and history, do not readily mix with *gaijins* ("foreigners"). Because of the homogeneity of Japanese society and its relative isolation from the outside world until the midnineteenth century, its people are less adept at living and working in a foreign environment. Through self-discipline and meticulous preparation, however, the Japanese who have been sent abroad to establish and manage foreign subsidiaries have succeeded in making Japan a formidable global economic force.

Although much of this success can be attributed to the quality and competitiveness of its products, the ingenuity of its work force also plays a pivotal role in ensuring that its products are effectively marketed in foreign countries. As Dr. Jiro Tokuyama, then executive director and dean of the Nomura School of Advanced Management, said, there appears to be a general thirst or quest for global information on the part of many executives:

"Many of the Japanese executives not only follow many Japanese magazines and newspapers, but read at least a few of the following periodicals: *Newsweek, Time,* the *London Economist,* the *Wall Street Journal,* the *New York Times,* and the *Financial Times.* We are making such an effort to understand the global market. As you know, we live in an information-oriented era when countries with valuable pieces of information or intelligence win. So-called industrial policy is not necessarily the cause of our competitive position in world markets. The economic 'miracle' of Japan is attributable in part to our eagerness to gather and analyze available information on world markets. I recommend that American executives do the same if they want to remain intact in the highly competitive global market."[2]

This is where the human factor comes into play. Without a highly developed and trained core of interna-

1. Rosalie L. Tung, *Key to Japan's Economic Strength: Human Power* (Lexington, MA: D. C. Heath, Lexington Books, 1984).

2. Ibid., p. 31.

tionally oriented human talent, the competitiveness and, indeed, the viability of a multinational are greatly jeopardized.

In this article, I will present findings concerning how 18 Japanese multinationals prepare and train their people for operating in the global environment. These findings are part of a larger research on international human resource management practices and policies in Japanese multinational corporations.[3] These Japanese multinationals come from a wide range of industries and services, including finance and banking, electronics, heavy industrial manufacturing, general trading companies, textiles, and chemical manufacturing.

FINDINGS

While the nature and content of the training programs provided by the 18 multinationals varied, there were certain common denominators. In general, these programs consisted of the following components: language training, field experience, graduate programs abroad, in-house training programs, and outside agencies. Each of these components will be elaborated on in the following pages.

Language training

Many Japanese multinationals consider language an important criterion in the selection of a candidate for overseas assignment, although its rank ordering has decreased relative

to technical and administrative skills.[4] According to Dr. Tokuyama, "In the past, language abilities took precedence over technical competence, but a mere linguist proved to be inefficient in many cases. Of course, language is an important criterion, but it is no more than a means to achieve the objectives."[5] Many Japanese executives are of the opinion that if Westerners simply confine their business interactions to those Japanese who speak fluent English, they may be "dealing with the wrong person" because the individual may merely be an "eigo-ya, an English specialist, who doesn't know much else."[6] Thus English-language proficiency cannot be equated with seniority or authority within a Japanese organizational hierarchy.

The foregoing discourse is not intended to downplay the significance of the need to assess and develop language proficiency. Rather, it is intended to highlight the emphasis Japanese multinationals, in general, place on developing the whole repertoire of technical and human relational skills to ensure maximum performance in operating in a global context. As a Japanese executive puts it, "'The concept of adaptability is comprehensive and consists of various components. Adaptability could be closely tied to language ability and personality.'"[7] Since the Japanese

4. *Human Resource Development in Industry*, Japan Industrial Relations Series no. 10 (Tokyo: Japan Institute of Labor, 1983).

5. Tung, *Key to Japan's Economic Strength*, p. 9.

6. *Fortune*, 6 Nov. 1989, p. 74.

7. Tung, *Key to Japan's Economic Strength*, p. 9.

3. Tung, *Key to Japan's Economic Strength*.

language is seldom used outside of Japan, in order to conduct international business the Japanese have to speak English, the lingua franca of international business transactions. Although Japanese schoolchildren study English from grade seven on, the emphasis is on reading and writing, not conversing. In the opinion of many Japanese, this method of instruction has made them poor linguists and explains why many have difficulty with oral communications.[8] Consequently, training in the language of the target country is fundamental to an orientation program for international assignments among all Japanese multinationals.

Most of the multinationals I studied provided in-house intensive language-training programs, ranging from three months to a year, prior to departure. Furthermore, many employees participating in the programs continue to immerse themselves in language training after their arrival in the host country. In fact, many of the Japanese multinational corporations I studied select ten to twenty of their elite trackers to attend graduate programs in engineering, business, or law abroad every year. Such graduate training programs may extend for four years because the individual spends the first year abroad in intensive language training in preparation for the subsequent graduate program.

Besides in-house training programs, many of the Japanese multinationals utilize external agencies that specialize in developing foreign language proficiency. Two such institutes are the Japanese American Conversation Institute (JACI) and the Institute for International Studies and Training (IIST). Each of these programs will be examined briefly here.

The Japanese American Conversation Institute. The JACI was established in November 1945 to serve the needs of the Ministry of Finance and other governmental agencies to provide English-language training to young government employees who had to communicate with the Allied Occupation authorities. Today, the institute serves a broader audience; its student body is drawn from the financial, business, and governmental sectors.

JACI offers day programs, which meet five hours a day for five days a week, and evening programs, which meet three hours a day. The day program lasts from 11 to 20 weeks, and the evening program lasts up to two years.

As noted earlier, a principal limitation of the way in which English is taught in Japanese schools is the emphasis on writing. Consequently, many Japanese have difficulty conversing with foreigners. According to the chairman of the institute, Mr. Namiji Itabashi, in order to be fluent in a foreign language, trainees need a comprehensive understanding of the foreign culture. In his words, "A language has been developed on the soil of a culture while a culture has been advanced with the language as

8. *Nippon: The Land and Its People* (Tokyo: Nippon Steel, 1982), p. 153.

its blood, and the two are inseparable."[9] Consequently, the training in both must go hand in hand. Mr. Itabashi contends that a good method for improving oral English skills is to help students "think in English." A portion of the program is therefore devoted to a course entitled "Thinking in English."

In my opinion, this recognition represents a major strength in international development education programs offered by this and other Japanese institutes. The programs provided by some U.S. multinationals to prepare trainees for international assignments may sponsor a crash course in a foreign language, but the trainees are generally not exposed to the nuances and subtleties surrounding the use of the language. In a conversation, such superficial knowledge of the language may result in insulting the other party. In the Chinese and Japanese languages, for example, there are various levels of formality in the spoken language depending upon the person with whom one is conversing. Furthermore, according to an executive from Dentsu advertising agency, "The Japanese communicate in almost telepathic ways: through gesture, nuance, inflection."[10] This is what Hall has referred to as the "silent language" of international business negotiations and transactions.[11] In-

appropriate use of certain terminologies, which stems from an inadequate understanding of cultural norms, may do the speaker more harm than good in attempts at conversation in a foreign language.

Institute for International Studies and Training. In 1967, in line with Japan's growing involvement in the world economic arena, the Japanese government enacted special legislation authorizing the establishment of the IIST, whose mission was to "provide graduate-level training for selected qualified persons contemplating careers in the international field" with the ultimate goal of developing a "body of rising young leaders who will eventually play a key role in international affairs."[12] The IIST offers two types of programs: regular and practical trade. Both are residential, full-time programs. The former program extends for a full year, while the latter runs for three months. Both types consist of several components, language training being one of them. The focus here will be on language training. Other aspects of the programs, designed to develop different types of international business skills, will be explored in a subsequent section of this article.

In the regular program, the number of instructional hours devoted to English language is 540, excluding the courses in international management and economics, which are also conducted in English. English language is taught in the first eight weeks of the program by native speakers; the emphasis is on listening and

9. Namiji Itabashi, "Adult Education: English Teaching at a Language School," in *The Teaching of English in Japan* (Tokyo: Eichosha, 1978), p. 173.

10. *Fortune,* 1 Nov. 1982, p. 68.

11. Edward T. Hall, *The Silent Language* (Garden City, NY: Doubleday, Anchor Press, 1959).

12. *IIST Brochure* (Tokyo: Institute for International Studies and Training, 1980-81).

speaking skills. Besides learning the language through formal lectures and laboratory training, the trainees are given ample opportunity to practice their English with exchange students who are native speakers of the language. Every year, such exchange students from major industrialized countries are brought in for three months to share the same dormitory as the Japanese trainees. This intensive three-month interaction not only permits the Japanese trainees to practice their foreign language skills but provides an opportunity for them to observe foreign cultures in action and to interact with foreign nationals.

In the practical trade program, the number of instructional hours in English is 230, and the first six weeks of the program are devoted to English-language training. The trainees in the practical trade program also share the dormitory with foreign exchange students.

In the regular program, another eight weeks is set aside for training in a second foreign language, such as Spanish or German, or advanced English. The selection of the language is based on the country or region to which the trainee will be assigned.

Field experience

Many of the Japanese multinationals surveyed send select members of their career staff to serve as trainees for one year in their overseas subsidiaries. As trainees, their primary mission is to observe closely and learn about the company's foreign operations. The trainees also try to acquire as much information as possible about the foreign country, including noneconomic variables. This kind of training prepares them for an eventual overseas assignment, which is viewed as part of one's career development.

This type of training can best be illustrated by the following example. A large general trading company sends a trainee to Spain for one year to learn how to play the Spanish guitar. During that time, the person does not have to engage in other types of productive functions in the foreign subsidiary. When I asked the company executive how the company could justify the expenses associated with sending a person abroad just to learn a musical instrument, the response was, "You have to understand how important music is in the Spanish context." Despite my agreement, I still had questions about the cost-efficiency of such an assignment. The executive then explained,

In order for the person to be a good producer, he must first and foremost be a good consumer of the culture. In order to come up with a product that will be in demand in a foreign culture, the person has to first consume and understand what the likes, dislikes and tastes of people in that country are. Only then, can he be a good producer of products with local demand and appeal.

This philosophy helps explain, in part at least, why Japanese products have met with such great success in many parts of the world. While the Japanese employees serve in the capacity of consumers rather than producers in the one-year overseas job-training programs, the companies do not feel that this is a waste of money; the reason for this attitude is the Japanese belief that in order to become better producers later in their careers, the employees need to have an adequate understanding of all factors, both economic and noneconomic, that could influence a society's functioning. This philosophy is in contradistinction to the typical American assumption that what sells well in Peoria, Illinois, for example, will also have a ready market abroad.

A small but growing number of U.S. executives are beginning to share this Japanese sentiment. Last year, a cover story of the *Wall Street Journal* was devoted to an examination of the attributes of the chief executive officer of the year 2000. The article profiled the requisites of the future corporate chief as follows: the person "must have a multienvironment, multicountry, multifunctional, maybe even multicompany, multiindustry experience."[13] Ways to develop these skills and perspectives include several stints of overseas assignment in strategic locations around the world and course work in non-business-related subjects.

Williams College, for example, pioneered a five-week summer program for middle-management executives from IBM, General Electric Corporation, and Polaroid Corporation. The participants were slated as fast trackers by their respective companies. During the five-week program, these executives studied subjects ranging from film criticism, politics, art, classical music, and literature to human behavior. These companies were willing to invest $5200 per employee in the program

because they believe that candidates for top management positions must sharpen their powers of inquiry and reflection and have a deeper understanding and awareness of social issues.

Corporations are increasingly cognizant that these skills may not be adequately conveyed through business or technical courses. In order to become a successful chief executive officer, Irving Shapiro, former chairman and chief executive officer of Dupont, believes that it is imperative for a person to have a broad understanding of world issues "beyond the provincial limits of his own business."[14] This sentiment is similar to that espoused by Japanese executives who contend that in order to become better businesspersons, it is necessary to understand the social, economic, and cultural factors that make up a society.

Graduate programs abroad

Every year, many of the Japanese multinationals that I surveyed send ten to twenty career staff to attend graduate business, law, and engineering programs overseas. The company pays tuition and all expenses in addition to the employee's regular salary. As noted earlier, these graduate programs may sometimes extend for four years. In the first year, the trainee is immersed in intensive English-language training in the foreign country. This is followed by two years in a master's program in business administration and a fourth

13. Amanda Bennett, "The Chief Executives in Year 2000 Will Be Experienced Abroad," *Wall Street Journal,* 27 Feb. 1989.

14. Errol T. Louis, "Williams College Summer Course for Executives Stresses Liberal Arts, Shuns Job-Related Subjects," *Wall Street Journal,* 26 Aug. 1983.

year in field experience. While attending graduate school, the Japanese employee is exposed to foreign principles of management. Furthermore, during the two-year period, the Japanese employee gains a better understanding of the broad functioning of other societies. Thus the study-abroad programs serve a function similar in many ways to that of the overseas job-training program described in the preceding section.

In-house training programs

Besides language training, many Japanese multinationals offer in-house courses in international finance and economics. Expatriate employees are also given environmental briefings about their country of assignment.

In the past, the emphasis of pre-departure training was on language. As noted earlier, many Japanese companies now realize the importance of developing the management or administrative skills of their expatriates to ensure success abroad. I have found that a principal reason for failure is the inability of the expatriate to cope with the larger responsibilities of overseas work.[15] Many Japanese expatriates may initially encounter status shock when they have to operate pretty much on their own, isolated from corporate headquarters. Although they maintain daily contact by telephone and other means of telecommunication, they cannot have the kind of close interaction that they are accustomed to at home. There are

15. Rosalie L. Tung, "Selection and Training Procedures for U.S., European and Japanese Multinationals," *California Management Review*, 25(1):57-71 (1982).

many subtleties and nuances of the Japanese language that can be conveyed only through face-to-face interactions. While abroad, the expatriates find themselves burdened with added responsibility as overseas representatives, a role they are generally not used to performing alone. To a Japanese who has been used to working in a group, the adjustment problem may be tremendous. Consequently, a number of the Japanese executives interviewed for the study feel it is imperative to develop the management skills of expatriates to prepare them for the added responsibilities as representatives of a Japanese firm. An executive-development program designed to foster these administrative and management skills is provided by the Nomura School of Advanced Management.

The Nomura School of Advanced Management. This school, established in 1981, is part of the Nomura Group. The participants in the program are drawn from the ranks of senior management in leading Japanese companies. The program is developed jointly with the Harvard Business School and uses the case-method approach.

As Dr. Jiro Tokuyama, dean of the Nomura School of Advanced Management, noted, a principal objective of the school's program is to develop the skills of senior management with respect to strategy formulation, an area in which Japanese executives are presumably weak. The purpose of the three-week program at the Nomura School is to prepare senior management personnel to take on "general management responsibilities including the development and implementation of corporate strategies." Apparently, these are skills required of an expatriate while serving as the company's representative or liaison person abroad.

Outside agencies

As noted previously, language represents one of the components of the training program provided by IIST. The other aspects of the regular and practical trade programs offered by the institute are examined here.

Regular program. Besides the 540 instructional hours in English, there is a 22-week segment in international management and economics, area studies, and Japanese studies. The courses in international management and economics are designed to provide trainees with skills in functional disciplines so that they will be prepared to handle the broader duties associated with an overseas assignment. As indicated previously, status shock is a principal cause of expatriate failure among Japanese multinationals. Consequently, knowledge in the functional disciplines is considered essential.

The area studies program is designed to provide trainees the knowledge required to live in the geographic region to which they may be assigned. The first section of the program covers North America and Western Europe; the second section covers the socialist-bloc nations, the Middle and Near East, Latin and South America, and Southeast Asia. For each region, the trainee learns about the history, culture, socioeconomic, and political characteristics of each country and the country's relationship with Japan. Although the course content is primarily factual, the program stresses adaptation and interaction with members of a foreign culture.

The course material is presented through a combination of lectures by overseas instructors, the use of case studies, interaction with foreign exchange students, and seminar discussions with invited speakers, among them ambassadors and ministers, foreign businesspersons who live in Japan, and overseas researchers. The seminars provide the trainees an opportunity to interact with experienced practitioners from other nations. The seminars are usually conducted in the evenings, after class hours, which run from 9 a.m. to 4 p.m. After the seminars, the trainees have homework and other preparation for the following day's lectures. Most of the trainees study until 2 a.m.

The trainees are also taught about Japanese society, its position in the world economic system, and how to explain the distinguishing characteristics of Japanese culture and society to non-Japanese. According to a survey conducted by the *Japan Economic News*,[16] which examined the problems encountered by 612 expatriates during their overseas assignments, only half of the expatriates —54.3 percent—and a third of their spouses—33.9 percent—had sufficient information about various aspects of Japanese society. Given the increasing interest in Japan on the part of people of other nationalities, more

16. *Japan Economic News,* 24 June 1982.

and more foreigners want to speak to Japanese about Japan, yet many Japanese lack sufficient knowledge to discuss with them the subjects of Japanese martial arts, Japanese life and culture, floral arrangements, and the tea ceremony. Hence the Japanese studies program fulfills a special need in an overseas assignment.

Practical trade program. Besides the 230 instructional hours in English, the practical trade program concentrates on intercultural communication, fostered through an understanding of the culture behind English expressions. As noted previously in the section on the JACI, this is a very useful approach because without comprehension of the cultural roots behind the development of certain expressions, a nonnative speaker of English cannot hope to acquire a good command of the language.

Another segment of the program deals with practical training in the areas of international business transactions, foreign exchange management, and other related subjects. Courses are taught in international trade theory, trade administration regulations, documentation, marketing abroad, and so on. The information is conveyed through lectures, case studies, and seminars.

CONCLUSION AND DISCUSSION

In my comparative analysis of international human resource management practices and programs in U.S., European, and Japanese multinational corporations, I found that European and Japanese multinationals tend to experience high incidences of success in expatriate assignments as compared to their U.S. counterparts.[17] In general, it appeared that the Europeans have an innate advantage. Given the smaller size of the domestic markets and the geographic contiguity of European countries, Europeans have a greater awareness of the need to learn a foreign language and to adapt to foreign ways of living. In the case of Japanese multinationals, there appears to be an acquired advantage. Because of the country's recognition of the need to acquire resources from abroad and to sell overseas, the Japanese multinationals invest heavily in training programs to teach their people to operate effectively in the international arena. The highlights of the training programs provided by many leading Japanese multinationals have been discussed in this article. U.S. multinationals appear to possess neither the innate advantage of the Europeans nor the acquired advantage of the Japanese.

This advantage does not mean that the Japanese do not encounter problems in operating abroad. There are problems associated with the prolonged separation of husband and wife that may be brought on by international assignments. This situation arises because under the Japanese educational system, children who are educated abroad can experience difficulty in passing admission examina-

17. Rosalie L. Tung, "Expatriate Assignments: Enhancing Success and Minimizing Failure," *Academy of Management Executive,* 1(2):117-25; idem, *The New Expatriates: Managing Human Resources Abroad* (Cambridge, MA: Ballinger, 1988).

tions to leading universities at home. Thus it is not uncommon for Japanese expatriates with children in high school to go abroad alone so that their wives can supervise their children's education at home. This and other related problems will not be elaborated upon here, however.

Furthermore, this discussion of Japanese training programs for international assignments does not imply that the provision of such training is solely responsible for the low rate of expatriate failure abroad. There are other factors that can account for the higher rate of success. These include the overall qualification of the candidates for overseas assignments, the longer duration of overseas assignments, the support system provided by corporate headquarters, and the selection criteria and process for overseas assignments. While space limitations do not permit examination of each of these factors here, it is important to note that they are all directly or indirectly related to the importance attached to an international assignment by Japanese corporations. In general, Japanese multinationals place a heavy emphasis on international assignments because of the significance of international sales to a company's overall profitability. Thus Japanese multinationals tend to send abroad those with high potential for subsequent career advancement. For example, among Japanese general trading companies, it is known that the person who will eventually assume the position of chairman of the board will have served in either the London or the New York office.

In contrast, an international experience is not considered a very important criterion for promotion to senior management positions in U.S. companies. In a study I conducted with Edwin L. Miller of management succession in 123 U.S. companies, the majority of which had annual gross operating revenues in excess of $1 billion, over 93 percent of the companies did not consider "international experience or perspective" an important criterion for promotion or recruitment.[18] In many U.S. multinationals, some repatriates may even find that their career progression has stagnated. In fact, some high achievers refuse an overseas assignment for fear that it may result in a negative career move. According to a survey by Moran, Stahl, and Boyer, Inc., only 4 percent of the U.S. companies surveyed judged overseas assignments as having a "positive effect on career advancement."[19] This finding is consistent with that by Korn/Ferry, in which only 0.5 percent of the junior executives surveyed considered an international route as a fast-track option. This percentage was a decrease from 2.0 percent in 1979.[20]

This analysis suggests that the barriers hindering internationalization in the United States are perhaps more deep-rooted. Before corporations are willing to invest in language

18. Rosalie L. Tung and Edwin L. Miller, "Managing in the Twenty-First Century: The Need for Global Orientation," *Management International Review,* 30(1) (1990).

19. Selwyn Feinstein, "Labor Letter," *Wall Street Journal,* 30 June 1987.

20. Bennett, "Chief Executives in Year 2000." The Korn/Ferry study was conducted in the late 1980s.

training and other programs, such as the ones described in this article, to prepare their people for operating in the global environment, there has to be recognition of the importance of the international marketplace. Without such an awareness, much of the effort toward globalization will prove futile.

ANNALS, *AAPSS*, 511, September 1990

Foreign Language Needs in
the U.S. Government

By RAY T. CLIFFORD and DONALD C. FISCHER, Jr.

ABSTRACT: The federal government has a great number of designated positions that require foreign language competence. The scope of these positions is quite broad and encompasses such diverse fields as intelligence collection, treaty and commercial negotiations, and individual survival skills. The language-competence levels required by these positions are just as varied, ranging from survival to professional skill levels. Many of these needs go unfilled. The government's foreign language jobs can be divided into two categories. The larger includes jobs where the foreign language skill is an adjunct to a professional skill or preparation. In the smaller, the foreign language ability is the critical skill. The number of federal agencies with foreign language requirements is great; the needs of the government's major foreign language employers are described briefly. Due to the significantly changing world and our growing economic interdependence, linguistic needs are growing tremendously. To meet these needs the education system would have to lengthen the instructional sequences and increase tenfold the number of languages taught. Foreign language instruction should move to a proficiency-based system at all levels. Better communication between the educational community and government agencies is also needed.

Ray T. Clifford has been provost of the Defense Language Institute Foreign Language Center since 1981. He holds a Ph.D. in foreign language education.

Colonel Donald C. Fischer, Jr., is commandant of the Defense Language Institute Foreign Language Center. He has had key management and leadership positions in the Department of the Army and NATO organizations. He holds master's degrees in logistics management and in military arts and sciences.

ONE needs only to refer to the Constitution to see that foreign language capabilities are in the interest of the United States. The federal government's responsibilities of providing for the general welfare, promoting the common defense, and securing liberty's blessings—all gen- erate requirements for foreign language competence. The constitutional task placed on Congress to regulate commerce with foreign nations also cannot be accomplished without foreign language skills. Like it or not, we have violated President Washington's guidance on entangling alliances. Such alliances are not only political; they also have military, commercial, and technological implications.

The foreign language needs of the United States government are broad and diverse, and no nationwide systemic improvements have been made in the decade since the President's Commission on Foreign Language and International Studies declared that our nation's incompetence in foreign languages was "nothing short of scandalous."[1] In general, there remains an unfilled need for individuals with the professional levels of language expertise needed to handle sensitive foreign intelligence collection, diplomatic exchanges, treaty and commercial negotiations, foreign military liaison, and overseas deployment. There is also a large demand for the functional language ability necessary for handling informal daily

1. President's Commission on Foreign Language and International Studies, *Strength through Wisdom: A Critique of U.S. Capability* (Washington, DC: Government Printing Office, 1979), p. 5.

activities as well. This is especially apparent as family members of government personnel assigned overseas become the day-to-day, face-to-face ambassadors for our nation.

Foreign language jobs in the government can be divided into two categories. The first and larger category includes jobs where the foreign language skill is a necessary adjunct to professional preparation and skills in another substantive area, such as engineering or international relations. The second category of jobs is typified by translation, interpretation, and teaching assignments. Here additional skills are needed beyond those of simply being proficient in a foreign language, but the use of the language itself is the critical factor. In both categories the highest demand is for skills in Russian and other Slavic languages, followed by Middle Eastern and Asian languages. Spanish is becoming increasingly important, and, although the current demand is small, there is likely to be a greater need for African language skills in the future.

PROGRAM OVERVIEW

The number of federal agencies with foreign language requirements is larger than may be generally recognized. The major employers are the Department of Defense, the Department of State, the Central Intelligence Agency, the National Security Agency, the U.S. Information Agency, the Federal Bureau of Investigation, the Foreign Broadcast Information Service, the U.S. Joint Publications Research Service, the Peace Corps, and the Voice of America. Other agencies, such as the Department of Commerce, Radio Liberty, the Department of Agriculture, the U.S. Agency for International Development, and the Library of Congress, also have foreign language requirements for some positions. All of these agencies are members of the Interagency Language Roundtable.[2]

The following summaries are offered to the reader as an overview rather than a definitive statement concerning those government agencies with significant foreign language requirements. The synopses are presented in alphabetical order by agency.

Central Intelligence Agency

The Central Intelligence Agency (CIA) has need for a variety of linguists, many of whom should possess knowledge of specific subject matters as well as of language at high levels.

In general, job requirements at the CIA are for professional-level linguists, that is, those with Level 3 or higher proficiency in the skills of reading, speaking, and listening, as measured by the Interagency Language Roundtable proficiency scale. (For an example of the proficiency scale, see Table 1.) In addition to being able to read, translate, or summarize both concrete and abstract ar-

ticles, one must be able to understand subtleties and idioms that carry meaning beyond the words printed on the page. Analysts must also be able to read technical documents in substantive areas such as international trade, finance, and technology, including specialized areas such as offshore drilling and narcotics.

In order to communicate effectively, employees need to know the history, politics, and ethnic and religious customs of the country and region where the language they are studying is used. Because typical college language courses do not provide the level of language proficiency required to meet these higher levels of ability, additional in-house training is required to qualify individuals for job assignments after hiring.

For individuals with native or near-native language skills, many job opportunities exist in teaching, transcribing, and translating. Those seeking to work as transcribers and translators should recognize that the work will reflect a wide range of both printed and video materials. For those interested in teaching, the minimum requirements are a college degree with training in linguistics or a related field. Applicants with prior experience teaching a foreign language to adults are given preference.

The CIA recognizes the importance of foreign language skills and has employee pay incentives for learning, maintaining, and using foreign language skills.

Agency positions require U.S. citizenship, a background investigation, and a polygraph interview.

---

2. Additional information can be obtained by contacting the member agencies directly or by writing the Interagency Language Roundtable at this address: Chair, Interagency Language Roundtable, c/o DLI Washington Office, 1111 Jefferson Davis Highway, Suite 507, Arlington, VA 22202-4306.

TABLE 1

INTERAGENCY LANGUAGE ROUNDTABLE LANGUAGE-SPEAKING SKILL LEVELS

Speaking 0: Unable to function in the spoken language.

Speaking 0+: Able to satisfy immediate needs using rehearsed utterances.

Speaking 1: Able to satisfy minimum courtesy requirements and maintain very simple face-to-face conversations on familiar topics.

Speaking 1+: Can initiate and maintain predictable face-to-face conversations and satisfy limited social demands.

Speaking 2: Able to satisfy routine social demands and limited work requirements.

Speaking 2+: Able to satisfy most work requirements with language usage that is often, but not always, acceptable and effective.

Speaking 3: Able to speak the language with sufficient structural accuracy and vocabulary to participate effectively in most formal and informal conversations on practical, social, and professional topics.

Speaking 3+: Is often able to use the language to satisfy professional needs in a wide range of sophisticated and demanding tasks.

Speaking 4: Able to use the language fluently and accurately on all levels normally pertinent to professional needs.

Speaking 4+: Speaking proficiency is regularly superior in all respects, usually equivalent to that of a well-educated highly articulate native speaker.

Speaking 5: Speaking proficiency is functionally equivalent to that of a highly articulate well-educated native speaker and reflects the cultural standards of the country where the language is natively used.

SOURCE: U.S. Department of Defense, Defense Language Institute, Program Evaluation, Research, and Testing, *Interagency Language Roundtable Language Skill Level Descriptions*, 1985.
NOTE: Similar ratings are available for listening, reading, and writing skills.

Department of Defense

The Department of Defense has over 15,000 military positions with documented needs for foreign language skills. The majority of those positions support the intelligence community, and, due to the positioning of forces outside, but in relatively close proximity to, key foreign nations, emphasis has been on listening to radio broadcasts and to reading printed materials. Now, recent changes in Soviet policy are leading to a new Warsaw Pact configuration, and previously inaccessible areas of the world are opening their borders. The major official document exemplifying this new openness is the Intermediate Nuclear Forces Treaty, which, with its on-site inspection provisions, has set the patterns for all future accords.

A significant result of this expanded accessibility is likely to be a shift from military to economic and technological competition. In any case, there will be a greater requirement for foreign language skills, since there will be a greater need to speak—in order to express opinions, debate issues, and ask in-depth questions—and a greater need to listen and read, in order to stay abreast of complex issues, know what others are capable of doing, and assess what they intend to do.

Other key foreign language positions are responsible for security assistance, such as attachés or instructors of another country's military personnel.

Besides positions with formal foreign language requirements, there has always been a need for soldiers and families overseas to be able to understand and express themselves. All officers and noncommissioned officers need some familiarity with European, Middle Eastern, and Asian languages because of the probability of their going to these areas.

Finally, technical functions performed in foreign countries require foreign language competence. For instance, as the number of U.S. depots overseas is reduced, we will rely more on in-country sources as opposed to costly pipelines of supplies, and in-country procurement specialists will need foreign language capabilities.

The National Guard and Reserves also provide a storehouse of linguists for use in the event of contingencies. Language training provided by public schools and colleges could go a long way toward meeting our requirements. To motivate linguists to enhance and maintain their foreign language skills, the armed services have instituted special pay incentives for their linguists. The actual plans vary somewhat from service to service, but, depending on their language proficiency, military linguists may earn up to $100 extra pay each month.

The Defense Language Institute Foreign Language Center provides language instruction for the Department of Defense and other federal agencies. The Institute currently has over 900 civilian faculty and academic staff positions that require high degrees of language proficiency. These positions are devoted to curriculum development, teaching, and testing at the Institute's facilities in Monterey, California.

Drug Enforcement Administration

The Drug Enforcement Administration (DEA) uses practically every foreign language in its worldwide operations. As the title of the agency implies, its mission is to combat international narcotics smuggling. Emphasis now is on Central and South America. Spanish and the dialects of these regions are especially sought after. There will be a continuing need for skills in Southeast Asian languages such as Thai, Burmese, and Malay as well as the more commonly taught Asian languages: Korean, Japanese, and all dialects of Chinese. There is also a pressing need now for Turkish, Greek, Farsi, Urdu, and all dialects of Arabic.

DEA personnel assigned overseas are collocated with U.S. embassies and work as criminal investigators, intelligence research specialists, general investigators, or administrative and clerical employees. The minimum speaking skills required to apply for these positions are Level 2+ in the Romance and Level 2 in other languages.

The DEA has just begun a foreign language bonus program for employees that provides cash bonuses for individuals with high levels of language proficiency who are assigned to jobs that require use of that language in conducting agency business. For employees who meet these qualifications, it is anticipated that bonuses will range from 6 to 12 percent of annual salary.

Federal Bureau of Investigation

In the Federal Bureau of Investigation (FBI), positions requiring foreign language skills are generally divided into three categories: special agent linguists, language specialists, and translators.

The FBI is charged with protecting the security of the United States through identifying and countering efforts by foreign intelligence services and agents to conduct espionage activities against the United States. Foreign counterintelligence requires individuals with high levels of foreign language skills.

The FBI also has the duty to protect the United States from acts of terrorism committed by individuals or groups against the country or its property throughout the world. Many of these terrorist activities are conducted by individuals who use languages other than English.

Thanks to Hollywood, the best known of the FBI's responsibilities is its charter to fight organized crime. Languages other than English are frequently used by some of the major organized crime groups.

The FBI works with the DEA to prevent unlawful distribution and use of illegal drugs and controlled substances. Again, much of this illegal activity is conducted in languages other than English.

Finally, general criminal activities, such as kidnapping, bank robbery, extortion, and interstate transportation of stolen property, often require the FBI to communicate in languages other than English.

Individuals must speak one or more languages critical to the FBI at Level 3 or better to qualify for the position of special agent linguist. Individuals wishing to be considered for language specialist or translator positions must speak their first language at least at Level 4 and their second language at least at Level 2+. Exceptions to the Level 4 standard are sometimes made if the individual is able to achieve Level 3 or 3+ in both first and second languages.

The FBI has a foreign language incentive program for its employees. One segment of this recognizes special agents who make significant use of foreign language skills in the performance of their duties. Another segment of the program recognizes the linguistic performance of language specialists and translators. Employees are also rewarded when their foreign language expertise significantly facilitates official investigative efforts not addressed in the other two program elements. For those qualifying, the incentive program provides lump-sum payments of 3 to 11 percent of the employee's base salary on an annual or one-time basis. In addition to these language-use awards, there is also a foreign language achievement program, which provides for one-time, lump-sum bonus payments to individuals who raise the level of their language proficiency. For individuals who learn a new language and bring their language skills to Level 4, these bonus amounts may total $14,500.

National Security Agency

The National Security Agency (NSA), part of the Department of Defense, is one of the largest employers of linguists in the United States. It uses dozens of languages on a daily basis. Most of the language jobs are in transcription or translation. There are also a smaller number of positions in such fields as language teaching, research, and scientific or computational linguistics. The form of the language encountered in most assignments is not literary or classical but today's spoken and written vernacular. Topics covered include such diverse areas as military, economic, and scientific subjects.

The typical person entering the NSA language field has a B.A. in a foreign language and a passing score of Level 2 on the entry-level Language Proficiency Test or Language Transcription Test in that language. The new employee is then expected to progress to Level 3 and above through a combination of work assignments, on-the-job training, and formal language instruction at the NSA school—the National Cryptologic School—or at local commercial language schools.

The starting grade for a person with a B.A. in language or comparable experience is a GG-7. Higher grades are available for people with advanced degrees or additional experience, and advancement to GG-12 has become routine for most NSA lin-

guists. Professional certification is a requirement for promotion to GG-13 and above. To complete this program, one must pass both unclassified and classified reading or listening tests and have a certain amount of work experience, formal education, and training in related fields. The creation of a strong technical-track career program now allows linguists to remain in the language field and enjoy further advancement. Many linguists are now in grades 13-15, and there are even a few supergrade working linguists.

While many new hires work in the languages they studied in school, others learn a new language at NSA. Employees with majors in commonly taught languages such as French or German are often placed in full-time, year-long courses in another language. This training may take place at the National Cryptologic School or at one of the nearby commercial facilities.

In addition to the foregoing, there are many other language-training opportunities for NSA employees. Tuition assistance is provided to those individuals taking after-hours university language courses. Full-time undergraduate scholarships and graduate fellowships are available to those majoring in foreign languages. Opportunities to attend summer immersion programs in the United States and overseas are also available. In addition to formal schooling, agency linguists have an opportunity to serve overseas, usually for tours three years long.

Finally, NSA has a foreign language incentive program whereby linguists receive additional pay for achieving Level 2 in listening or Level 3 in reading. Extra money is given to those working in more than one language and to those who study and reach Level 2 in a contingency language.

All agency employees have top-secret clearances, which require a full background investigation, including a polygraph interview. NSA also hires a small number of native-speaker language instructors on one-year renewable personal-services contracts. These are uncleared positions that require U.S. citizenship, a background investigation, and a polygraph interview.

Peace Corps

The Peace Corps currently has more than 6000 volunteers serving in 67 countries worldwide. The Peace Corps's mission is to help countries meet their needs for trained men and women and to help promote better understanding between Americans and other people. In most of the countries served by the Peace Corps, foreign language skills are absolutely necessary for these grass-roots-level interactions to be accomplished.

The Peace Corps works in the areas of education, health, agriculture, natural resource preservation, urban development, and small business assistance. For example, there are more than 100 education volunteers in West Africa, who need French-language skills of at least Level 3 to teach math, science, vocational skills, and other subjects in secondary schools and teacher-training institutions. Unfortunately, the corps is consistently unable to supply the

requested number of volunteers in such areas as agriculture, education, and home economics due to a lack of people both qualified in these areas and with the prerequisite French-language skills.

Because volunteers with the language skills required are not available, language-training programs have been established in all Peace Corps countries. These do a good job of developing survival and social language skills during the volunteers' preservice training period, but there is not sufficient time to provide advanced language skills in technical areas. Moreover, while many volunteers come with a book knowledge of French, they commonly have been found to be unable to carry on a conversation. Their schooling has been focused on the structure of the language, the syntax, and the literature; while they are knowledgeable about the language, they are unable to use it in everyday conversation. For these individuals, the Peace Corps provides language training that stresses the speaking proficiency and communicative skills essential for Peace Corps work.

As with all government agencies, the Peace Corps would clearly benefit if it were able to recruit people who have basic communicative proficiency in foreign languages. The 8 to 10 weeks of intensive technical training given to volunteers in-country at the start of their service is inadequate to provide them with the linguistic, technical, and cultural skills they will need to perform their jobs. If volunteers with developed fundamental language-proficiency skills could be found, the time available for training could focus on technically oriented language skills.

The Peace Corps also requires language skills of staff personnel and consultants who assess and evaluate Peace Corps programs. In hiring staff, it is unfortunate but true that language requirements must be slighted in order to acquire substantive skills. It is also difficult to locate consultants with the proper mix of technical expertise and the level of language proficiency necessary to interact with host-country officials.

State Department

The Department of State posts several thousand Americans abroad at U.S. diplomatic missions. Some of the overseas positions are language designated, that is, the person filling the position is required to have a designated proficiency in a given language. At present, over 1900 positions, involving 46 languages, carry such proficiency designations. Other positions are described as language preferred. Persons assigned to these jobs often receive some language training as time permits. Adult family members accompanying employees to overseas assignments are also eligible for language training as resources permit. Thus foreign language requirements range from language preferred—no specific proficiency required—to Level 3 in the speaking and reading skills on the Interagency Language Roundtable proficiency scale.

Training is available in various formats, locations, and durations. Training for language-required positions is full-time—four to six hours per day, five days per week—and includes an area studies component. The length of training is a function of the speaking and reading requirements and the difficulty of the language. Training for language-preferred positions is also full-time, but it usually lasts only 7-10 weeks, depending on the language. Training is conducted at the Foreign Service Institute in Rosslyn, Virginia; for advanced Chinese, Arabic, Japanese, and Korean, there is a second year of study at advanced Foreign Service Institute schools abroad.

Foreign Service personnel use their language skills in a variety of tasks related to State Department reporting and support functions. Broadly, these include negotiation, representation, and reporting as well as language use inherent in living abroad. Many Foreign Service personnel acquire more than one foreign language during their careers as they move from region to region. Efficient learning and effective use of foreign languages is one of the primary attractions of a career in the Foreign Service.

A limited number of positions as language-training supervisor are available in the State Department's Foreign Service Institute School of Language Studies. Applicants for these teaching positions must possess a high level of language skills and should have experience teaching foreign languages to adults, curriculum-development experience, and, preferably, supervisory experience as well as experience living abroad.

Language-teaching positions at the Foreign Service Institute are normally filled with native speakers of the language in question. Experience in teaching foreign languages is preferred.

The State Department also has a foreign language incentive pay program. This program rewards employees with salary increases of 10 to 15 percent if they learn specified languages in conjunction with assignments to countries where those languages are spoken. The department also offers pay incentives to new employees who bring requisite language skills into the Foreign Service.

U.S. Information Agency

The U.S. Information Agency has a sizable Foreign Service Information Officer Corps working in press, cultural, and public affairs positions at embassies abroad. These positions typically require designated levels of language proficiency. The U.S. Information Agency also has limited positions in Washington for translators, interpreters, and editors with language skills. Some opportunities exist for specialists to accompany exhibitions and for short-term contract interpreters.

U.S. Joint Publication Research Service

The U.S. Joint Publication Research Service has numerous opportunities for free-lance translators to work on a contract basis. Payment is made per unit of work according to a scale based on language difficulty, the quality of the product, and the complexity of the source material. U.S. citizenship and security clearances are not required but an agency check is conducted on all qualified candidates.

Voice of America

The Voice of America offers multiple positions for broadcasters and support personnel in 42 languages. In order to qualify, one must pass stringent translating, writing, and broadcasting tests. Qualified candidates are placed on a standing register from which selections are made when appropriate vacancies occur. Professional positions start at level GS-9 or higher. Trainee and intern positions start at GS-7.

PROFICIENCY ORIENTATION

The preceding summaries reveal that there are significant needs in the federal government for Level 1 (survival), Level 2 (limited, working ability), Level 3 (professional), and higher language skills. It is also apparent that agencies with major requirements have had to create their own schools to fill these positions because the needed language skills are not provided by our public education system. We need a better match of school learning to national needs.

The education system at all levels should move to a proficiency-based orientation. Language-use situations and linguistic tasks such as those defined by the *Proficiency Guidelines* of the American Council on the Teaching of Foreign Languages[3] should become the focus of instruc-

3. *ACTFL Proficiency Guidelines* (Hastings-on-Hudson, NY: American Council on the Teaching of Foreign Languages, 1986).

tion.[4] Evaluation systems related to those situations and required levels must be developed and used.

Before and after World War II, when the United States was the major source of developed industry goods and our best and primary customer was ourselves, survival-level skills for tourism or troops in residence were adequate for most of our needs. The world has changed, however, and our linguistic needs have grown. Certainly, tourist or survival-level usage remains an appropriate goal for short, school-based programs, but it should not be the end objective for all students. Unfortunately, we have not kept pace with the expanding language-proficiency requirements caused by our alliances and economic interdependence.

The world has changed significantly since World War II and so have our reasons to communicate with other nations. Japan, Germany—in fact, almost all European and Asian nations—have well-developed education systems and their literacy rates and foreign language capabilities are higher than our own. The U.S. consumer's preference for foreign goods is a fact of life. Diplomacy is now more complicated. Our allies are more demanding, and they wonder more and more openly about the quality of our international leadership. We need to communicate better and more accurately, both to share our views and experiences and to learn from theirs.

A world with smaller military establishments requires better intelli-

gence, and this presumes better language skills. The so-called war on drugs will require competence in formal language styles, as well as considerable ability in dialect forms and gutter slang. Drawing up agreements will require technical competence in many languages since the native language always has precedence in courts of law. Our ability in translation and interpretation must increase dramatically to ensure the full participation of our leaders in the negotiation and planning set in motion by recent world changes.

We must recognize language as the means to enter markets, to communicate our philosophies, to learn, to foster peace, to exploit technologies, to cooperate in the process of raising the quality of life around the globe, and to prevent destruction and conflict. Above all, we must increase understanding to reduce the degree to which we feel threatened by a changing world and the emergence of new players in international relations. It is obvious that our needs have taken us beyond tourist survival as the desired level of language proficiency to be reached. The future will require even greater levels of competence.

Ideally, the U.S. educational system could provide fully competent, professional linguists in adequate numbers to meet our national needs. This would require, however, significant changes in our educational system.[5] To meet national needs, there ideally would be at least a tenfold increase in the number of languages

4. Theodore V. Higgs, ed., *Teaching for Proficiency, the Organizing Principle* (Lincolnwood, IL: National Textbook, 1984).

5. John B. Carroll, *The Teaching of French as a Foreign Language in Eight Countries* (New York: Halsted Press, 1975), p. 275.

taught; creation of 8-year to 10-year instructional sequences, beginning in elementary school and continuing progressively through secondary and higher education; preparation of a pool of qualified teachers large enough to support these increases; and expansion of the current school calendar to provide the time for these added language classes.

A more realistic approach would be to articulate a partnership between the academic community and the government language schools. The education system's responsibility would be to prepare students with the fundamental knowledge, skills, and attitudes necessary for continued linguistic development. Central to this fundamental preparation would be learning any foreign language to a level that allows successful interpersonal interaction to meet real communicative needs. This would not only provide the basis for later refinement of skills in that language but also prepare students linguistically and attitudinally for learning other languages.

Consideration should also be given to reducing our national linguistic isolation by providing a general introduction to world languages and cultures. One of the authors remembers an eighth-grade pre-language course where basic greetings and phrases, common grammatical concepts, and cultural awareness were taught in five languages. This course has had a lasting impact on his personal life and his career. While it is not realistic to expect public schools to provide full programs in all of the world's major languages, they could offer appreciation courses that would include an introduction not only to European languages but to African, Asian, and Middle Eastern languages as well. The objective of such courses would be to get students beyond their initial negative reaction to things foreign and to make them more aware of the vagaries of their first language.

Advances in communication have made the languages of the world accessible through our telephones and satellite dish receivers. The news media bring the sights and sounds of foreign lands into our homes daily. We purchase products that come with instructions in the major languages of the world. Yet, while the motivation and interest in learning other world languages is growing, the system is generally not in place to provide needed foreign language skills to those who must work in an ever shrinking world.

It may be because proficient linguists make communicating in another language look easy that we have not yet recognized the time and effort needed for people to develop high levels of language proficiency. It remains a reality nonetheless that while—just as with musicians and artists—some language students may learn faster than others, even the best students require more time to develop competence in another language than is currently offered in standard instructional sequences. Neither the educational system nor the government agencies that teach foreign languages have sufficient time and resources to accomplish the task alone. Better communication between the educational community and the government agencies, who are this nation's largest employer of personnel with skills in foreign languages, would be the first step toward solving our problems with international communication.

ANNALS, *AAPSS*, 511, September 1990

International Education for Engineers: A Working Model

By HOWARD L. WAKELAND

ABSTRACT: An overview is provided of the need for a portion of science and engineering graduates to have language and cultural backgrounds for international involvement. The nature and educational background of engineering students, which have changed measurably in recent years, are reviewed. The experimental international engineering programs developed in the College of Engineering at the University of Illinois are described. These include active programs in Latin America, Europe, Asia, and the Pacific Rim. A variety of experimental programs has been tried, and experiences from these efforts have provided a basis for establishing future goals and direction.

Howard L. Wakeland serves as the associate dean of the College of Engineering and professor of agricultural engineering at the University of Illinois, Urbana-Champaign. He has served on educational missions to the Pacific Rim, Micronesia, Europe, Africa, Australia, and Latin America. He has been a leader in developing international programs for technical students at his university and in forming an alliance of U.S. universities—the Engineering Alliance for Global Education—to develop international programs for technical students from the entire nation.

WHY should an engineering educator be concerned about establishing international capability in engineering graduates? Primarily because the engineering educator believes that these graduates are an increasingly important manpower resource in maintaining the technical competitiveness of our society and, in turn, our standard of living.

Ten years ago, American employers had virtually no interest in U.S. engineering graduates' having second- and third-language capabilities. We now find them ferreting out such capabilities. Also, for the first time in our history, foreign industry is coming to the United States to hire engineering graduates to work in companies abroad. Global competitiveness has created an increasingly interdependent and international world.

The United States has maintained technical leadership most notably through continued emphasis upon development and research. Our creative competitiveness through research and development is, however, already under challenge from Japanese and European countries. This challenge will increase further with the developing economic alliances such as that of the European Economic Community and others that will follow in Southeast Asia, Micronesia, and Latin America, all of which will provide broader, more stable foundations for their productive and creative capabilities. Senator Paul Simon has said, "You can buy in any language, but you can't sell in any language." The challenge that the United States faces today reaches far beyond sales, however. Increased worldwide competitiveness has challenged and will continue to challenge our productive, creative, and marketing capabilities.

Today's engineering graduate most likely will have some foreign assignment or will be involved with foreign counterparts within the first three years of employment. Further, the number of industrial executives coming from technical backgrounds has increased in recent years, and industry forecasts predict that the percentage will continue to grow. Technical manpower will be sought not only for productive and creative endeavors but more and more for leadership roles as well. We must prepare our engineering students to meet these challenges. This means providing undergraduates opportunities to gain much-valued international experiences and training.

It will be vital for graduates, if placed in these roles, to have more than a technical background. Without knowing the cultures of world markets—including their history, language, and values—they may easily misdirect their efforts. Clearly those best able to improve U.S. competitiveness are those skilled both technically and culturally. Typically, our college graduates are either one or the other. Can we produce graduates with both qualities? Perhaps not in large quantities or with complete backgrounds in each area, but we can produce hybrids—a combination of the two—though this requires more time and effort on the part of the student and the educator.

Engineering schools can find inventive ways to add nontechnical courses to a crowded curriculum and to fund programs that involve overseas experiences. If international training is to have a larger role in engineering education, it must start at the earliest possible level, reach more students, and deal with a broader selection of languages and cultures.

Teachers of language and culture are needed by the technical community now more than ever before. The reverse is also true. The technical community can bring to the linguists' and culturalists' classrooms the very brightest of our students, who will be future leaders in our societies—local, national, and global.

THE ENGINEERING STUDENT

Currently, engineering schools in the United States are attracting more than their share of freshmen enrollees in both number and quality. It is a time when many of our brighter youths see the future in technology and pursue engineering, physics, chemistry, or other math- or science-based fields. The vast majority of these students, however, come from what has typically been known as the college preparatory spectrum in our high schools. Not only do they have strong math and science backgrounds, but the vast majority also have had strong language preparatory course work. At the University of Illinois at Urbana-Champaign (UIUC), for example, about one-third of the entering freshmen in the College of Engineering have had four or more years of foreign language in high school, and 90 percent or more have had two or more years.

Engineering schools are also receiving more than their share of first-generation immigrants, particularly from Asian and Hispanic cultures. These students are both bright and accomplished, and they have strong language capabilities in their native or near-native tongues.

Engineering colleges have been pleased to enroll these students and have had a high regard for their high school or native language background. Nevertheless, we typically have not encouraged the students to continue language studies in engineering schools. Engineering students represent a great reservoir of language training that has essentially been truncated as they enter college.

Though the freshmen entering engineering at UIUC have a strong language base, the languages of preparation are heavily biased toward the Western European languages—German, studied by 17 percent of the freshmen; French, 24 percent; Latin, 7 percent; and Spanish, 40 percent—with little exposure to other languages. Fifteen years ago we had more than 10 percent of our freshmen presenting Russian as a high school language, but that has now dwindled to approximately one-tenth of 1 percent. We should encourage students to continue in the Western European languages, but we should also make a major effort to move some of them into other languages—Chinese, Russian, Japanese, and Hindi, for example.

Engineering students in most other leading U.S. institutions will have nearly the same academic profile and interests as those at UIUC.

Thus UIUC is representative of trends and developments that are likely to be found in many leading U.S. engineering institutions.

PROGRAM DEVELOPMENT

A number of innovative initiatives have been made in the College of Engineering at UIUC to develop international capabilities in some of our students. To the extent possible, use has been made of regularly offered language and cultural courses and exchange programs serving primarily liberal arts students. These offerings tend to emphasize European studies and Western European languages with far fewer opportunities available for experiences in the developing world. Though other initiatives described herein have been successful, the major portion of our internationally oriented course work and exchanges are still gained through the regularly offered liberal arts programs.

Three developments within the College have had a major impact on our international programs: the development of an international minor in engineering, a special fund to support undergraduate international experiences—the Elmendorf Travel Award—and the greater use of work-experience programs.

International minor

The UIUC College of Engineering has developed an international minor in which courses in the language, history, economics, and politics of a non-English-speaking country or region are combined with regular engineering studies. The program allows students to obtain an international minor in Asian studies, European studies, Chinese studies, and so on as a part of their mechanical, electrical, or other engineering degree. Engineering accreditation policies require college engineering programs to have at least one-half year of studies in the social sciences and humanities, and the policies thereby serve as a base for the development of an international minor.

The international minor at UIUC requires that a student complete at least the equivalent of two years at college-level foreign language study in the chosen country or region and at least nine semester hours—three in advanced course work—of culture and political science and/or economics course work related to his or her chosen minor field. Additionally, the student must spend at least eight weeks working or studying in the chosen region or country. In recognition of the completion of these requirements, the international minor, with identification of the geographical region, is recorded on the student's transcript, for use in gaining employment or in the continuation of his or her education.

Elmendorf Travel Award

The College of Engineering received a small donation from an alumnus, Armin Elmendorf, to start a student travel fund for international experiences. Other sources now provide these funds. A travel grant is awarded to any engineering student who undertakes overseas educational or work experience. Grants vary from $250 for students studying in the United Kingdom to $1000 for those going to Pacific Rim countries. Last year the College awarded 85 such travel grants to its students. These grants help students offset the anticipated loss of income from summer jobs, encouraging students to make the financial sacrifice necessary for overseas experiences. UIUC students usually receive some academic credit for a portion of their overseas experiences—other than work experience—and this increases their willingness. The results of the availability of such funding have been very positive; despite the costs, UIUC now has more potential participants than places to send them.

Work experience

Since 1970 UIUC has worked closely with the International Association for the Exchange of Students for Technical Experience (IAESTE), one of the programs of the Association for International Practical Training. Through our association with IAESTE, UIUC has placed more than 350 students in practical training positions throughout the world.

Typically, IAESTE places technical students in internship-type employment positions overseas. These are most often summer jobs, lasting 8-12 weeks, but positions are available for up to 12 months of experience. During this period the students receive, from their employers, maintenance wages and assistance in locating housing.

Technical students achieve great improvement in language and cultural skills and a better technical understanding through these experiences abroad. Recognition of this has caused us to develop programs that combine academic and work experience.

These three developments—the international minor, the Elmendorf Travel Award, and work experience—have served as guides in the development of our programs. A fourth concern, financial support, is a continuing one, and we are now seeking innovative ways to increase support.

ENGINEERING PROGRAM OFFERINGS

In our commitment to the international preparation of our engineering students, the College has, in the past 10 years, placed over 800 students in practical work or study experiences throughout the world. The program emphasizes undergraduate involvement and focuses upon conversational language ability as a primary goal. Engineering students may now choose from a smorgasbord of programs taking them to Latin America, Europe, Asia, or the Pacific Rim. Currently, 4 percent of UIUC engineering students are involved in international programs, and the immediate goal is to raise the level to 10 percent.

Our experiences have led us to believe that international programs for engineering students should

- emphasize conversational capability in a second or third language;

- offer cultural course work paralleling the language study;
- expose the student to foreign cultures through on-site study or work experience; and
- expose the student to the foreign technical community, also through on-site study or work experience.

With these principles in mind the college has developed the following range of opportunities for its students.

Europe

Study opportunities and work experiences in Europe have been well developed primarily by liberal arts educators. This wide variety of opportunities also serves technical students adequately in many cases. In some instances, though, technical students find they pay a lot, in money and time, to lose a year's worth of schooling. UIUC engineering students participate every year in standard liberal arts programs of this and other institutions that involve them in nearly every European country.

Separate from these liberal arts programs the College has developed exchange study programs of a technical nature with three technical schools in France, two in Germany, and one in Portugal.

Typically, the U.S. engineering student is behind the French student in theoretical mathematics but ahead in application-related subjects. Also, few of our students are really proficient in the French language. We have found that we need to prepare students better for the leading French technical institutions. Specifically, our students need stronger theoretical mathematics backgrounds and greater proficiency in French.

The transition to German schools is more moderate, and our students make the transition more easily. In a majority of cases, the students will complete an intensive German course such as those offered by the Goethe Institute prior to the academic year abroad. Through a variety of programs, more than 50 UIUC engineering students are involved in Europe each year.

China

In 1986, the University initiated targeted area programs in Asia and Latin America. The term "targeted area" was descriptive of our efforts to develop some type of a program in a given geographical region. Targeted area programs require students to spend one-half of each day in practical work experience at the foreign location. Typically, students work for a consulting engineering firm, a power company, university research labs, or a manufacturing plant. The other half of the day is spent in language instruction. The assignments are arranged by the foreign sister institution. We, in turn, provide an opportunity for our sister institution's faculty to study at UIUC with financial support.

An agreement with universities in the People's Republic of China trades a slot for one Chinese graduate student—with assistantship support—at UIUC for summer opportunities —including room, board, and tuition— for five American undergraduates.

This financially innovative technique allows our students to study and work in countries short of hard currencies. Since 1986, we have had 86 UIUC students spend the summer in China in this type of program. The program was canceled in 1990 for political reasons but will resume in 1991.

UIUC students participating in this program are not required to have any previous language training. They are, however, required to complete a five-semester-hour, intensive Chinese-language course, stressing speaking ability, during the spring semester before the summer trip to China. While in China, they continue with Chinese-language study half days for eight weeks and gain daily exposure to Chinese society through concurrent half-day experience in Chinese industries or research labs. Students then spend two additional weeks traveling in China.

The design of the program seeks to gain a 30-40 percent fluency level in conversational Chinese and enough background for growth in the future should the student be involved in further Chinese interactions. The design also includes introductory cultural course work and on-site experience.

Colombia and Argentina

In 1987, UIUC targeted Colombia as the location for its first Latin American program. Twenty-seven students have since participated in a Spanish-language program at the University of the Andes in Bogotá. The Colombian program is similar to the Chinese program; it places stu-

dents in engineering work experience half days for eight summer weeks followed by travel in South America. Participation is limited to students with four years of high school Spanish or the equivalent, and they must complete a five-semester-hour, intensive Spanish course prior to the summer in Bogotá. Students completing this program achieve excellent Spanish capability. The Colombian program was also canceled in 1990 for political reasons; we hope it will resume in 1991.

Realizing that Colombia may be politically unstable for several years, we expanded the Latin American program to Argentina for 1990. A program similar to the University of the Andes program was initiated with the University of Belgrano, Buenos Aires, Argentina, for the summer of 1990. Upon reestablishment of political stability in Colombia we intend to continue both programs.

Brazil

In the summer of 1989, a program was initiated in Recife, Brazil, for UIUC students. Limited to students with four years of high school Spanish or the equivalent, it is open to engineering and science students from other U.S. universities. The eight-week program emphasizes work experience in addition to Portuguese-language training at the University of Pernambuco in Recife. UIUC students were also asked to complete a "Portuguese for Spanish Speakers" class on the UIUC campus in the spring semester prior to their summer involvement.

Australia

Exchange agreements have been made with three Australian institutions: the University of Sydney, the University of Melbourne, and the University of New South Wales. Initially, six to eight students will be exchanged each year starting in 1990. It is a one-semester program emphasizing engineering, science, and/or liberal arts courses and is open to engineering and science students from other universities.

Japan

Programs for our students interested in Japan have proven to be especially difficult. Introductory and intermediate Japanese is taught in a four-course sequence of five semester hours each, a program that has proven too demanding for engineering students, who typically must balance language study with the other requirements in a very full curriculum. The engineers performed in Japanese-language courses as well as the other students did but opted out as the course work became increasingly demanding on their time. Of those engineers starting the first-level Japanese course, one-half advance to the second course, one-fourth ultimately to the third course, and one-eighth to the fourth course. Though there is great interest on the part of engineering students, the demands are such that nearly 90 percent drop out after the first, second, or third course.

We have also had difficulty in arranging work experience with Japanese employers.

We are now developing a second sequence of Japanese courses for technical students. It requires an intensive 10-semester-hour summer course after the freshman year to be followed by four 3-semester-hour courses in hopes of retaining more students. Summer internships in Japan will also be a feature of the program. This language sequence will be further augmented with three additional cultural courses. The program will have its first group of students in the spring of 1991. The initial target is to graduate 20 students from this program each year.

UIUC has an excellent program with Konon University, and a few technical students have participated in it. The requirement of a full year in Japan and its attendant expense have discouraged more students from participating. Those that have participated have achieved very good Japanese language and cultural levels.

Russia

A new summer program is being initiated with the Siberian Institute of Terrestrial Magnetism, Ionosphere, and Radio Wave Propagation, part of the USSR Academy of Sciences in Irkutsk, Russia, in 1990. The first group of six students will have mixed Russian-language preparation—from poor to very good. The program model will be similar to those in China and in Colombia, namely, a Russian course at UIUC during the spring semester followed with an 8- to 10-week stay in Russia that includes language instruction half of the time and work experience the other half, followed with a 2-week travel period.

PROGRAM OBSERVATION

As mentioned earlier, many of the needs for technical students can be met through standard liberal arts study and exchange programs. There are, though, many students who will never be involved in or meet their goals through these programs. Following are some observations that have been made in designing UIUC programs for technical students.

Based on our experience at UIUC, the following concerns should be considered in designing international programs for technical students.

1. Foreign languages are the heart of international understanding. A sense of cultural values, history, traditions, geography, and the like are important, but the ability to communicate is vital. If a choice must be made between cultural and language courses, for the technical student, it should be made in favor of language.

2. Some language capability is better than none. One may occasionally hear, "It's better to speak no Japanese than to speak poor Japanese." This is nonsense. Native speakers of Japanese and other languages may be sensitive on some points concerning their languages, but the poor foreign speaker will always receive greater acceptance and understanding than the nonspeaker.

3. Consistent with this concept and realizing that technical students are loaded with course work, it may be desirable to design a program to

achieve 40-50 percent language proficiency. If the student is later placed in a full language environment, he or she will have the basics necessary to achieve full proficiency.

4. Based on experiences at UIUC, I believe that it is more important for technical students to gain conversational ability than written ability. It is more important to have general conversational ability than technical language ability in most cases, the exception being primarily in the research and advanced technical areas. The foundation for written capability must, obviously, be put in place, and it will have potential for improvement if the conversational ability has been developed.

5. Most engineering students are capable of language studies and are more often discouraged by course load than by course difficulty. For example, a five-semester-hour course requires major daily commitment, whereas a three-semester-hour course provides some breathing space. Retention for our students will be greater in three-hour sequences.

6. Typically, freshman and sophomore summers are McDonald's-restaurant-and-grass-mowing employment periods. It is during these periods, when the technical students' summer earning capabilities are low, that we must start intensive beginning language study.

7. Technical students are willing to take summer courses, hours beyond degree requirements, and semester-long internships if they are convinced of the value of the experiences. They are seeking an education for the future.

As the quality of entering freshmen in technical studies has increased dramatically in the past twenty years, the family economic level from which they come has also increased dramatically. Most now come from middle- and upper-income families. Many can now afford summer studies and offshore travel.

Encouraging students can make vast differences. Each year the dean writes all entering freshmen encouraging them to continue studying the foreign language that they started in high school or to start a new language. As a result of the first letter ever sent, the enrollments increased fourfold in German courses, from 20 to 80 students, and from 10 to 75 in Japanese.

THE FUTURE

Currently the College of Engineering envisions that 10 percent of its students—140 graduates per year—will have backgrounds for international involvement, primarily through the international minor. Many more will have language capability. Approximately 20 percent of our graduates have college-level course work that provides them with second-language fluency or near fluency.

The College has implemented a new three-year high school language requirement for admission in order to further strengthen students' language backgrounds. We hope that in the near future 50 percent of our graduates will have second-language fluency. The major portion of these capabilities now lie in the Western European languages, and heavy emphasis must be placed on non-Western European languages, such as Japanese, Chinese, and Hindi.

The overseas work experiences and the combination of work experience and educational experience have been highly successful and will be expanded. Efforts will be made to provide greater financial assistance for students in overseas experiences.

The College has benefited greatly from a strong liberal arts faculty, including language faculty, and an international studies office that has had the interest and willingness to work with technical students and to provide innovative courses and programs. There is also a recognition that the importance of language and cultural studies has never been greater for technical students. If language and cultural faculties seize the opportunities, they will bring to their classroom some of the brightest, most dedicated students preparing for industrial, society, and world leadership roles.

International competitiveness requires cultural awareness, international experience, and language skills. We are attempting to integrate international capabilities into undergraduate engineering curricula. U.S. engineering colleges now attract many of the nation's most capable high school graduates. We provide them with excellent technical training, but technical training alone is not enough. In this age of global technical competitiveness, engineering educators owe it to their students, and to the nation, to help them become not only good engineers but also potential world leaders.

ANNALS, *AAPSS*, 511, September 1990

The Translation Profession in the United States Today

By DEANNA LINDBERG HAMMOND

ABSTRACT: Translators represent a small part of the population, yet their services are in high demand. Working with the printed word, they can be found in the service of government, industry, and science. Recently requirements for entry into the profession have become exacting, with an in-depth knowledge of technical subject matter often the key to success. Modern technology has changed the life of translators, since sophisticated equipment makes their task less laborious and at the same time allows them a geographical freedom they never had in the past. Whereas traditionally many entering the translation profession did so by chance, the new generation of translators will come in large part from American universities. Although foreign language programs do not as a rule provide the necessary competency in written skills, some U.S. universities now offer well-established translator- and interpreter-training programs. As the need for translators continues to grow, it is to be hoped that the U.S. education system will be able to respond effectively.

Deanna Lindberg Hammond is president of the American Translators Association. She holds a Ph.D. in Spanish linguistics from Georgetown University, an M.A. in teaching English as a second language from Ohio University, and a B.A. in history from Washington State University. A Spanish teacher for many years at the high school and university levels, since 1977 she has been the head of the section of the Congressional Research Service that provides translations for the U.S. Congress.

TRANSLATING is not a new profession. It is at least as old as literature itself. Through the work of translators, cultures have been spread beyond their borders. As small children, many of us enjoyed the characters of Hans Christian Andersen, the tale of Hansel and Gretel, the story of Heidi, and numerous other memorable works written in another language and brought to this country in translated form. Later, in school, we learned of great scientific discoveries and voyages, of inventions and philosophies, many of which became known to us through translations. Certainly the Bible, laboriously translated into countless languages, represents one of the greatest achievements of translators. On today's ever shrinking planet, ways of thinking and scientific advances are crossing borders at an unprecedented rate, via satellite, telefax, television, newspaper, and other means, in large part thanks to translators. It is no wonder that translators have been called builders of bridges between nations in the name of rapprochement and friendship.[1] Nevertheless, translators, particularly those of nonliterary works, rarely become well known to the public. They tend to be the people behind the scenes who relay the ideas of others. Their profession is often misunderstood or neglected, in spite of the rising demand and pressing need for their services.

PUBLIC PERCEPTION OF THE TRANSLATOR

A translator renders materials in one language into written form in another, whereas an interpreter works with spoken communication. Few professionals do both, as the skills required are quite different. In the mind of the general public, however, the two terms are often used interchangeably. Television networks help to perpetuate the confusion every time they show interpreters speaking for foreign dignitaries and flash the words "voice of the translator" on the screen. Whenever I tell someone I am a translator, the inevitable response is, "Oh, how many languages do you speak?" A German colleague has noted that when he says that he works in two languages, it is not uncommon to see the disappointment of persons who respond, "What? Only two languages?" Then, either "I always wanted to learn languages myself," as if that would automatically have made them good translators, or "I was never cut out for foreign languages," as if some ethnic blessing beyond our sphere of influence were to blame.[2] To make matters worse, those enlightened citizens who know that interpreters speak and translators write often tend to envision the two as stereotypes. They think of the glamorous life of interpreters, meeting heads of state and

1. Victor Borissov, "Literature Brings People Together," in *La traduction et la coopération culturelle internationale: Colloque international* (Sofia: International Federation of Translators, 1979), p. 143.

2. Manfred Schmitz, "Statutory Regulation of the Practice of the Profession and the Use of the Title 'Translator/Interpreter,' " in *Translation, Our Future: Proceedings of the XIth World Congress of FIT*, ed. Paul Nekeman (Maastricht, The Netherlands: Euroterm, 1988), p. 272.

traveling around the world, and of the solitary life of those eccentric translators, who work by themselves and avoid human company. Even those who hire translators often fail to appreciate what is involved in the job. All too often a client who briefly studied a foreign language assures the translator, "I'd do it myself but I don't have the time." Nevertheless, misunderstood though translators may be, they are finding an unprecedented demand for their services and recognition of their contributions.

HISTORICAL IMPORTANCE OF SCIENTIFIC AND TECHNICAL TRANSLATIONS

Although literary translation is a very important and perhaps more recognized sector of the profession, the vast majority of translators work with semitechnical and technical texts. Translation has long played a major role in the dissemination of scientific information, particularly since the invention of movable type around 1500. It is in the last 100 years, however, that the full force of translation has been brought to bear on the transfer of scientific knowledge. Since then science has become more dependent than ever on the translator for its dissemination and development.[3]

In the United States a pressing need for translations came about shortly after World War II, with the release to the public of German research reports containing a wealth of

scientific information.[4] The only problem for Americans was that the documents were written in German. Consequently, the government and private sector had large numbers of the reports translated, often calling upon immigrants who possessed translation skills not found among the general American populace. A few years later, with the launching of *Sputnik* in 1957, a flurry of requests for translations of Russian documents ensued.

In spite of such complications, however, in the postwar years American exports and technology flourished without much assistance from translators, since English had emerged as an international language. Americans expected the world to know English. Today the situation is dramatically different.

DEMAND FOR TRANSLATIONS TODAY

Everyone is aware of the unprecedented increase in contacts between nations in the past few decades. With foreign travel more common and with increased communications through satellites and other products of modern technology, it has become easier and faster to learn about what is happening outside our borders. The exchange of ideas and printed matter between different linguistic communities has meant an unprecedented amount of translation. In the last

3. Henry Fischbach, "Translation, the Great Pollinator of Early Medicine—A Historical Flashback," in *Translation, Our Future,* ed. Nekeman, p. 362.

4. Ildiko Nowak, "World Scientific and Technical Literature and the NTC," in *Across the Language Gap: Proceedings of the 28th Annual Conference of the American Translators Association,* ed. Karl Kummer (Medford, NJ: Learned Information, 1987), p. 18.

several decades the need for translations has continued to rise until it is estimated that the global marketplace now reaches approximately $20 billion a year.[5] Much of the translating reflects the needs of businesses with offices or marketing efforts overseas and the needs of the scientific, industrial, and research community, although translations are by no means limited in these areas.

TRANSLATION FOR BUSINESS NEEDS

Foreign trade and international business have become an important part of the American economy. One-third of all corporations in the United States are either owned or based abroad; more than 6000 companies have at least some of their operations abroad; one of every six production jobs in the United States depends on foreign trade; more than 5 million current jobs in the United States rely on imports and exports; four of every five jobs are generated as a result of foreign trade.[6]

Yet America's position in the world economy is one of deficit. One reason often given is the inability of Americans to understand the culture and language of the nations for whom U.S. products are intended. In order to remedy that situation, more and more companies have turned to translators to render advertisements into the language of the client. Although anecdotes on mistranslations

of advertising materials abound, in reality successful marketing efforts are being carried out around the globe. One U.S. soft-drink company now has different advertisements prepared for each country of Latin America, each presentation adapted to the particular Spanish and culture. A colleague of mine translated an ad into Chinese. When pronounced, the words he chose sounded something like "coca cora," but with characters saying, "make man mouth happy." Such creativity is especially important in the translation of advertisements for the business community.

In what the *Wall Street Journal* has called an "explosion in demand for business and technical translation,"[7] American companies are also calling on translators to provide them with information that will enable them to find out what their competitors are doing to improve their products. With the rise of the multinational corporation, a company may also depend on translators to facilitate communications with its subsidiaries. Company publications, such as employee manuals, safety regulations, and company policy, are often written at headquarters and then translated, facilitating coordination and saving an unnecessary duplication of effort. Information on research or marketing efforts within the company must be provided to foreign subsidiaries in order to promote the technological advancement of the firm as a whole. And, needless to say,

5. *Machine Translation of Natural Languages, the TOVNA MTS Solution* (Washington, DC: TOVNA Translation Machines, 1989), p. 2.

6. Mary Conroy, "Foreign Languages: Critical Skills for Your Child's Future," *Better Homes and Gardens*, May 1988, p. 64.

7. Christian Hill, "Language for Profit: More Firms Turn to Translation Experts to Avoid Costly, Embarrassing Mistakes," *Wall Street Journal*, 13 Jan. 1987.

the countless letters, telegrams, and telefaxes sent from one subsidiary to another must be translated.

A sign of the important link between translators and export firms is the noticeable increase in contact between translators and international trade groups. In 1989, on the occasion of an international trade symposium cosponsored by the Mid-America Chapter of the American Translators Association and the International Trade Association, the governor of Missouri and the mayor of Kansas City proclaimed 21-28 August Translators' Week in order to recognize the vital role of translators in successful international trade efforts. Other cities and states are likely to follow suit.

TRANSLATION FOR SCIENTIFIC AND RESEARCH NEEDS

In the not-too-distant past, U.S. researchers and scientists generally felt that anything worth reading would automatically appear in English. That attitude has all but vanished. Advanced technologies, including data bases, have made scientists more aware than ever of the vast amount of material being produced outside the United States. Currently one-fourth to one-half of all scientific scholarly production is in languages not handled by U.S. scientists, and only about 20 percent of the 10,000 technical journals published annually in Japan are translated into English.[8] Not only has the percentage of technical journals published in En-

glish declined, but many new ones are written in languages that have not traditionally received much attention in the United States, such as Japanese, Russian, Portuguese, and Chinese.[9] In other words, even those researchers who may be able to understand documents written in German, French, or other more commonly studied languages find themselves relying on translations more than ever.

In science and technology, as in world trade, the United States has lost its unquestioned leadership. The fact is that other countries are outspending the United States with respect to research. For example, in 1985 Japan outspent the United States on nondefense research, which consumed 2.6 percent of the Japanese total economic output as compared to 1.9 percent of the U.S. total economic output; furthermore, whereas Japan quadrupled its research expenditures between 1965 and 1985, spending on research in the United States increased during the same period by less than 50 percent.[10] As a result, in 1981 Japan put more new drugs on the market than any country, and it has now taken the lead in biotechnology.[11] This means

8. Suzanne Fedunok, "Translations in Science and Technology Libraries," in *Across the Language Gap*, ed. Kummer, p. 455.

9. Karl-Heinz Brinkmann, "The TEAM Multilingual Terminology Bank," *Technical Communication*, 29:4, 6-7 (1982).

10. Tomoyuki Satoh, "The Evolution of the Japanese Technical Information Service: Reversing the Flow of Information—Japan to the U.S.," in *Across the Language Gap*, ed. Kummer, p. 135.

11. Josephine B. Howe, "Translating Japanese in the Field of Pharmaceuticals: The Japanese and U.S. Pharmaceutical Industries' Changing Translation Needs," in *Across the Language Gap*, ed. Kummer, p. 153.

translators are needed so that Americans can reap the benefits of breakthroughs taking place overseas.

Translation of patents has become a big business due to the increased proportion of patents being granted to individuals and firms from other countries. Nearly 50 percent of the U.S. patents granted in 1986 were to non-U.S. residents, and, among these, Japanese companies received the most, about 14,000, or 40 percent, which was greater than those of the West German, British, and French companies combined.[12] Among the top U.S. patent recipients, including giants like General Electric and IBM, four were Japanese companies.[13] Through patents, researchers can evaluate the state of the art, predict trends and tendencies, and learn who their competitors or prospective clients are. Thanks to data bases, information is available on patent applications pending in such countries as the Federal Republic of Germany and Japan, allowing firms timely access, with the assistance of translators, to information that was once limited to patents approved long after the filing of the applications.

To anyone observing the international marketplace, it should be no surprise that a language in growing demand in translations for industry is Japanese. At firms such as Dupont, the number of translation requests by researchers has been on the rise for all languages, but, whereas in the past the largest number of requests was for translation of German docu-

ments, it is now for Japanese.[14] Japanese advances have not gone unnoticed by the U.S. government. In 1987, the U.S. Congress, aware of the importance to the public and private sectors of Japanese materials, passed the Japanese Technical Literature Act in order to ensure the prompt translation of important technical documents from Japanese to English. Although a team of experts has been meeting regularly through the auspices of the Department of Commerce in order to implement the act, funding is still pending. Furthermore, to help meet the need for technical translations, particularly from Japanese, the U.S. government is showing interest in machine translation. Prompted by the growing commercial implications of Japanese technology and the awareness that Japan is heavily committed to the development of machine translation, the National Research Council's Office of Japan Affairs held a one-day symposium on Japanese-to-English machine translation at the National Academy of Sciences in Washington, DC, in December 1989.

TRANSLATION FOR OTHER NEEDS

Translation services are listed in the Yellow Pages of the telephone directories of virtually every American city. Clients vary widely. Persons seeking U.S. citizenship may have to have their birth and marriage certif-

12. Tsuneichi Takeshita, "Japanese Translation in the Field of Polymer Chemistry," in *Across the Language Gap,* ed. Kummer, p. 135.
13. Ibid.

14. Alexander Shkolnik, "Some Advice on Translation of Patent Specifications," in *Building Bridges: Proceedings of the 27th Annual Conference of the American Translators Association,* ed. Karl Kummer (Medford, NJ: Learned Information, 1986), p. 241.

icates and other relevant documentation put into English. People seeking to know more about their roots may have old documents translated. Scholarly papers to be presented abroad may require translation. In bilingual cities and states, information on the area, ballots, driver's licenses, and a variety of other materials are translated into other languages, especially Spanish. Spanish is also becoming very important for advertising in the United States. For example, in 1982 Coca-Cola spent $166 million on advertising aimed at Hispanics, and by 1984 the amount had jumped to $228 million.[15]

GROWTH OF THE TRANSLATION PROFESSION

Not surprisingly, the number of translators worldwide has increased considerably in recent years. Generally speaking, the social position and payment levels have risen. In addition, a sense of professionalism has become evident. In many countries, translators have formed professional associations, such as the American Translators Association (ATA). Founded thirty years ago by a handful of translators, ATA's membership is now over 3000. ATA is a member of the International Federation of Translators (FIT), which has about fifty member societies around the globe. FIT hosts international congresses every three years, the next one to be held in 1990 in Belgrade, Yugoslavia. A Regional Center for North America, under the auspices of FIT, also offers congresses every three years for translators and interpreters of Canada, the United States, and Mexico. ATA has many well-established committees, such as Accreditation, Continuing Education, Client Education, Ethics, Interpretation, Rates Guidelines, Terminology, Translation Studies, and Dictionary Review. Within the association are Scientific-Technical, Literary, and Japanese Language divisions, all of which produce their own informative publications. ATA chapters throughout the United States also hold regular meetings and workshops. All of the committee work, the annual conference, and ATA publications are intended to increase the professionalism and competence of the translator. The same can be said for other associations founded for translators and interpreters in recent years, such as the American Literary Translators Association, the National Association of Judiciary Interpreters and Translators, and The American Association of Language Specialists.

TRANSLATORS AND LINGUISTS

All translators are linguists, but few linguists are translators. In the U.S. government, of the more than 40,000 linguists using foreign languages in the performance of their duties, only a few hundred are classified as translators.[16] For example, hundreds of Library of Congress staff members use foreign language skills

15. Irma Herrera, "U.S. Advertisers Talking Hispanics' Language: Nation's Fastest-Expanding Market Is Courted in Its Native Tongue," *Washington Post*, 28 Aug. 1985.

16. Deanna Lindberg Hammond, "Washington Notes: Foreign Language Careers at the Library of Congress," *Modern Language Journal*, 65:387 (Winter 1981).

regularly in their work as area specialists, foreign analysts, foreign law experts, catalogers, reference librarians, copyright specialists, and researchers, but they do not provide a word-for-word translation for someone else's use. That is the task of the translator. By any estimate, the number of translators is very small in comparison to other better-known professions. The U.S. Census Bureau and the Department of Labor Statistics have no category for translators, claiming in fact that there are too few to be statistically significant.[17] No accurate count has been made of translators in the United States today, in part because many persons translate part-time or sporadically. Nevertheless, the number of translators is increasing and is certainly in the thousands.

CLASSIFICATIONS OF TRANSLATORS AND SOURCES OF EMPLOYMENT

Translators generally work as either in-house or free-lance translators. Most are free-lance translators, who either find their own clients or translate for firms or translation bureaus, for which they are generally paid according to the length and difficulty of the translation. Fees may also reflect supply and demand for a given language and subject. Many free-lance translators rely on translation as their only source of income, while others translate on a part-time basis. Free-lance translators have

the advantage of being able to work at home and generally set their own hours. They can limit themselves to one foreign language and can live virtually anywhere, thanks to advances such as electronic mail, the fax machine, and the modem.

Salaried translators are part of the in-house staff of a number of agencies, firms, and institutions. They are commonly found when the company or institution has enough of a need for translations on a regular basis to justify full-time staff. For the vast majority of such translators, specific areas of subject-matter expertise, such as chemistry, economics, engineering, and patents, are a must. In-house translators are paid a regular salary unrelated to the number of pages they translate or their languages of expertise. Unlike the freelancer, they receive insurance, vacation, retirement, and other benefits. They may be called upon to do foreign language research, oral translations for staff, and other language-related duties since they are readily available on-site. In-house translators may need to translate from several foreign languages. For example, translator positions in the U.S. government require the ability to translate from at least two foreign languages, and World Bank applicants must know three. Full-time positions are quite limited in comparison to opportunities for contract work.

Other translators own agencies or provide translations for agencies. Translation agencies can be found in most major cities. An increasing number of translators, both literary translators and scientific and technical translators, are also university

17. Patricia Newman, "Profile of the American Translator," in *Languages at Crossroads: Proceedings of the 29th Annual Conference of the American Translators Association,* ed. Deanna Lindberg Hammond (Medford, NJ: Learned Information, 1988), p. 5.

professors of translation and foreign languages.

The leading employers of translators are the U.S. government; U.S. and foreign multinational corporations and their subsidiaries; U.S. importers and exporters; commercial and nonprofit research institutions; pharmaceutical, chemical, machinery, and other manufacturers not covered by the foregoing; engineering and construction firms with foreign connections; patent attorneys; the publishing industry; the news media; municipal governments in bilingual U.S. cities; graduate schools of U.S. universities; the United Nations and other international organizations; and foreign, diplomatic, commercial, scientific, and other representatives in the United States.[18]

QUALIFICATIONS OF A COMPETENT TRANSLATOR

Although the belief persists that all that is needed to translate is a speaking knowledge of a foreign language, such is not the case. Being bilingual does not make one a translator. In fact, speaking the language is not even relevant compared to literacy and the possession of the other necessary skills.

Translators need to understand the language from which they are translating and to be able to write well in the one into which they are rendering the translation, which is normally their native language. This

18. American Translators Association, "Profile of a Competent Translator and an Effective Translator Training Program" (Manuscript, American Translators Association, 1987).

means an understanding of nuances, regional terms, and subject-specific terminology as well as an awareness of style and grammar. One of my greatest frustrations in teaching Spanish-to-English translation at the university level was the inability of many students, as fluent as their oral skills might have been, to write clear and proper English.

Translators also need to understand the technical areas in which they are working. They are often expected to possess an in-depth knowledge of highly specialized subjects. Subject matter is becoming so important, in fact, that the European Economic Community has recently changed its language-specific translation divisions into subject-matter ones. For example, the English Division no longer exists as such. Translators who work with economic, legal, and marketing terminology, regardless of the language into which they are translating, are now placed in the same division.

Translators must keep up to date with respect to terminology. For technical vocabulary, they should frequently consult articles published on the given subject matter, maintain access to new glossaries, and have contacts with experts in the given fields. For more commonly used words and idiomatic expressions, translators need to be equally diligent in their choice of reading materials, as expressions tend to enter the language rather quickly. When I returned to the United States after just two years in the Peace Corps, I could not for the life of me understand what people meant when they referred to someone's "hang-up." Although it would be years before the term appeared in a dictionary, reading American newspapers, including the comic strips, helped update my vocabulary very quickly.

Translators must be able to look at a text for meaning and not necessarily translate literally. For example, in my office we once had a request for a translation of "Where's the beef?" into 11 languages. That phrase, translated literally, would not only have been meaningless in many cultures but misunderstood in countries such as India, where much of the Hindu population does not eat meat. The sensitivity and creativity often required of the translator are not easily taught.

Translators, particularly those doing free-lance work, must have access to a personal computer, word-processing equipment, a fax machine, and a modem. While this equipment may require a considerable initial investment, translators receive many benefits in return. The days of typing and retyping manuscripts are a thing of the past, allowing more efficient and productive use of time. With access to terminological data bases and the rapidly increasing use of computer-assisted translation, the future promises even more tools for translators.

The qualifications that translators must meet cannot be overemphasized. Foreign language graduates with what is described as no other skills come to our doors all too often to say they want to be translators. One applicant who came to my office had majored in Russian, with hopes of entering the Foreign Service.

When he failed the English examination, he decided he should become a translator. The unfortunate part is that a number of such unqualified people do enter the profession every year. Some may actually succeed, since the client is often unable to judge the quality of the translation rendered. The passage rate of just 40 percent on the ATA accreditation examination is one indication that not all translators are sufficiently qualified. It is to be hoped that as the profession is recognized and understood to a greater extent, unqualified persons will be discouraged from entering it.

THE AMERICAN TRANSLATOR TODAY

In 1987 ATA undertook a survey, with a response rate of over 50 percent of its membership. Results of that survey indicated the following:

1. Whereas only 6.2 percent of the U.S. population is foreign-born, 49 percent of the members were born outside the United States, with Germany as the most frequently listed place of birth, followed by France, Argentina, Cuba, and Japan.

2. Among the American-born respondents, over 50 percent have been abroad for more than one year and 17 percent for more than five years.

3. Over half have reached the master's degree or doctoral level, and 91 percent have completed four or more years of college, considerably higher than the average for the general population.

4. One of every four scientific or technical translators has a formal education in science or engineering.

5. English is the language most cited as the language into which they translate, followed by Spanish, French, and German.[19]

Many translators who joined the profession in the last couple of decades were American-born persons who wanted to do something besides teach languages and who fell into translation without any prior training or experience. Today, a significant number of those entering the profession have received formal training in translation studies.

TRAINING TO BECOME A TRANSLATOR

In response to a multitude of needs of today's world, foreign language enrollments have been increasing in high schools, colleges, and universities. Translation courses are part of the curriculum of a number of universities, whether as separate classes or part of certificate or degree programs. The first courses in the relatively new field of translation study date back just a few decades. Although it appeared in the mid-1980s that the number of institutions offering courses or programs in translation was increasing, such may no longer be the case. In a 1986 ATA survey, 240 institutions claimed to have some type of program in translator training.[20] In 1989, questionnaires were sent to those 240 schools and 35 additional ones; results

showed that some programs had been dropped altogether, and it was only possible to verify translation courses in about 80 universities.[21] The institutions that have been the leaders in establishing translator- and interpreter-training programs still have high enrollments and are greatly respected in the field. Other schools are in the process of establishing carefully worked-out degree programs in translation, but, for the most part, translation courses are part of the offerings of foreign language departments. As Krawutschke has noted, a discipline such as translation, which takes from and builds on other disciplines, may require a generation of scholars before becoming firmly established.[22] It would appear that many of the introductory courses in translation are taught by professors of literature who may or may not have had any substantial experience translating.

Where translation classes have emerged, they may have replaced literature courses that were faced with declining enrollment, as many students have learned that a literature major is not the most marketable degree outside the field of education but that an additional skill such as translation is. This is particularly the case when the student combines foreign language studies with a major in an-

19. Patricia E. Newman, "Profile of the American Translator," p. 4.

20. American Translators Association, *Survey of Schools Offering Translator and Interpreter Training* (Ossining, NY: American Translators Association, 1986).

21. American Translators Association, *Survey of Schools Offering Translator and Interpreter Training* (Ossining, NY: American Translators Association, 1989).

22. Peter Krawutschke, "The Place of Translation in U.S. Postsecondary Education," in *Proceedings of the Second North American Translators Congress*, ed. Jean-François Joly (Montreal: Imprimerie Trandek Limitée, 1989), p. 174.

other field. For example, at Rose-Hulman University, officials have noticed that the graduates of its engineering program who know German and Russian are getting twice the job offers of those who do not.[23] Other students are combining foreign languages with such fields as Latin American studies, business, or international relations.

A major source of frustration to the translator community, however, is that foreign language majors rarely graduate with translation skills because the emphasis on language instruction in the classroom continues to be on oral proficiency. Even the best-known advocate of foreign language competency, Senator Paul Simon, to whom we all owe a great deal as language professionals, seems to equate foreign language skills with the ability to speak the language. In a recent article, he stated, "For diplomats, scientists, and business personnel, they must be able to speak other languages with fluency."[24] In advocating the multi-disciplinary approach, he states that we need "the development of accountants who speak French, engineers who speak German, and so on."[25] Absolutely no mention is made of written skills. Yet, in today's business world, understanding a text and being able to use it in one's work or reproduce it for the benefit of others

is a skill greatly needed. An engineer in the United States is much more likely to be called upon to read and understand a foreign language text than he is to make a transatlantic phone call.

Since oral proficiency is the goal of most foreign language programs, reading and writing skills do not receive a lot of attention. Teachers of modern languages who use translation for the purpose of foreign language acquisition employ methods quite different from those used in training translators. In translation programs, reading and writing become the primary language skills, and a comparatively high level of proficiency in them is required of the students. In fact, the written skills needed by a competent translator exceed those expected in the proficiency examination provided by the American Council on the Teaching of Foreign Languages, considered by many to be the standard for language competence.[26] Furthermore, translation classes emphasize the theory of translation, the marketplace, and issues involved in translation, which are neglected in language courses.

Although the annual meetings of foreign language teachers' associations have in recent years tended to include a session or two on translation, they, too, emphasize literature and oral skills above all. For exam-

23. Sally Reed, "New Surge in Demand for Language Skills," *New York Times,* 12 Oct. 1986.

24. Paul Simon, "A Decade of Change to a Decade of Challenge," *Newsletter of the Northeast Conference on the Teaching of Foreign Languages,* 27:22 (Feb. 1990).

25. Ibid., p. 23.

26. Jerry W. Larson, "Using the ACTFL Proficiency Guidelines to Assess Reading and Writing in the Translation Programs," *Translation Excellence: Assessment, Achievement, Maintenance,* American Translators Association Scholarly Monograph Series, no. 1, ed. Marilyn Gaddis Rose (Binghamton, NY: University Center, 1987), p. 48.

ple, the 1990 program of the North-east Conference on the Teaching of Foreign Languages, one of the largest associations for foreign language teachers, included just one session on translation in its total of more than 75 presentations. Interestingly, the session was titled, "Translating—But How? The Neglected Skill in the Proficiency Movement."

To assist would-be translators in preparing for a career in translating, ATA has outlined some suggestions in its "Profile of a Competent Translator and of an Effective Translator Training Program."[27] Recommendations include the following curriculum:

- courses that provide an extensive knowledge of, and ability to reason in, the subject matter of the translation: mathematics, pure sciences, social sciences, history, business administration, and economics;
- courses that provide a sound reading knowledge and grasp of the language or languages from which one will be translating;
- four years of a major language, two years of a minor language, and as many basic language courses as possible, including at least two years of Latin;
- courses that provide the ability to express oneself in lucid and straightforward English: writing courses, including one in

newspaper writing and one in technical writing; and
- periodic participation in advanced postgraduate workshops, notably in the specialized subject-matter area.

CONCLUSION

The demand for competent translators is at an all-time high. In part this is because of the lack of foreign language capabilities of most Americans, but even for those persons who have fluency in another language, translations are still necessary. With the internationalization of science and the global market, materials are being produced in many languages, just as American products are being marketed in numerous countries. Because of the advanced state of science, subject-matter specialization is a must for the translator, as are highly developed writing skills. Whereas a few years ago, the United States could rely on its immigrant population to do much of the translating, in the future it will have to rely much more on the educational institutions of this country to prepare students in technical subjects, excellent writing abilities in English, and translation skills. Much will depend on the education system as a whole, but until more attention is given to developing written skills of foreign language students, as well as competence in the more uncommon languages, there is likely to be a shortage of qualified translators entering the much-needed profession.

27. American Translators Association, "Profile of a Competent Translator."

ANNALS, *AAPSS,* **511,** September 1990

Interpretation in the United States

By WILHELM K. WEBER

ABSTRACT: This article attempts to outline the field of conference interpretation as the most advanced and difficult language profession in the United States. Aptitudes, preparatory studies, training, job opportunities, and the supply and demand situation are outlined. The author lists a number of recommendations in an attempt to improve both sides of the equation: the market of international conferences and meetings on the demand side and an increase of interest in the interpreting profession as well as training on the supply side. Funding possibilities to achieve these goals are briefly discussed, as are the potentially disastrous consequences of complacency and inaction for the profession in the next millennium, because of the effects of aging and natural attrition of the present population of interpreters.

Wilhelm K. Weber is dean of the Graduate Division of Translation and Interpretation, Monterey Institute of International Studies. He graduated in translation and conference interpretation from the University of Geneva, Switzerland. Between 1964 and 1978 he worked as a free-lance conference interpreter for most of the specialized agencies of the United Nations and for several heads of state and government. In 1978 he joined the Monterey Institute of International Studies. He still interprets regularly and is a contract conference interpreter with the U.S. Department of State.

IN contrast with translators, who operate exclusively within the written medium, interpreters attempt to transpose statements given orally by speakers representing one culture into the spoken form that is characteristic of the culture of those listening to the interpretation. Ideally, therefore, a good interpretation makes listeners forget that the speakers express themselves in a different language.

There are several types of interpretation. One is community interpretation, which includes work for the armed forces; emergency services, such as 911, police, and ambulance companies; hospitals and doctors' practices; attorneys' offices; and tourism. Other types are court interpretation, interpretation for the hearing impaired, and conference interpretation.

Although this article will deal mainly with the most difficult form of interpretation, conference interpretation, the other forms of the profession will be explained briefly.

Community interpretation has seen a spectacular development in recent years. It still needs to be defined as a professional activity with its own standards for training and qualifications. Although it is an easier form of interpretation, excellence of service is of the essence, as both human lives and large sums of money may be at stake. Modern technology makes it possible to have access to an interpreter in any language instantly over the phone. Several companies specialize in this kind of service.

Court interpretation has become a full-fledged profession since the passing of the Federal Court Interpreters' Act in 1977. The quality of court interpretation still remains largely unchecked, however, and, with the exception of some laudable instances, leaves much to be desired at the municipal and state levels. Moreover, training programs are very rare. Nonetheless, the awareness of the importance of good court interpreters is rising, especially in those states with a large population of recent immigrants, such as Florida, New York, California, and Arizona.

Interpretation for the hearing impaired can often be observed on television and is fast gaining the recognition it deserves, both politically and by members of the interpreting profession at large. The first graduate training program for American Sign Language interpreters and interpreter trainers has only recently been established, however; it is located at Western Maryland College.

Conference interpretation can be performed in two modes: simultaneous interpretation and consecutive interpretation.

Simultaneous interpretation is the faster form of interpretation. It requires technical equipment, as interpreters work in soundproof booths in which they listen to the speakers through earphones. Their interpretation is spoken into a microphone and can be heard by their listeners through earphones on the appropriate language channel. This form of interpretation is the preferred mode for meetings involving more than two languages and whenever time is of the essence. Well over 90 percent of the work of all conference interpreters is done in this mode nowadays.

Consecutive interpretation is considered to be the most accurate and the most refined form of interpretation. It is often called an art. In this mode, the interpreter takes notes during a speech and interprets segments of up to 10 or 15 minutes. It is the preferred mode for so-called diplomatic interpretation, the interpretation that takes place at high-level meetings between government officials and heads of state and government.

Although some of the techniques, aptitudes, skills, and training methods are essentially similar for the different types of interpretation, the rest of this article will pertain to the field of conference interpretation exclusively.

THE SITUATION IN
THE UNITED STATES

Compared to other parts of the world, especially Europe, conference interpretation is still relatively poorly known in the United States. Several factors have contributed to this state of affairs. These include the size of the continent, which constitutes a linguistic monolith; lack of educational programs at all levels with a foreign language requirement; a propensity of immigrant parents to have their children totally assimilate into the American mainstream rather than keep some of their ethnic identity and languages; few international conferences; the ability of many foreigners to conduct business in English; the incorrect impression that all language-related professions are poorly paid; a lack of opportunity for the public at large to observe the art of conference interpretation; and, last but not least, the myth that becoming an interpreter is an almost impossible goal unless one grew up with more than one language.

This combination of factors has led to several phenomena: students interested in foreign language studies often do not know about interpretation as a career—neither do their parents or even their foreign language teachers, for that matter; and good professional training programs are scarce, thereby perpetuating the misconception that the only places to study interpretation are in Europe. These factors, together with the resulting small number of available interpreters, have led to a very low turnover in the profession, thereby inverting the age pyramid in favor of older interpreters and seriously endangering the future of the profession in this country.

Moreover, good interpreters are hard to find by Americans who are suddenly confronted with the awesome challenge of organizing an international meeting. This often leads to the once-and-never-again syndrome that develops after a bad experience with mediocre interpreters. Unsatisfactory experiences can occur because the organizers do not know where to find good interpreters or, worse, because they automatically take the lowest bidder without realizing that the saying "You get what you pay for" is particularly relevant in the interpreting profession.

Recruiting a team of interpreters requires particular skills and a profound knowledge of both the profession and the requirements of the particular meeting. This task should be entrusted only to an experienced professional and under no circumstances to firms that rent equipment, translation agencies, language schools, or foreign language departments at universities. An exception could be made for university foreign language departments if they have an accredited training program for conference interpreters with a teaching staff of practicing interpreters who have an excellent track record of organizing language services.

The U.S. Department of State

The single largest employer of conference interpreters in the United States besides the United Nations is the Office of Language Services at the U.S. Department of State. A short analysis of the services offered by this government agency and of their personnel resources is indicative of the situation in the whole country.

Besides the Department of State and the White House, this agency provides interpretation services for roughly thirty agencies, congressional leaders, the judiciary, and other entities, such as U.S. negotiating teams abroad, in particular those involved with the arms-control negotiations in Geneva. The department's Office of Language Services provides over 40,000 days of interpretation each year.

In order to perform this awesome task satisfactorily, the State Department has only roughly 25 staff positions for conference interpreters. Of

these positions, 10-18 percent on average are vacant each year, making it necessary to farm out 87 percent of the work to outside contractors. By comparison, the United Nations, which has a much larger workload, uses outside contractors for only 48 percent of its volume. The State Department suffers a highly undesirable lack of control over the quality of the interpreting services provided and over the availability of interpreters.

While all 25 conference interpreters at the State Department are U.S. citizens and have a top-secret security clearance, more than half are foreign-born. Two-thirds were trained in foreign countries, only one-third in the United States. Most have received additional training of some kind by the department to meet the very high quality requirements.

Contrary to the other market segments, 70 percent of the work at the State Department is in consecutive interpretation and only 30 percent is in simultaneous. For staff interpreters the percentage of consecutive interpretation is as high as 80. This is mainly due to the requirements of diplomatic interpretation.

Although the State Department does not require university degrees if candidates are otherwise qualified, staff members generally hold at least an M.A. degree. Interpreters need to be generalists, not specialists.

The supply

Superior conference interpreters in the United States are usually members of one or both of the following professional associations: the International Association of Conference Interpreters and The American Association of Language Specialists (TAALS).

The International Association of Conference Interpreters, better known by its French acronym AIIC, is headquartered in Geneva, Switzerland, and constitutes the only worldwide association for conference interpreters alone.[1] Its membership consists of about 2500 practicing conference interpreters on all five continents, both staff interpreters, so-called permanents, and free-lancers. It has very stringent admission criteria because it guarantees the quality of the work of its members. Membership in AIIC is tantamount to an international accreditation. To be admitted, candidates must show at least 200 days of work and have five sponsors. This association lists 115 active members in the United States.

As its name indicates, the membership of TAALS[2] comes from the Americas and comprises, besides conference interpreters, other language specialists, such as translators and précis writers. It claims to apply the same criteria for the admission of conference interpreters as does AIIC. TAALS lists 49 conference interpreters in the United States who do not appear in the AIIC yearbook.

Both associations publish a code of ethics that is binding for members, as well as a yearbook with the names, addresses, telephone numbers, language combinations, and professional domiciles of members.

The languages most often represented are English, French, and Spanish. Rare languages for which there is a high demand are Chinese, German, Japanese, and Russian. It is especially rare to find interpreters who are equally fluent in any of these languages and English. Language competencies that are difficult to find when they are needed but for which there is limited demand include Italian, Korean, and Portuguese.

When the European Communities tried to finance a special training course at the Monterey Institute of International Studies for conference interpreters capable of working into English from Portuguese and one other of the Communities' official languages, the program fell through because only three candidates responded to advertisements in five major newspapers in the United States. All three were found to be deficient in their language skills when tested.

Interpreters' languages are divided into A, B, and C languages. They are defined as follows:

1. A language. The interpreter's native or principal language, into which he or she works from his or her B and C languages.

2. B language. The interpreter's strongest foreign language, into which he or she works consecutively but rarely simultaneously from his or her A and C languages. An interpreter may have more than one B language.

---

1. The AIIC's address is as follows: Association internationale des interprètes de conférence, 10, avenue de Sécheron, CH-1202 Geneva, Switzerland.

2. The address for TAALS is Suite 9, 1000 Connecticut Avenue, NW, Washington, DC 20036.

TABLE 1

LANGUAGE COMBINATIONS OF
ALL CONFERENCE INTERPRETERS IN THE UNITED STATES

	A Language		B Language		C Language	
	FL	ST	FL	ST	FL	ST
English	28	19	52	25	20	16
French	19	22	13	5	50	29
German	13	1	2	0	11	5
Spanish	32	26	5	7	22	18
Chinese	4	0	0	0	0	0
Japanese	3	0	0	0	0	0
Russian	6	1	2	0	5	9
Italian	3	0	0	1	10	2
Portuguese	4	2	2	2	9	10

SOURCES: *The AIIC Yearbook* (Geneva: Association internationale des interprètes de confér-ence, 1990); *The TAALS Yearbook* (Washington, DC: The American Association of Language Specialists, 1988).

NOTE: "FL" stands for free-lance interpreters, "ST" for staff interpreters.

3. C language. The interpreter's passive language, of which he or she has a perfect understanding but into which he or she does not work. The interpreter may have more than one C language.

Table 1 shows language combinations of conference interpreters in the United States. From Table 1 we go to a picture of the availability of free-lance interpreters in the United States working into and out of various languages (see Table 2).

Observations

As conference interpreters usually work into their native languages only, the picture is even bleaker than the tables indicate. Only 28 free-lance conference interpreters in the United States are native speakers of English. Among these, American-born interpreters are a small minor-ity. There are, however, 52 interpreters who transpose into English as a foreign language. This practice invariably leads to a lesser quality of interpretation and is frowned upon by professionals in Europe.

Very few Japanese interpreters belong to the associations. They command much higher fees than other interpreters and feel that they can do without both the prestige and the protection of association membership. On the other hand, this makes it extremely difficult for users and sometimes even for experienced consultant interpreters to locate the few truly excellent Japanese interpreters.

By way of comparison, here are some figures about interpreters working into English as their native language who live and work in countries where English is not the main language: 89 such interpreters live in France, 83 in Switzerland, and 41 in Belgium.

TABLE 2

AVAILABILITY OF FREE-LANCE INTERPRETERS IN THE UNITED STATES

	Number Working into the Specified Language			Number Working out of the Specified Language*
	As A language	As B language	Total	
English	28	52	80	20
French	19	13	32	50
German	13	2	15	11
Spanish	32	5	37	22
Chinese	4	0	4	0
Japanese	3	0	3	0
Russian	6	2	8	5
Italian	3	0	3	9
Portuguese	4	2	6	10

SOURCES: *AIIC Yearbook; TAALS Yearbook.*

*Number of interpreters who work out of these languages as their C and B languages only. This column does not include interpreters for whom these languages are A languages and out of which they may work into their B languages at times.

Many smaller countries have a much larger staff of conference interpreters working for their governments.

The most serious danger for the interpreting profession in the United States is that, conservatively speaking, over one-half of the currently available conference interpreters are expected to leave the profession within the next ten years. The present output of training programs is greatly insufficient to fill the resulting gap.

MYTHS AND REALITY ABOUT
CONFERENCE INTERPRETING

One myth is that an interpreter must grow up with at least two languages. Although growing up with more than one language used to be quite frequent among conference interpreters of the first generation —that is, those who worked for the League of Nations between World War I and World War II and those who joined the ranks of the profession from other backgrounds, mainly former diplomats or children of foreign service families at the end of World War II—less than 3 percent of all interpreters today are true bilinguals in the sense that they possess more than one A language.

AIIC lists 13 interpreters in the United States with a double-A combination. This, however, actually represents a high percentage of the total number of interpreters in the United States, compared to other world regions.

Another myth is that an interpreter must know many languages. Although most conference interpreters possess at least three languages, the number of languages very much depends on the marketability of their skills. Most interpreters of Chinese and Japanese, for instance, have English as their only other language.

Also, job opportunities for the Spanish-English combination are excellent in some states, and many interpreters work with those two languages only. But this is true for court interpretation only and not necessarily for conference interpretation.

The U.S. Department of State will hire interpreters with only one foreign language provided that they are able to work into their one foreign language both consecutively and simultaneously.

For languages paired with English other than Chinese, Japanese, and Spanish, in the realm of both international organizations and conventions using more than two languages, a minimum of three languages is generally required to be successful. The European Communities, the world's largest employer of conference interpreters, now even requires four languages to start.

It is often thought that interpreters must be born and cannot be trained. This misconception arose from the fact that most interpreters in the early days were self-trained, because there were no training programs. Moreover, the skills and aptitudes of conference interpreters were somewhat mysterious to the uninitiated.

In the last twenty years or so, members of this profession have established themselves and their art as a full-fledged academic discipline in most countries where good training programs are available. The particular mental processes that are at work during simultaneous and consecutive interpretation have been and continue to be extensively researched by teachers of interpretation in collaboration with psycholinguists, neurologists, and other academics. This research has resulted in some extraordinary progress in the understanding of the processes involved in interpreting and has resulted as well in a considerable improvement of teaching techniques.

There is also the myth that interpretation is never as good as the original. Unfortunately, many users of interpreters have had to cope with mediocre or even bad quality. As the name "interpreter" is as yet legally unprotected in most countries, anyone with some knowledge of a foreign language can claim to be an interpreter. Often clients do not know where to turn to find the few really excellent interpreters, and they abandon the idea of ever using interpretation again after just one bad experience.

In fact, the record of the profession proves that a good interpretation is often even better than the original because interpreters are trained to express a speaker's ideas more clearly if necessary.

Finally, there is the myth that an interpreter's career is limited by age. The contrary is the case, however. Medical studies have shown that interpreters have an unusually long and satisfying professional career. It is not uncommon to find colleagues in their seventies still doing an admirable job. In fact, older colleagues are known to maintain unusually fresh and agile mental abilities, compared to noninterpreters of the same age group. Although it would be fair to say that someone over 50 years of age might experience difficulties in acquiring the skills of interpreting, once these skills have been learned, they can be maintained for a very long period of time, provided they are regularly used.

Most of what is perceived as unusual stress by the layperson really becomes very much part of the interpreter's daily life and is no longer experienced as stress. Much of the stress, in fact, stems not from the practice of the profession but from frequent traveling, which entails jet lag and other extraneous factors, such as change in food and sleeping habits, that may contribute to some health problems in the long run, unless they are carefully monitored.

In the past, overwork was also an omnipresent danger in interpreters' lives. Improved working conditions, which have been obtained and are carefully monitored by professional associations, have virtually eliminated this source of potential health problems, however.

SKILLS AND APTITUDES

In most people's minds conference interpretation is nothing but a language profession. The more languages one knows, the better one's chances of becoming an interpreter.

Nothing could be further from the truth! In actual fact, conference interpretation is an act of interpersonal and intercultural communication. Both the interpreter's native language and his or her foreign languages are merely part of his or her skills. They are to be taken for granted, very much like instrumental techniques or being able to read a score for a musician. This is the reason why, ideally, an interpreter-training program no longer teaches languages but only concentrates on imparting the skills necessary to perform interpretation.

Among the natural aptitudes that future conference interpreters must possess are a good voice, good communicative skills, analytical skills, intellectual curiosity, a high degree of intercultural sensitivity, and a stable personality paired with excellent nerves.

Among the skills that need to be learned and constantly refined are the following:

— perfect understanding of the cultures expressed in the interpreter's foreign languages, in all their varieties and accents;
— the skill of making someone else's ideas one's own and expressing them, as if they were one's own ideas, in a different cultural setting; and
— the more mechanical skills involved in consecutive and simultaneous interpretation, such as note taking, memorizing, and handling voice and equipment.

Ideally, a conference interpreter is perceived by his or her listeners as one of their own, someone representing their own culture, thereby making them forget that in fact they are listening, through the interpreter, to a person speaking in another language. In the best of all possible situations, interpreters will remain unnoticed.

As conference interpreters normally do not specialize, they must demonstrate an unusually keen intellectual curiosity and keep abreast of current events and progress in science and technology.

THE FOREIGN LANGUAGE FACTOR

Although, as stated previously, excellent foreign language skills are to be taken for granted for conference interpreters, some brief observations are, of course, in order in this context.

Students whose foreign language skills can be called good enough to enter a training program for conference interpretation are extremely rare in the United States. Some of the deficiencies encountered in students of interpretation are found in grammatical correctness; idiomatic language; the ability to think and express thought as a native speaker of the language would; understanding of all accents, at any speed; and reading and writing skills, especially in Asian languages.

Excellent foreign language skills in this profession may be defined as the ability to comprehend any statement about any subject, including all linguistic and cultural shades of meaning and inferences. Obviously, this level of competence cannot be attained through studies in a typical language and literature program, even at the graduate level. Such studies must be complemented by extensive sojourns in the countries where the languages are spoken within their natural cultural context. In the case of some languages this may imply as many as three or six years abroad, especially for Asian languages. A typical junior-year-abroad program is definitely going to be insufficient.

Nevertheless, many American students are able to attain this high degree of fluency and knowledge. Once they discover the love for a foreign culture, they are usually willing to make many sacrifices to spend as much time as needed in a foreign country.

TRAINING

The education of conference interpreters has become a well-defined academic field in the last twenty years or so.[3] The University of Paris now offers a doctoral degree in conference interpretation. This implies, of course, that this type of education can be given only in a university setting, at the graduate level.

Depending on whether they include additional foreign language training abroad or not, training programs usually are between two and five years long.

Although many foreign language departments in American universities attempt to offer courses in interpretation, there are only two institutions with full programs that concentrate on conference interpreting exclusively. Georgetown University offers a one-year program leading to a certificate, and the Monterey Institute of International Studies offers the only master's degree in conference interpretation at the present time.

When choosing a program, care should be taken by applicants to find one whose teaching staff is com-

3. This section of the current article is based on Wilhelm K. Weber, *The Training of Translators and Conference Interpreters* (Orlando, FL: Harcourt Brace Jovanovich, 1984).

posed exclusively of practicing conference interpreters with a proven track record both in the professional field and in teaching. The best programs in the world are members of the International Association of University Schools of Translation and Interpretation.

JOB OPPORTUNITIES

When discussing the topic of job opportunities for conference interpreters in the United States, a distinction needs to be made between present opportunities and potential opportunities.

The reason for the scarcity of good conference interpreters in the United States is actually threefold:

1. Potentially interested candidates hesitate to invest in an education program lasting two years or longer because the present job opportunities are scarce.

2. The field is still not well known among parents, foreign language teachers, and business corporations.

3. Potential users of conference interpreters do not realize their usefulness until they have suffered financial losses because they used an in-house staff person with only a vague knowledge of a foreign language and no training as an interpreter.

One may add to this list the fact that most conference interpreters do free-lance work, a life-style that does not appeal to everyone, although it has definite advantages, both financial and otherwise.

Employment opportunities in the United States may be found in three sectors. One comprises international intergovernmental organizations, such as the United Nations, the International Monetary Fund, the World Bank, the Organization of American States, and the Panamerican Health Organization. The official languages of the United Nations are Arabic, Chinese, English, French, Russian, and Spanish; however, not all of the specialized agencies use all of these languages. The second sector is composed of the U.S. Department of State and other government agencies, and the third is the so-called private sector, which includes conventions and business meetings.

The first two sectors can be accessed directly whereas work in the private sector is normally handled through consultant interpreters, through translation agencies, or through firms that rent equipment for simultaneous interpretation. Colleagues in the profession formally discourage the use of teams of interpreters assembled by equipment dealers, who normally do not know enough about the intricacies of putting together such teams. Assembling a good team is a job that can be quite tricky. It requires extensive knowledge of the types of meetings and the available interpreters, their language combinations, their possible specializations, as well as their quality. Moreover, any agency will normally take a profit margin that is much more substantial than that charged by a consultant interpreter.

Conference interpreters in staff positions normally earn salaries ranging from $25,000 to $70,000, depending on experience. Fees for free-lance interpreters vary but range from $375 to $1000 per day, depending on language combination, staffing patterns, duration of the meeting, mode of interpretation, and so on. In the United States, free-lance conference interpreters work between 100 and 130 days per year on average. Many of their European counterparts work up to 200 days per year.

ACCESS TO THE PROFESSION

Access to the profession in this day and age will be through a university degree in conference interpretation and subsequent testing by the employer. It would be unrealistic, however, to expect to obtain a staff position as a conference interpreter right after graduation, without prior professional experience. In the case of rare language combinations, the United Nations sometimes will give a beginner additional in-house training before offering him or her a staff contract.

In any event, it must be remembered that conference interpretation is a truly international profession and that employment is not necessarily limited to one's own country. For the United States, this is a problem, as many trained American interpreters prefer to work in Europe, where the volume of conferences generates much more work than in the United States.

RECOMMENDATIONS

What can be done to overcome the present shortage of good conference interpreters and, concurrently, to increase employment opportunities?

As the enormous success of Chinese and Japanese interpreters in recent years has demonstrated, once a real need is created, interpreters are hard to come by and may command fees that are quite substantial—between $500 and $1000 per day for Japanese interpreters, for example.

The potential for enlarging the conference interpreters' market in the United States is practically unlimited. The awareness of the corporate world, in particular, however, must be raised to the dangers of losing substantial amounts of money unless communication with foreign business partners is flawless. Moreover, it must be clearly understood that conference interpretation has become a profession distinct from all other language professions and that it requires many years of training. To expect any untrained person, even though that person may be fluent in a foreign language, to perform well as an interpreter in difficult negotiations can only lead, at best, to frustration on both sides in the negotiations and, at worst, to substantial financial losses.

Some lawmakers have long recognized the need to promote foreign languages and international studies in the United States. Paul Simon and Leon Panetta may suffice as role models in this respect. Much remains to be done, however. The present publication is a laudable step in the right direction, and it is to be hoped that it will contribute to the nation's awakening.

Furthermore, the field of conference interpretation must be made eligible for grants from major government and private foundations. Funds are needed to enable gifted students to spend more time in foreign countries to absorb as much of these cultures as possible, thereby enabling them, once they have become interpreters, to communicate to their American clients the true and full meaning of statements by people of other countries. Moreover, subsidies are needed to sustain training programs in languages that are critically important for the nation but may attract few students at times.

Incentives need to be created to enable persons with the right background to take time off their usual jobs and undergo training in conference interpretation. Short and intensive training programs for special purposes need to be conducted in parallel with the regular, longer training programs to enable adults who are ready for and capable of a career change to receive the necessary training. This solution is quite realistic if participants can expect to find employment at the end of such a program.

The Monterey Institute of International Studies conducted a four-week intensive training program in consecutive interpretation for the Department of State in the summer of 1988. Participants were chosen from a group of volunteers from the Foreign Service. All of them had a high level of fluency in Russian and had been carefully screened and tested for their aptitudes to interpret. Similar programs should be funded to ensure a sufficient number of well-trained interpreters, especially for critical languages.

In conclusion, here is a list of recommendations that may prove instrumental in assuring that excellent conference interpreters will be available in the United States for the foreseeable future.

1. Reinstate foreign language requirements in high schools and colleges.

2. Raise the awareness of all Americans that learning a foreign language and culture improves both the understanding and the usage of their own language and will eventually contribute to better business opportunities abroad, based, inter alia, on an improved foreign policy conducted by foreign service personnel and politicians who possess an outstanding knowledge of foreign languages and cultures.

3. Develop more and better-funded study-abroad programs, enabling students to spend more time in the countries and cultures of their foreign languages.

4. Raise the awareness of all Americans, especially parents and elementary school teachers, that learning a foreign language is not like learning the Morse code but involves great cultural sensitivity and constitutes a lifelong learning process.

5. Raise children's awareness that not the whole world speaks English. Awaken interest, rather than suspicion. Churches should teach early on that, contrary to what children may naturally assume, Jesus did not speak English and that the Bible had to be translated into many languages for the message of Christianity to be understood around the world.

6. Raise the salaries of foreign language teachers.

7. Compensate corporate and government employees with foreign lan-

guage skills adequately. They should receive additional bonuses, as these skills are part and parcel of their educational background and not merely ancillary skills.

8. Seek funds for professional associations and training programs to conduct information campaigns about the profession. Besides written materials, speakers' bureaus could be established so that speakers could be made available to educational institutions at all levels, corporations, gov- ernment agencies, convention and visitors' bureaus, chambers of commerce, hotel chains, city halls, and so on.

9. Advise students who are interested in the interpreting profession early on about what studies best will prepare them and on how much time they must expect to spend abroad.

10. Organize demonstrations of conference-interpretation skills.

11. Stress the importance of an excellent and unusually broad general education. Interpreters' assignments vary constantly and include scientific and technical meetings, labor negotiations, business negotiations, diplomatic interpretation, working with sports federations, and the like.

ANNALS, *AAPSS,* 511, September 1990

Bilingualism in the Workplace

By MARY E. McGROARTY

ABSTRACT: This article discusses occupational bilingualism from the perspective of speakers of other languages who need to acquire English to be able to work. Most of the data are drawn from information on the language-use patterns of recent immigrants, a group that has been the focus of much policy research, though the situation of workers from indigenous language minority groups and those involved in the border economy are also mentioned. Data on immigrants' job experiences show that the relevance of English skills to employment varies by geographical location, occupational sector, gender, and ethnic background. Three case studies of occupational language use—in a restaurant, in small retail businesses, and in hospitals—illustrate the job-specific nature of second-language skills in these settings. Evidence indicates that bilingualism, defined as the addition of some level of English to previous native-language skills, plays an active role in the American economy.

Mary E. McGroarty is associate professor in the applied linguistics program of the English Department at Northern Arizona University. She received the B.A. from Macalester College, the M.A. from Tufts University, and the Ph.D. from Stanford University. She was on the faculty at the University of California, Los Angeles, where she and her students investigated aspects of occupational bilingualism. She has taught in Latin America, worked in vocational training programs for limited English speakers, and consulted for local, state, and federal agencies concerned with provision of bilingual services.

BILINGUALISM has always been a part of the American workplace, but its relevance is specific to locations where contact between people who use different languages is a regular part of the occupational setting.[1] Historical and contemporary patterns of settlement and immigration have shaped the nature of occupational bilingualism all through American history; the types of bilingualism observed today are no different in kind, though they may well differ in the component languages involved, from those that have occurred earlier in our history.

Today, as in the past, workers endeavor to develop the language skills that will allow them employment and mobility whenever developing those skills is imperative for participation in the economy. Nevertheless, the relationship between labor market participation and language and ethnicity is now more complicated than it has been in the past because of changes in both immigration patterns and the American economy.[2] Investigation of occupational bilingualism has important implications for both social science theory and public policy. In a capitalist society, the relationship of human capital factors —level of education, language skills, specialized occupational qualifications—as well as traditional capital—economic assets such as property, credit, and money—to a worker's ultimate success in the economic sphere is a critical issue but one too often ignored or oversimplified by theorists and policymakers alike.[3]

This article examines the question of the relationship of bilingual skills to workplace success by means of sur-

1. Throughout the article, I use the term "American" to refer only to the United States of North America. This usage is strictly for economy, and no slight to other countries is intended. I am aware that, for Spanish speakers, "America" refers to all of North and South America and that North America includes Canada as well as the United States. The subject of occupational bilingualism in all countries of North and South America deserves extensive further study; for the sake of brevity, this article concentrates on the situation in the United States.

2. Marcia Freedman, "Urban Labor Markets and Ethnicity: Segments and Shelters Reexamined," in *Urban Ethnicity in the United States,* ed. L. Maldonado and J. Moore (Beverly Hills, CA: Sage, 1985), pp. 145-47.

3. As Marxist or world-system views of immigration have become more carefully explicated by social scientists and historians, some of these factors have begun to assume greater salience; see, for example, Lucie Cheng and Edna Bonacich, *Labor Immigration under Capitalism: Asian Workers in the United States before World War II* (Berkeley: University of California Press, 1984). As these sources show and as I will argue here, it is the dynamic and reciprocal relationship between, on the one hand, variation in immigrant control of both human capital factors—which include language—and economic resources and, on the other, the social and economic networks characteristic of the immigrants' new places of residence that accounts for some of the differential economic outcomes observed. With respect to the present discussion, this means that a worker's control of two languages, a human capital characteristic, will not have an invariant relationship to economic success but will come into play to the degree that such skills enhance employability in a specific geographical location or occupational sector. The diversity of background found in the foreign-born labor force and the variable match with local resources is a major theme of current research and policy interest; see Demetrious G. Papademetriou et al., *The Effects of Immigration on the U.S. Economy and Labor Market,* Immigration Policy and Research Report no. 1 (Washington, DC: Department of Labor, 1989).

veying available data on the economic performance of nonnative English-speaking groups within the U.S. economy. Most of the discussion deals with the language skills and occupational performance of the foreign-born immigrant population for three reasons: (1) the public policy questions related to immigration reform have generated considerable discussion and some pertinent research; (2) the number of workers involved here is large, and more data are available regarding their occupational paths; and (3) these workers represent a substantial portion—averaging 22 percent per year in the years 1980-87—of the growth of the U.S. civilian labor force.[4]

I then look briefly at the questions of occupational bilingualism that arise in conjunction with two other groups: members of indigenous language groups who currently use, or have in the past traditionally used, a language other than English, and workers in the U.S.-Mexico border industries. After addressing the questions related to occupational bilingualism pertinent to each of these groups, I note some of the unanswered questions that emerge and then consider the public policy implications of the data available so far.

BASIC CONCEPTS: POWER AND RESOURCES

The dual concepts of superordinate-subordinate relations, drawn from political science and sociology, and the ethnic-enclave economy, drawn from economics, are the keys to understanding the role of bilingualism in the American workplace. Each sheds light on the question of who needs to speak which language at work and why.

Political scientists examining the social relations attendant on bilingualism have distinguished between superordinate and subordinate groups. Joshua Fishman, a sociologist noted for decades of work on language distribution in the United States, has noted that in contemporary America, the term "bilingual" is "a euphemistic code word for ascribed membership in a minority ethnolinguistic group,"[5] and he has emphasized that such use highlights the minority-majority intergroup conflicts that arise over access to societal resources and to decisions regarding their allocation.[6] His emphasis on the social meaning of bilingualism echoes the observation of Norwegian American linguist Einar Haugen, who remarked over thirty years ago that social and economic prestige determined the answer to the question, Who learns whose language?[7] Thus the social connotation of bilingualism includes an understanding of power relationships within a society.

The general pattern in recent American occupational bilingualism has been for the subordinate group to be non-English speakers who must

4. Papademetriou et al., *Effects of Immigration*, tab. 2.7, p. 41.

5. Joshua A. Fishman, "Bilingualism and Separatism," *The Annals* of the American Academy of Political and Social Science, 487:170 (Sept. 1986).

6. Ibid.

7. Einar Haugen, *Bilingualism in the Americas: A Bibliography and Research Guide* (University, AL: American Dialect Society, 1956), p. 97.

conform to the language demands of the English-speaking superordinate group in order to participate in the economy. Monolingualism in English for members of the dominant group is not perceived as an occupational or social problem; in contrast, monolingualism in a language other than English is interpreted as an economic and social obstacle.[8] Occupational bilingualism, or mastery of some level of English in addition to the native language, is thus seen as essential for successful participation in the American economy.

At certain periods in our history, however, non-English-speaking groups have achieved the status of what might be called coordinate groups. In the nineteenth century, the Germans in the Midwest and, on the contemporary scene, the Cubans in the Miami area and Spanish speakers in some other parts of the country have controlled sufficient economic and political resources to promote the use of their mother tongue in occupational as well as educational settings. Study of the Cuban experience led to the development of the concept of an ethnic-enclave economy, or realization that, when an immigrant group possesses a critical mass of economic and social resources, its members may establish for themselves a protected economic sphere revolving around the use of ethnic resources, including language, the social and familial connections of members, and cultural traits that support economic activity.[9]

The influence of enclave economies on patterns of occupational language acquisition is ripe for scholarly exploration. On the one hand, the possibilities of obtaining work and advancing without knowing English may lessen the motivation to acquire the language. On the other, the need to comply with business regulations and the desire to expand one's market for goods or services beyond coethnics may demand the use of English. It is as if enclaves allow an initial level of economic survival to those without high levels of English proficiency, but, once participants wish to move beyond the enclave or establish a broader business base, they need some use of English.

Moreover, the presence of large numbers of non-English speakers in a certain area and the viability of ethnic economies that sometimes arise in these circumstances have created a reciprocal need for English speakers to acquire some skills in the non-English language in order to provide products or services. Efforts by English speakers to learn Spanish to provide consumer, legal, or medical services to those who speak that language reflect this trend. Because many of the articles in this issue of *The Annals* describe efforts of English speakers who already possess certain occupational qualifications to learn a language in addition to English, I will not go into detailed discussion of such trends. Nevertheless,

8. That data do not always substantiate such an interpretation is a separate matter.

9. Kenneth L. Wilson and Alejandro Portes, "Immigrant Enclaves: An Analysis of the Labor Market Experiences of Cubans in Miami," *American Journal of Sociology*, 18(2):295-319 (1980).

it is instructive to note that, whenever there is an economic or political payoff to knowing two languages, English speakers, even in the historically ethnocentric and monoglot United States, will strive to acquire relevant skills in a language other than English. Other articles in this issue describe some of the many special language programs, often conducted at great cost, aimed at giving English speakers the second-language skills they need to deploy their occupational training more effectively in the domestic as well as the international economy.

Instead, in this article I will concentrate on the efforts of groups who do not speak English as a native language to acquire the level of English needed for economic participation or advancement. As we shall see, whether or not a worker in fact needs English to get a job or advance in an occupation once employed is a function of the worker's geographic location and the sector of the economy in which he or she is employed.

EFFECTS OF LOCATION: IMMIGRANT NETWORK STRENGTH

Let us examine the effects of the first factor mentioned, geographic location of the person seeking work. For non-English speakers, the relevance of English to employment depends in part on where they reside. If they reside in an area with many other conationals who speak the same language, they may not need to know English, at least not for initial employment. If, however, they find themselves in areas with few speak-

ers of their own language, they will need some English even to find a job. Hence the necessity for occupational bilingualism, or skills in English in addition to a non-English native language, is partially a function of the potential worker's location in areas with or without many other compatriots.

The first pattern, immigrant clustering rather than dispersion, is by far the more typical. Immigration history shows that immigrants have always been concentrated in certain areas, and their concentration has given them additional impact on local labor markets.[10] Though the 1990 census will provide more accurate figures, all available evidence reinforces the marked geographic concentration of immigrants. Even data from the mid-1970s showed that 40 percent of all immigrants lived in the 10 largest U.S. cities, where immigrants represented a proportion of the population higher than their share of the U.S. population at large.[11] Between 1970 and 1980, 40 percent of new immigrants settled in either the Los Angeles or New York greater metropolitan areas, with another 20 percent going to one of four

10. The relationship of immigrant clustering to the learning and use of English in occupational and domestic spheres is a subject nearly untouched by historians and social scientists. Substantial work on immigrant clustering in the labor market has been done, however; see John Bodnar, *The Transplanted: A History of Immigrants in Urban America* (Bloomington: Indiana University Press, 1985), esp. chaps. 2, 6.

11. Saskia Sassen-Koob, "Immigrant and Minority Workers in the Organization of the Labor Process," *Journal of Ethnic Studies,* 8(1):7 (Spring 1980).

other cities: Chicago, San Francisco, Houston, or Miami.[12] The settlement patterns of post-1965 Asian and North American—mainly Mexican and Central American—immigrants show that they, too, are concentrated in certain areas, mainly in western and southwestern states.[13] Other Spanish-speaking groups have strong historical links to a particular area and demonstrate contemporary residential clustering as well, with Puerto Ricans in the New York and New Jersey area, Cubans in Miami, and Mexicans and Mexican Americans living all along the current border and in the area of historic Old Mexico that is now part of the United States.[14]

What does this residential concentration mean for the process of finding employment? Labor market analyst Marcia Freedman notes that most job vacancies in the United States are filled not through public media but through the operation of informal information networks; immigrants, often brought into the country by a family or kinship network, use those same associations to find employment.[15] Thus, if a worker goes to a place where many compatriots are already employed, it may be possible to find initial employment without knowing any English. Incentive to acquire English for occupational advancement will then depend on the worker's perceptions of the need for English to hold or advance in the job. First-person narratives from immigrant workers demonstrate the value of bilingual skills —in these cases, adding English to Spanish—for purposes of occupational survival and mobility. These include such short-term needs as protecting oneself from harassment by the Immigration and Naturalization Service and longer-term outcomes such as attaining supervisory positions involving the oversight of work crews made up of non-English speakers.[16]

OCCUPATIONAL SECTOR:
WHO DOES WHAT FOR WHOM?

In determining the need for occupational bilingualism, the effects of geographic location interact with those of the occupational sector involved. Freedman observes that, once immigrants enter the country,

12. Thomas Muller, "Economic Effects of Immigration," in *Clamor at the Gates: The New American Immigration*, ed. N. Glazer (San Francisco: ICS Press, 1985), p. 115.

13. Morrison G. Wong, "Post-1965 Immigrants: Demographic and Socioeconomic Profile," in *Urban Ethnicity in the United States*, ed. Maldonado and Moore, p. 68.

14. For discussion of the current operation of the social networks underpinning Mexican immigration to the United States, see Douglas S. Massey, "The Social Organization of Mexican Migration to the United States," *The Annals* of the American Academy of Political and Social Science, 487:102-13 (Sept. 1986).

15. For descriptions of the importance of informal kinship networks in finding employment for immigrants in the nineteenth and early twentieth centuries, see Bodnar, *Transplanted*, chap. 2. For information on the contemporary picture, see Freedman, "Urban Labor Markets," pp. 145-46.

16. See accounts of Miguel Torres and Jaime Alvarez—both pseudonyms—in *American Mosaic: The Immigrant Experience in the Words of Those Who Lived It*, ed. J. Morrison and C. F. Zabusky (New York: New American Library, 1980), pp. 349, 358.

their labor market participation is dependent on three factors: how much English they know; the specific occupational skills they already possess; and the nature of the industries where their compatriots already work.[17] The two latter forces are related to the effect of occupational sector—the nature of the enterprise in which a worker is employed; for example, manufacturing, service, or public employment—on employment. Although prior occupational skills are an individual attribute, their relevance to the new country is partially determined by whether or not they fit the occupational possibilities, or opportunity structure, available in the new environment.

The effect of occupational sector on immigrant labor force participation and the consequent need for English-language skills on the job depends mainly on the sector in which immigrants find work. This, again, depends on their previous skill levels as well as their geographic location. Immigrant participation in different occupational sectors shows dramatic variation and interacts in interesting ways with the restructuring of the global and U.S. economy.[18] How does the occupational sector affect the press to develop English-language skill? Recall that 40 percent of all new immigrants between 1970 and 1980 went first to New York or Los Angeles, two areas with long histories of immigrant involvement in the local economy. A brief look at immigrant involvement in two sometimes overlapping sectors in these two metropolitan areas, manufacturing as represented in the apparel trades and small business ownership, provides an initial perspective on the continued relevance of fluency in the native language and the variable importance of English-language skills for occupational success.

Apparel manufacture: New networks for the needle trades

Roger Waldinger's recent study of Chinese and Dominican immigrant apparel contractors in the New York City area demonstrates the importance of coethnic networks in sustaining economic viability in an increasingly competitive national and international production force.[19] As the children of Jewish and Italian immigrant entrepreneurs who historically had run the apparel subcontracting shops moved into professional jobs, they created opportunities for would-be entrepreneurs drawn from among the new—that is, post-1965—immigrants to try their hand at aspects of clothing manufacture. The relatively low cost of going into business for oneself and the high failure rate of these firms, which operate on a very slim profit margin, create continuing opportunities for small independent contractors. Because of the changing patterns of production in the American apparel industry, many more entrepreneurs have started small workshops cater-

---

17. Freedman, "Urban Labor Markets," p. 157.

18. See discussion in Papademetriou et al., *Effects of Immigration*, esp. chaps. 1, 2, 6.

19. Roger D. Waldinger, *Through the Eye of the Needle: Immigrants and Enterprise in New York's Garment Trades* (New York: New York University Press, 1986).

ing to highly specialized segments of the clothing market, such as production or finishing of ladies' handbags, belts, and notions or manufacture of individual sportswear items rather than full-scale coat, suit, or dress manufacture.[20]

Although we do not have detailed accounts of language use in such firms, some inferences regarding the nature of occupational language skills can be derived from descriptions of the work force and production processes. These small shops often draw on readily available immigrant labor pools composed mainly of coethnics for their work force; workers are likely to be recruited by word of mouth by present workers. For machine operators or garment assemblers in such settings, where both owner and employees share a home language other than English, there is little reason to learn English, except to change the nature of one's employment, and little opportunity or incentive to learn English on the job. Essential communication in the factory can be handled in the immigrants' native language. Owners of small contracting firms need some English to deal with the manufacturers for whom they work, but the level of English skill required is apparently not high. In interviewing manufacturers who did business with immigrant

contractors, Waldinger reported that communication was not a major difficulty. Though communication with immigrant contractors in English was at times stilted, the manufacturers did not perceive it as a problem. If the contractors did not understand what was to be done, the manufacturers simply showed them what to do, probably using some relevant props such as patterns, finished versus unfinished items, and so on.[21]

At the same time, the contractors' limitations not only in English but in awareness of the culture of American business were among the factors that kept them dependent on the personal contacts of their ethnic networks.[22] Thus the native language remains a vital means of communication for dealing with the contractor's labor force and creating and maintaining the business contacts with coethnics that presumably contribute to successful operation of a small apparel enterprise in the American market. Bilingualism becomes an issue only when contractors deal with the larger, nonethnic manufacturing firms that generate demand for their services.

Language use in
small businesses:
Who is the customer?

One sector of lively and continuing interest in terms of immigrant economic progress has been that of entrepreneurship, or ownership of small businesses, as an avenue of economic mobility. Historically, some

20. The increasing internationalization of clothing manufacture has had a major impact on availability of apparel-related jobs in both major American apparel centers, New York and Los Angeles. For a description of changes in the production process in Los Angeles with special emphasis on the labor force effects, see John Laslett and Mary Tyler, *The ILGWU in Los Angeles, 1907-1988* (Inglewood, CA: Ten Star Press, 1989).

21. Waldinger, *Through the Eye of the Needle*, pp. 145-46.

22. Ibid., pp. 144-45.

immigrant groups have used entrepreneurship to establish themselves and advance within the economy of the host country as a result of a combination of internal resources—levels of available capital, education, language skill, support from an ethnic community—and external obstacles to other ways of making a living—lack of some relevant skills such as the language of the host country, discrimination in the wider community, and so on.[23] Work on contemporary American immigration, particularly the line of theory and investigation begun by sociologist Ivan Light, confirms the value of entrepreneurship for many language minority groups that establish strong identification with particular enterprises in various cities.

Light and other scholars have suggested that, given relatively high levels of general education and occupational skills but low proficiency in English and limited access to mainstream institutions such as banks, recent Asian immigrants find the opening of a small business an attractive alternative to seeking wage employment.[24] If one has white-collar qualifications from the country of origin, as many new immigrants do, but lacks the English skills to use them in the United States, it is more palatable to start one's own business than to seek wage employment. Furthermore, because the new immigrants are better educated in general than those who took this route in the nineteenth and early twentieth centuries, it is easier for them to become successful faster; they are more sophisticated at obtaining and using information about the American workplace. If they were professionals such as accountants or lawyers in their own country, they may be able to open a business that provides related services to their compatriots. Thus, while lack of English skills may prevent some immigrants from using their specialized occupational training when they first arrive in the United States, continued use of their ethnic language may facilitate their integration into the ethnic business network that can support them in taking the risks of entrepreneurship.

When, if ever, does the lack of English skills affect the success of an ethnic entrepreneur? There are two junctures where bilingualism is of interest here. The first has to do with the language skills needed to start a business and the second with those needed to expand one's labor force or market.

To open a business, one must find financial backing and comply with the business practices and commercial codes of the host country. At this point, ethnic entrepreneurs find assistance through their own rotating credit associations and get advice from coethnic intermediaries whose command of English is sufficient to

23. Edna Bonacich, "A Theory of Middleman Minorities," *American Sociological Review*, 38(5):583-94 (Oct. 1973).

24. The pioneering work in this field is that of Ivan H. Light. See his *Ethnic Enterprise in America: Business and Welfare among Chinese, Japanese, and Blacks* (Berkeley: University of California Press, 1972). More recent treatments appear in Ilsoo Kim, *New Urban Immigrants: The Korean Community in New York* (Princeton, NJ: Princeton University Press, 1981); Ivan H. Light, "Immigrant Entrepreneurs in America: Koreans in Los Angeles," in *Clamor at the Gates*, ed. Glazer, pp. 161-78.

decipher rules and regulations. If the business is dependent on wholesale distribution, an entrepreneur can choose to deal with only distributors who know the ethnic language; if there are enough of them, it may not be necessary to learn much English to get started.[25] In the initial phase of entrepreneurship, then, it is the ethnic language that provides access to many necessary resources. English is useful for dealing with institutions outside the ethnic community, but the need to use English varies in proportion to the possibility of carrying out necessary functions without it.

As soon as the business expands to the point where either the potential employee pool or the market includes more than coethnics, however, the need for the use of English in addition to the native language is inescapable. The business owner must then learn English or hire workers who know it to continue successful operation. As noted in the case of the apparel industry, as long as contractors employed mainly coethnics, there was no need for extensive use of English in the production process. At the same time, comments from the Spanish-speaking immigrant who achieved a supervisory position on a hospital cleaning crew because of his bilingualism in Spanish and English show that addition of English to native-language skills can help workers advance.[26]

For small, family-run retail businesses, the younger relatives or children who know English may provide the initial language links with customers who do not speak the ethnic language. Owners who serve many customers who are members of various language groups may need more English-speaking employees to serve their clientele effectively, however. Moreover, in some areas, small-business owners may want to hire English speakers of the same ethnic backgrounds as their customers to maintain good community relations; this is of particular importance when the immigrant business owners conduct trade in heavily minority communities. Korean business owners in south central Los Angeles, a largely black and Hispanic area, have made special efforts to hire members of the community to staff their stores, in part because of linguistic necessity and in part from the desire to lessen the tensions between the two communities. Once an immigrant business seeks to sell goods or provide services to others in addition to those who speak the same language as the owner, English is critical. In assessing the impact of differences between immigrant and native workers, economist Thomas Bailey points out that immigrants' lack of English proficiency becomes a relatively greater disadvantage as the importance of retail trade increases in the sector in which they are employed.[27]

Occupational bilingualism, characterized here as continued use of the native language plus English, may

25. On the importance of rotating credit associations and the interlocking of ethnic wholesale and retail networks, see Light, *Ethnic Enterprise in America;* Kim, *New Urban Immigrants.*

26. See the account of Jaime Alvarez in *American Mosaic,* ed. Morrison and Zabusky, pp. 357-58.

27. Thomas R. Bailey, *Immigrant and Native Workers: Contrasts and Competition* (Boulder, CO: Westview Press, 1987), p. 82.

contribute to economic success in the unconventional as well as the conventional sectors of the American economy. Light has pointed out that the relationship between immigrant communities and some of the less favorable manifestations of unconventional entrepreneurship, such as ethnic gambling and racketeering industries, reflects the effort to attain economic success when starting with unequal resources.[28] Fluency in English may help immigrant entrepreneurs evade as well as comply with accepted business practices and American laws, while continued use of the native language may be useful for exercising illicit as well as licit activities within ethnic enclaves. Bilingual language skills are simply additional means to achieve the goal of financial success whatever the nature of the enterprise.

Other relevant variables:
   Gender and ethnic
   background

Thus far we have seen that geographic location and occupational sector affect the relevance of bilingualism for non-English-speaking immigrant workers. There is some additional evidence that other social factors—chief among them, gender and ethnic background—play a role in determining the relevance of bilingual skills to workplace participation and success. It appears that having bilingual skills may provide different sorts of opportunities for men from those available to women and different possibilities for white and nonwhite minority groups that have historically been targets of discrimination in employment. Such differences coexist with the factors of geographic location and occupational sector already discussed.

Among the economists who have done substantial work on characteristics of the immigrant labor force is Barry Chiswick, whose investigations shed some light on the relative value of English-language skills as reflected in the earning patterns of immigrant men. Chiswick's analyses, based mainly on decennial census data, show that while, for the first 5 years or so after immigration, immigrants may lag behind native-born workers with comparable educational and ethnic characteristics, they typically catch up to native-born workers after that time and surpass native-born workers within 11-14 years after migration.[29] The economic progress of self-selected or voluntary migrants is much different from that of involuntary migrants, or refugees, who generally arrive with much lower levels of resources and transferable skills.[30]

Chiswick's investigation shows that language, insofar as it has any

28. See Ivan H. Light, "Immigrant Entrepreneurs in Los Angeles," in *Clamor at the Gates,* ed. Glazer, esp. pp. 176-78; idem, "The Ethnic Vice Industry, 1880-1944," *American Sociological Review,* 42(3):464-79 (1977).

29. Barry R. Chiswick, "The Economic Progress of Immigrants: Some Apparently Universal Patterns," in *The Gateway: U.S. Immigration Issues and Policies,* ed. B. R. Chiswick (Washington, DC: American Enterprise Institute, 1982), pp. 119-58; idem, "The Effect of Americanization on the Earnings of Foreign-Born Men," *Journal of Political Economy,* 86:897-921 (Oct. 1978).

30. Chiswick, "Economic Progress of Immigrants," p. 128.

impact on labor market experiences of male immigrants, differentiates the progress of those who come from English-speaking countries from the progress of those who do not. Immigrants from English-speaking countries show patterns of economic returns on schooling more similar to their native-born counterparts who have similar ethnic backgrounds and levels of occupational skill than do comparable immigrants who do not come from English-speaking countries.[31] Nevertheless, language differences do not account for the most dramatic gaps in earning between immigrant and native-born men; Chiswick's analyses demonstrate consistent ethnic-group differences in the economic success of first- and second-generation Americans. Non-Hispanic whites, Japanese, and second-generation Chinese have been more successful than black immigrants, who have prospered more than Mexican and Filipino workers, at least according to the 1970 census.[32] While knowledge of English may give immigrant workers some advantage, other socially relevant variables such as ethnic-group membership are evidently more influential in predicting economic success.

Looking specifically at the experience of Hispanics in the U.S. labor market, economists George Borjas and Marta Tienda have noted that marital status and family conditions affect men's and women's labor force participation in different ways and

thus necessitate separate analyses for each.[33] They note the great variation in English skills that characterizes different national-origin groups —Cubans, Mexicans, Puerto Ricans, Central and South Americans—and indicate that these differences may or may not affect employment, depending on local opportunities.[34] Other economists have found that lack of the ability to speak English does not significantly affect wages for Hispanic women in the United States[35] but that English-language proficiency is positively and significantly related to the likelihood of working for Mexican and Cuban women, although not for Puerto Rican women.[36] All such investigations imply that bilingual skills are characteristics that interact with other social indicators in determining success in employment.

CASE STUDIES OF
OCCUPATIONAL BILINGUALISM

To get a close-up look at the need for English in American workplaces, we turn to three case studies of English-language use in occupa-

33. George Borjas and Marta Tienda, eds., *Hispanics in the U.S. Economy* (Orlando, FL: Academic Press, 1985), p. 4.

34. Ibid., pp. 3-12.

35. Cordelia W. Reimers, "A Comparative Analysis of the Wages of Hispanics, Blacks, and Non-Hispanic Whites," in *Hispanics in the U.S. Economy*, ed. Borjas and Tienda, pp. 74-75.

36. Frank D. Bean, C. Gray Swicegood, and Allan G. King, "Role Incompatibility and the Relationship between Fertility and Labor Supply among Hispanic Women," in *Hispanics in the U.S. Economy*, ed. Borjas and Tienda, pp. 235-36.

31. Ibid., pp. 134-35.

32. Ibid., p. 157.

tional settings by immigrant workers. Although these studies are not the result of random sampling and thus cannot be taken as necessarily illustrative of all trends in the occupational use of language, they are representative of some of the questions related to the need for English for occupational purposes. Examination of selected cases provides a vivid sense of the experience of individual workers that underlies the aggregate data used by sociologists and economists.

English for restaurant work:
Automaticity and attitude

In large cities, many immigrants begin their American employment career through work in restaurants. Bailey has noted that immigrants are employed in restaurants in a share far disproportionate to their numbers; furthermore, the restaurant industry, once characterized almost entirely by informal and on-the-job skill acquisition, has in the last twenty years developed to a point where occupational roles have become more differentiated, with an upper layer of personnel requiring formal training in cooking and in management.[37] Thus, because restaurants provide for such a large share of initial immigrant employment and because of the variety of occupational roles, some of which offer upward mobility in the form of access to higher-paying jobs that may provide more training, restaurants are a useful arena for ex-

amining the relevance of English-language skills.

How much English does it take to be successfully employed in a restaurant? In an ethnographic study of the difference between promoted and nonpromoted employees—that is, waiters versus busboys—at an expensive, full-service restaurant in Beverly Hills, it was found that a low intermediate threshold level of English-language skill was necessary but not sufficient to bring about promotion from busboy to waiter.[38] Interviews with the restaurant management showed that failure to learn even minimal levels of English—for example, failure to recognize table numbers when directed to give patrons more water—had been cause for dismissal of some workers in the past.

Nonetheless, the pattern of promotion indicated that mastery of the English language alone was not the decisive factor: the best employee was not the one with the best English. Instead, the star waiter was one who demonstrated the complex of attitudes and behaviors that enabled him to provide attentive service: remembering a patron's favorite dishes and special requests; refilling bread trays and water glasses without being told; emptying ashtrays after a single cigarette. His spoken English was actually difficult to understand at times, but his behavior showed what his employers interpreted as

37. Thomas R. Bailey, *Immigrant and Native Workers: Contrast and Competition* (Boulder, CO: Westview Press, 1987), p. 9.

38. Darcy Jack, "Linguistic and Cultural Aspects of the Communication of Limited-English-Proficient Restaurant Workers" (Master's thesis, University of California, Los Angeles, 1986).

interest in doing the job well. In fact, restaurant managers were so impressed that they were considering making him an assistant manager, thus recruiting him into a level of employees with more advanced training and greater earning capacity. Thus English-language proficiency, essential for the step to direct customer service, was only one of many factors affecting subsequent promotability within the restaurant.

English for small businesses:
  Knowing the product
  and the customers

The importance of immigrant small businesses as an avenue of economic mobility has already been noted. If immigrants become entrepreneurs, how much English do they need to be successful? The answer, of course, depends on their clientele; if they serve nearly all compatriots, they may not need to know very much English. Once they wish to provide a product or service to an ethnically or linguistically mixed community, however, English becomes more important. Another ethnographic study of the language skills needed by those who worked in small businesses—in this case, copy shops and watch stores serving English-speaking customers—showed that the interactional routines at each place had their own special requirements.[39]

The counter people at the copy shop had to be good at understanding and responding to quick questions,

often asked over the hum and whir of copy machines at work. Thus they had to be good at automatic recognition of numbers and recognition of customers' special requests, which tended to be constrained by the nature of the services offered, including finite choices in type of paper and in options such as collating, reduction, and blowup.

In contrast, the watch stores sold more expensive items, and customers sometimes had to be persuaded to buy. Effective salespeople were those who used a greater variety of techniques, not all of them including language, for getting customers to consider an item. Here the nonnative speakers actually used various linguistic selling strategies—including discussion of specific features of a certain model or a direct request about the customer's willingness to buy—more frequently than native speakers.[40] Furthermore, they also used gestures and props—physically demonstrating the properties of a watch, referring to printed material about the merchandise—to compensate for any linguistic difficulties that arose. Their communication strategies in English were tailored to the specific demands of selling a more expensive discretionary item.

English for hospital nursing:
  Talk in person and
  on the phone

The previous two case studies have dealt with English-language use within special sectors of the American economy where immigrant

39. Henry C. O'Roark, "A Language Needs Assessment of Two Public-Contact Occupations" (Master's thesis, University of California, Los Angeles, 1985).

40. Ibid., pp. 43-44.

presence is strongest. To round out the consideration of the nature of job-related English-language skills, we turn to discussion of the English-language proficiency required by a group of highly educated immigrants, Chinese nurses who work in American hospitals. This group is emblematic of the many highly educated new immigrants who have come to the United States with the requisite occupational qualifications but need English-language skills for American licensure and for dealing with English-speaking supervisors and clientele, in this case, patients and families. Because Los Angeles is home to a large number of Chinese speakers, the nurses in this study were occasionally called upon to provide professional services in their native language for Chinese-speaking patients. Thus their native-language skills could at times be utilized in their professional setting.

A survey of American health care professionals and Chinese nurses employed in Los Angeles hospitals revealed that the English-language communication of the nurses was on the whole viewed as relatively smooth. Problems sometimes arose, however, in certain areas of pronunciation, such as differentiation of /-l-/ and /-r-/ sounds as in "pulse" versus "purse," and in use of the telephone.[41] Additionally, the native-speaker supervisors mentioned the potential value of giving nonnative nurses some orientation to the psychological

needs and family relationships of American patients, two areas that, though more cultural than linguistic, influenced the effectiveness of nursing practice.

OTHER ARENAS FOR OCCUPATIONAL BILINGUALISM

Two other arenas for occupational bilingualism in the United States merit mention because of their difference from the immigrant pattern hitherto discussed: bilingualism as manifested in indigenous rather than immigrant populations—that is, in language groups of very long residence such as Native Americans or the Hispanos of the southwest mountain regions—and the bilingualism found in border areas, particularly along the U.S.-Mexican border. While the language-use patterns characteristic of these situations have not been as well documented as that corresponding to immigrants, they also reveal the variable relevance of two languages to work settings. Each of these bilingual or bidialectal situations challenges the frequent assumption that the learning of English and the concomitant loss of native-language skills represent keys to occupational mobility.

Indigenous language minority groups: A mixed language picture

The variation in language-use patterns in indigenous language minority communities is extraordinary, and the number of separate communities equally large. Such populations in the United States may or

41. Esther Sunde, "The Communication of Chinese Nurses in the American Hospital Setting" (Master's thesis, University of California, Los Angeles, 1986).

may not retain a language other than English for communication in the home. If they have shifted to English, we may well observe workplace bidialectalism, the use of a particular variety of English influenced by a different substrate language and other local developments, rather than bilingualism.

In indigenous language minority communities, then, the presumed link between English and job mobility, which we have observed to some degree in immigrant populations, is not as clear-cut. Such minorities are called "caste-like" by anthropologist John Ogbu because they have been incorporated involuntarily into the United States and, in the main, relegated to subservient economic roles.[42] The diversity of language-use patterns in such communities includes many that are monolingual in English, though the English may be a particular variety still influenced by characteristics of a substrate language.

Many of these communities, though marked by widespread or nearly universal use of English as the language of everyday communication, do not demonstrate great economic success; on the contrary, they show widespread un- or underemployment. Although they may have learned the language of the dominant culture quite well, members of such groups do not reap any particular

42. See John Ogbu, *Minority Education and Caste: The American System in Cross-Cultural Perspective* (New York: Academic Press, 1978); idem, "Minority Status and Schooling in Plural Societies," *Comparative Education Review,* 27(2):168-90 (1983).

economic rewards or have additional avenues to upward mobility that result from the use of English. Some of the lack of connection between the use of English as the language of everyday communication and occupational progress in such groups may be due to the fact that, because nearly all members of the community speak the language, its mastery is not remarkable and does not confer any special status or create a potential for employment as supervisors or middlemen.

The historical experience of such groups shows that, in occupational terms, just speaking English is not sufficient to guarantee advancement in the workplace. Paramount, instead, is the mastery of higher-level English-literacy skills, the skills that largely determine success in the American school system. High levels of English-literacy skills allow individuals to qualify for further training or for positions where entry is regulated by written tests as well as oral communication skills.

One could speculate that, for indigenous language minority communities, loss of the native language might in some circumstances have negative economic repercussions. First, if the native language is a language such as Spanish that is also the language of many economically vibrant minority language communities, loss of the ability to speak that language might indeed limit one's possibilities for employment requiring bilingual skills. Second, insofar as the native language can create in-group solidarity and hence provide a stronger support network, it is possible that a community's shift to English demonstrates not a step forward on the economic scale but the loss of a cultural resource, the native language, that could create a psychosocial disadvantage with economic ramifications. In short, some indigenous or caste-like language minority groups that have lost use of the native language may have lost with it a possible source of social strength and distinctiveness that might contribute indirectly to economic success. Such a line of reasoning is clearly speculative and deserving of further research.

Border areas:
  Bilingualism for
  international interaction

Another situation that differs from the immigrant language scene is that of border areas where two languages have coexisted for centuries. Linguist Guadalupe Valdés notes that language contact across national borders is recognized as qualitatively different from contact that occurs in immigrant settings because of the comparable status and range of function available to each language. Because each language is linked with a distinct polity, neither has minority status.[43] But Valdés observes that very little is known about why monolingual members of either group become bilingual. Are occupational considerations relevant to the question of who speaks which language to whom on the border?

Indeed they are. The border between the United States and Mexico is a particularly interesting context in which to ask questions about occupational bilingualism because of the intimate links between many cities along the border and the thriving *maquila* industry, which provides less expensive Mexican labor to produce goods later sold in the United States.[44] In the *maquila* work force, the norm is for the operatives to be monolingual Spanish speakers, while anyone involved in management is bilingual; some workers with highly technical skills, such as engineers, may not need to be fully bilingual, but most managers must be.[45] Although I know of no specific studies relating bilingualism, defined here as proficiency in English and Spanish, to labor market success along the border, some indirect evidence as well as anecdotal information about the language skills needed by those with different job classifications suggests that, other things equal, bilingual skills enhance earning power. Economic studies have documented relatively lower earnings for those employed along the border than for those employed in the interior of the United States but have noted, too, that the differential decreases dramatically with more years of education: college graduates earn more

43. Guadalupe Valdés, "Bilingualism in a Mexican Border City: A Research Agenda," in *Bilingualism and Language Contact: Spanish, English, and Native American Languages,* ed. F. Barkin, E. A. Brandt, and J. Ornstein-Galicia (New York: Teachers College Press, 1982), p. 4.

44. See Ellwyn R. Stoddard, *Maquila: Assembly Plants in Northern Mexico* (El Paso: Texas Western Press, 1987).

45. Telephone conversation with E. R. Stoddard, 16 Feb. 1990.

than high school graduates, who earn more than those with an elementary school education.[46] If we test the assumption that increasing years of education make it more likely that a person has acquired some bilingual skills—an assumption that bears empirical scrutiny—we may begin to illuminate the influence of bilingualism on earnings in this setting. Despite widespread observations of the importance of bilingualism along the border, little systematic work on the nature of job-related bilingual skills in this unique geographic area has been done.

UNANSWERED QUESTIONS

This brief survey of occupational bilingualism has left several questions unanswered. In terms of the experience of the individual worker, we need to know more about the relationship, if any, between English-language proficiency and occupational attainment over the course of a worker's career. In this regard, it is instructive to note that occupational use of English does not necessarily lead to loss of the first language in bilingual communities. Hence studies that document the dynamic relationship between the two languages

46. See Alberto E. Davila and J. Peter Mattila, "Do Workers Earn Less along the U.S.-Mexican Border?" *Social Science Quarterly*, 66(2):310-18 (1985). These economists note that it is difficult to calculate the "border wage differential" accurately because precise data are lacking on the relative cost of living in border areas versus other places; they conclude that much of the differential is a function of the "lower levels of education and experience and high proportions of Mexican Americans along the border." Ibid., p. 314.

in terms of their variable salience to an individual's economic activities over the course of a lifetime are needed. Second, again from the perspective of the individual worker, we would like to know more about whether and how the acquisition of English affects nonfinancial but economically and socially relevant indicators such as job satisfaction, relationships with coworkers, and possibilities for advancement.

Third, the extent and nature of English-language—and native-language—skills needed for survival and success in ethnic enclaves need to be better described. Thus far, we have had studies of mainly economic behavior and enclosure, and the linguistic concomitants of ethnic enclaves are not well documented. Fourth, in terms of the aggregate experience of language groups, we need to ask whether higher levels of bilingual skills—strong and balanced proficiency in both languages—in individuals translate into aggregate economic improvements for the group.

IMPLICATIONS FOR POLICY

Given the multifaceted relationships between occupational bilingualism and other social conditions, what actions, if any, should concerned government or private agencies take? These implications can be examined under the general rubrics of economic, social, and educational policy.

The continued vitality of languages other than English that function in tandem with English on the American economic scene means that those concerned with shaping the economy must realize the importance of bilingualism, not just the importance of English. In a capitalist society that aspires to pluralist ideals, we need to ensure that all language groups can participate in employment market choices through workplace and consumer behavior. Making information available in the appropriate language goes part of the way toward meeting this goal.

Labor relations, too, require application of bilingual skills to reach the appropriate audience. Current studies of the apparel trades show that lack of bilingual personnel able to do Chinese-language organizing in New York and Spanish-language organizing in Los Angeles has diminished the strength of garment workers' unions in both cities.[47]

In the economic sphere, we have seen that the nature of the link between English-language skills and employability varies considerably by geographic location and the sector of the economy in which a person is employed. Such variation suggests that it is still true that, in some areas of the United States and in some occupations, one can find work without knowing much English. Therefore the attempt to set a very high national standard of English-language proficiency for immigration purposes is not defensible on purely economic grounds. Although there may be other reasons for requiring an entrant to know English, the position

that it is necessary to know English well to obtain a job is not uniformly supported by the data.

Available data do suggest, however, that English assumes more importance as a worker considers either upgrading occupational qualifications or changing fields of work. Furthermore, workers who know only a little English and have no other occupational skills may be seriously handicapped in getting any but the very lowest-paying jobs in areas of the country where they have few compatriots; if they have little education and few other job skills, they will be unlikely to advance or even to break out of the poverty level. This, indeed, appears to be the situation of many Southeast Asian refugees in the United States;[48] given the great cultural and often educational as well as linguistic gap, the English-language training received under U.S. government auspices gave them only low levels of proficiency insufficient for all but entry-level jobs.[49] Hence, if the government is to support any language training, it should do so on the assumption that completion of the training will allow the participant to meet the appropriate economic objective, which we assume in this case to be not just survival but an income level above the poverty line.

What does the discussion of occupational bilingualism imply for the

47. See Bernard Wong, "The Chinese: New Immigrants in New York's Chinatown," in *New Immigrants in New York*, ed. N. Foner (New York: Columbia University Press, 1987), pp. 266-67; Laslett and Tyler, *ILGWU in Los Angeles*, pp. 63-65, 95-103.

48. Gail P. Kelly, "Coping with America: Refugees from Vietnam, Cambodia, and Laos in the 1970s and 1980s," *The Annals* of the American Academy of Political and Social Science, 487:138-49 (Sept. 1986).

49. James W. Tollefson, *Alien Winds: The Reeducation of America's Indochinese Refugees* (New York: Praeger, 1989), pp. 106-26.

educational system at large? As the United States becomes less able to ignore the world market, we expect that the potential economic benefits of bilingualism will attract more students to second-language study and will encourage students from immigrant backgrounds who already know a non-English language to maintain it.[50] If we do indeed feel that economic conditions require bilingual skills for occupational success, we need to ensure that the second-language education programs offered to students can deliver the requisite skills, both in terms of the language involved and the level of proficiency reached. The enrollment growth in classes in languages such as Spanish and Japanese testifies in part to students' recognition of the economic value of skills in each of these languages, one the most widely spoken second language in the United States and the other the medium of a world economic power. The changes occurring almost daily throughout the Eastern-bloc nations may well have important consequences for the kind of occupational bilingualism needed in the near future.

In sum, bilingualism is as much a part of the American workplace as it has always been. Although there are different languages now at play, we can observe dynamic relationships between the languages used when work involves two language groups in immigrant communities, in indig-

50. See Russell N. Campbell and Kathryn J. Lindholm, "Conservation of Language Resources" (Educational Report no. 6, Center for Language Education and Research, University of California, Los Angeles, 1987).

enous language minority groups, and along the border. In each of these situations, the nature of language contact, language behavior, and possible economic implications differs. The data so far available come from somewhat crude measures of actual language use, so it is difficult to develop a detailed picture of the varieties of workplace bilingualism. It is uniformly true that there is considerable variation in the necessity for English and the continued economic relevance of the native language according to geographic location, occupational sector, and personal circumstances. Additionally, while workers may demonstrate similar levels of second-language skill, it appears that mastery of functional control of language related to specific job activities is at least as important for occupational success as attainment of a prespecified level on any test of general English grammar and vocabulary.

This means that any proclamation of "English only" in the workplace is premature and potentially harmful. We have abundant evidence from the American immigrant experience that workers who do not know English can find jobs, particularly if they work within an ethnic economy. At the same time, an individual's limitation to skill in one language can have damaging economic consequences if that language is not English and the individual seeks upward mobility through job change or expansion of a customer base to include English speakers. Furthermore, there is evidence that, for some nonnative speakers, the addition of English skills to proficiency in another language is associated with economic progress.

Moving from the experience of the individual worker to that of businesses or institutions that rely on other languages for occupational purposes, we find that the favorable climate for the establishment of businesses in some nonnative English communities promotes some degree of occupational bilingualism for both the minority and majority. If they expand their markets beyond speakers of the same language, ethnic entrepreneurs find that the need to use English along with the native language grows; in turn, as such ethnic enterprises become more prosperous, they command more resources and thus create a larger market for goods and services involving the ethnic language as well as English. The relationships between languages used in occupational settings and economic outcomes are many; to date, few have been systematically described. Nevertheless, it is clear that many languages in addition to English will continue to play a part in determining the vitality of the American economy, domestic and international, of the 1990s.

Report of the Board of Directors to the Members of the American Academy of Political and Social Science for the Year 1989

MEMBERSHIPS AND SUBSCRIPTIONS
AS OF DECEMBER 31

Year	Number
1979	10,884
1980	10,059
1981	9,874
1982	9,536
1983	8,904
1984	6,564
1985	5,704
1986	5,606
1987	5,151
1988	4,674
1989	4,903

PUBLICATIONS
NUMBER OF VOLUMES OF THE ANNALS PRINTED (6 PER YEAR)

1979	71,513
1980	65,153
1981	69,313
1982	74,211
1983	68,236
1984	52,154
1985	52,800
1986	53,201
1987	43,629
1988	53,497
1989	40,269

FINANCES
SIZE OF SECURITIES PORTFOLIO
MARKET VALUE AS OF DECEMBER 31

1979	377,915
1980	368,926
1981	351,886
1982	390,119
1983	485,809
1984	384,312
1985	369,389
1986	373,320
1987	387,997
1988	345,634
1989	284,732

NUMBER OF VOLUMES OF THE ANNALS SOLD
(IN ADDITION TO MEMBERSHIPS AND SUBSCRIPTIONS)

1979	5,907
1980	8,751
1981	5,884
1982	7,562
1983	5,877
1984	5,230
1985	5,910
1986	5,119
1987	5,314
1988	13,283
1989	4,802

STATEMENT OF INCOME AND RETAINED EARNINGS FOR THE YEAR ENDED DECEMBER 31, 1989

Income
Royalty—Sage Publications	$110,000
Sales of review books	989
Royalties and reprint permissions	1,050
Annual meeting revenue	1,558
Contributions	5,530
Miscellaneous	9,481
Total Income	128,608

Operating Expenses
Salaries	80,985
Payroll taxes	6,735
Pension expense	20,221
Employee benefits	5,889
Annual meeting expense	18,329
Depreciation	1,839
Insurance	6,158
Postage	2,938
Repairs and maintenance	12,470

Professional and contracted services	19,760
Book review costs	4,046
Supplies	2,566
Utilities	12,433
Miscellaneous	1,048
Total Operating Expenses	195,417
Loss from Operations	(66,809)
Other Income (Expenses)	
Investment income (net)	26,738
Gains (loss) on sale of investments	(8,731)
Grant administration overhead	10,131
Total Other Income (Expense)	46,600
Net Income (Loss)	20,209
Retained Earnings—January 1	288,260
Retained Earnings—December 31	268,051

Report of the Board of Directors

During 1989, the six volumes of THE ANNALS dealt with the following subjects:

January *The Ghetto Underclass: Social Science Perspectives,* edited by William Julius Wilson, Professor, University of Chicago, Illinois

March *Universities and the Military,* edited by David A. Wilson, Professor, University of California, Los Angeles

May *The Quality of Aging: Strategies for Interventions,* edited by Matilda White Riley, Associate Director, National Institute on Aging, Bethesda, Maryland, and John W. Riley, Jr., Consulting Sociologist, Chevy Chase, Maryland

July *Peace Studies: Past and Future,* edited by George A. Lopez, Faculty Fellow, Institute for International Studies, University of Notre Dame, Indiana

September *The Pacific Rim: Challenges to Policy and Theory,* edited by Peter A. Gourevitch, Dean, Graduate School of International Relations and Pacific Studies, University of California, San Diego

November *Human Rights around the World,* edited by Marvin E. Wolfgang, President, American Academy of Political and Social Sciences, Director, Center for Studies in Criminology and Criminal Law, University of Pennsylvania, Philadelphia

The publication program for 1990 includes the following volumes:

January *Privatizing and Marketizing Socialism,* edited by Jan S. Prybyla, Professor, Pennsylvania State University, University Park

March *English Plus: Issues in Bilingual Education,* edited by Courtney B. Cazden, Professor, and Catherine E. Snow, Professor, Harvard Graduate School of Education, Cambridge, Massachusetts

May *American Federalism: The Third Century,* edited by John Kincaid, Executive Director, U.S. Advisory Commission on Intergovernmental Relations, Washington, D.C.

July *World Population: Approaching the Year 2000,* edited by Samuel H. Preston, Director, Population Studies Center, University of Pennsylvania, Philadelphia

September *Foreign Language in the Workplace,* edited by Richard D. Lambert, Director, National Foreign Language Center, Johns Hopkins University, Washington, D.C., and Sarah Jane Moore, Educational Research Specialist, Philadelphia, Pennsylvania

November *The Nordic Region: Changing Perspectives in International Relations,* edited by Martin O. Heisler, Associate Professor, University of Maryland, College Park.

During 1989, the Book Department published over 230 reviews. The majority of these were written by professors, but reviewers also included university presidents, members of private and university-sponsored organizations, government and public officials, and business professionals. Nearly 600 books were listed in the Other Books section.

Seventy-one requests were granted to reprint material from THE ANNALS. These went to professors and other authors for use in books in preparation and to non-profit organizations for educational purposes.

MEETINGS

The ninety-first annual meeting, which was held 28-29 April 1989, had as its subject *Human Rights around the World* and continued the tradition of our gatherings with respect to the diversity of organizations represented by delegates and the interest displayed by the audiences. Delegates were sent by American and foreign universities and colleges and international, civic, scientific, and commercial organizations. States, cities, and United Nations missions and embassies were also represented.

The ninety-second annual meeting, was postponed to 1991.

OFFICERS AND STAFF

The Board reelected the following officers: Marvin E. Wolfgang, President; Richard D. Lambert, Vice-President; Anthony J. Scirica, Secretary; Elmer B. Staats, Treasurer; Henry W. Sawyer, III, Counsel. Reappointed were: Richard D. Lambert, Editor, and Alan W. Heston, Associate Editor.

Respectfully submitted,
THE BOARD OF DIRECTORS

Elmer B. Staats
Marvin E. Wolfgang
Richard D. Lambert
Thomas L. Hughes
Lloyd N. Cutler
Henry W. Sawyer, III
Anthony J. Scirica
Frederick Heldring

Philadelphia, Pennsylvania
18 December 1989

Book Department

INTERNATIONAL RELATIONS AND POLITICS

DAHL, ROBERT A. *Democracy and Its Critics*. Pp. viii, 397. New Haven, CT: Yale University Press, 1989. $29.95.

It is difficult to conceive of a time when the allure of democracy has proven a more common and unifying motivator of political action than the present or of one when the term has had such numerous and diverse meanings. All the world, it seems, is an experiment in democratic theory, and all of its leaders, save perhaps Mr. Castro and a few widely scattered potentates, are democrats.

Alternatively, ours is a world devoid of true democracy, deprived by the scale of contemporary life of opportunities for meaningful, self-directed individual participation in the polity. Even in the seeming bastions of the liberal democratic state, elites and near elites guard the presumed core values of society against the baser urges, or—a rival hypothesis—the disinterest and lack of political skill, of those who supposedly espouse them, maintaining their positions of privilege through their own skills in purveying merely the symbols of democracy.

Which is it? That is the question—really a series of questions—that Robert Dahl addresses in *Democracy and Its Critics*.

In this capstone volume, Dahl interweaves normative and empirical notions in an effort to develop a broadly integrative theory of democracy, one that is at once historically grounded, context sensitive, true to its philosophical origins, and sustainable under scrutiny. His effort is both remarkable and, for the most part, successful.

Dahl's democracy is a dynamic entity, a ship of ideals steering a course across a sea of empirical realities, tossed here and there by human frailties but sailing bravely toward some unspecified destination. It is an amorphous entity, defined by rather than defining its content—taking the shape of its container. It is an entity in constant struggle, as much for definition as for survival. Above all, Dahl's democracy is instrumental, providing the democrats of nearly two millennia with both the rationale and the social technology to enrich political life.

Democracy and Its Critics is the product of literally decades of observation and analysis by one of the nation's premier political theorists, and in its breadth of vision and depth of insight it gives testimony to the quality of the author's mind. The book is well crafted, as Dahl's books always are, and is presented in a style that will prove accessible to the professional and the lay reader alike and to political scientists of both normative and empirical bent. One quibble is that the dialogues around which Dahl develops some chapters are not always productive and may, at times, detract from the unfolding of his argument.

This book represents a benchmark in the development of democratic thought at a time when clear thinking about the ideal and practical forms of democracy is especially in demand.

JAROL B. MANHEIM

George Washington
University
Washington, D.C.

VERNON, RAYMOND and DEBORA SPAR. *Beyond Globalism: Remaking American Foreign Economic Policy.* Pp. x, 246. New York: Free Press, 1988. $22.95.

COOPER, RICHARD N. et al. *Can Nations Agree? Issues in International Economic Cooperation.* Pp. x, 303. Washington, DC: Brookings Institution, 1989. $32.95.

The emergence of competitive markets to determine the international division of labor has raised pressing matters concerning cooperation and coordination between nation-states in such matters as monetary and fiscal policy, trade policy, international debt, direct investments,

technology transfer, and military arrangements. Both of the books under review are about the problems and prospects for successful cooperation on a wide range of international economic and political issues.

Raymond Vernon, an experienced and thoughtful expert on international economic arrangements, and his student, Debora Spar, have written a readable treatment of the international and domestic problems of achieving cooperation in the new competitive environment. Their book provides a historical perspective covering the years from the end of World War II to the present. They discuss the international monetary and trading system, the rise of the multinationals, the foreign-aid efforts of the United States, the rise and fall of multilateralism, and the past and current domestic political issues concerning all of these matters in Western Europe, Japan, the underdeveloped countries, and the United States.

The Vernon-Spar book provides a broad overview of the problems facing international policymakers, an approach of interest to the nonspecialist. On the other hand, Cooper and his colleagues address themselves to a more specialized audience of international experts.

This collection of essays begins with a thoughtful introduction by Ralph Bryant and Edith Hodgkinson. There are two instructive essays on monetary and fiscal coordination in the context of the 1978 Bonn Summit, one written by Robert Putnam and C. Randall Henning and the other written by Gerald Holtham. These case studies on the political and economic dimensions of macroeconomic coordination highlight the difficulties of coordination.

In his essay, Richard Cooper attempts to explain these difficulties. Applying the technique of studying a relatively structured and understandable situation in order to generalize to similar but less structured situations—a technique successfully employed by the late Ithiel de Sola Pool in his retrospective study on the spread of telephone technology—Cooper examines the history of successful international efforts to control the spread of contagious diseases in the nineteenth and early twentieth centuries.

Cooper concludes on a rather hopeful note, at least in principle. When the goal is well defined and the means of achieving the goal is agreed upon, international cooperation is achievable. Unfortunately for macroeconomic cooperation today, there is no agreement on means in the United States or abroad. In particular, the interventionist Keynesian model is in sharp conflict with the nonintervention-ist New Classical, or Lucasian, model. In the Keynesian model the government is a stabilizer. In the Lucasian model, it is just a meddler—at best, ineffective; at worst, destabilizing.

This brings us back to the Vernon-Spar analysis. For them, the difficulties of achieving international cooperation are organizational and political, not technical. In truth, common goals and shared understanding of technical reality are both essential. But policies always have losers as well as winners. If the losers cannot be politically outmaneuvered, they must be compensated. Unhappily, the slowdown in economic growth since the first oil shock contributed to a tax revolt. Under these circumstances, a budget-constrained government cannot easily buy off special interests who can often thwart international cooperation. Without internal economic growth, there is no foundation for international cooperation.

LEONARD A. RAPPING

University of Massachusetts
Amherst

AFRICA, ASIA, AND LATIN AMERICA

CHOUDHURY, GOLAM W. *Pakistan: Translation from Military to Civilian Rule.* Pp. 256. Essex, England: Scorpion, 1988. $29.95.

DUNCAN, EMMA. *Breaking the Curfew: A Political Journey through Pakistan.* Pp. 313. New York: Penguin Group, 1989. $22.95.

There are many similarities in these two books, one by a leading political scientist of East Pakistan and Bangladesh who was a member of the cabinet in Yahya Khan's brief administration in Pakistan (1969-71), the other by the South Asian correspondent of *The Economist*. The focus of each volume is the period of Zia ul-Haq's rule (1977-88). Choudhury's volume concentrates on the transition from military to civilian rule in 1985 and on Zia's attempt to blend Islamization and democracy. Duncan's book views the various groups that seem to be most important from the political and social point of view; she has separate chapters on businessmen, landlords, tribal chiefs, "urban upstarts," politicians, religious bodies, civil servants, and soldiers. By an interesting coincidence, both Choudhury and Duncan were among the last to interview Zia ul-Haq, only a few days before his death in an air crash in August 1988.

The differences in the two volumes are great. Choudhury has been a participant in as well as an observer of Pakistan's evolution as an independent nation. Because of his participation in Yahya Khan's administration and his subsequent book, *The Last Days of United Pakistan,* he was not allowed to visit either Pakistan or Bangladesh for more than a decade. He spent his years as a stateless person in the United States, with frequent trips to England and China. In 1984 he returned to Dhaka, and soon thereafter he renewed his contacts in Pakistan, including several meetings with Zia. His present volume includes a clear survey of Pakistan's political history, with two chapters each on the role of the military in politics and the state and religion—with special attention to the process of Islamization—and three chapters on the evolving nature of the political system. Duncan's book is more interesting and much less comprehensive. It is based exclusively on her "political journey through Pakistan" in the years 1986-88. She is obviously much less of an authority on Pakistan than Choudhury, but she demonstrates the value of first-class political reporting by probing deeply into the inner sources of Pakistan's political and social life.

Both Choudhury and Duncan present interesting comments on Zia ul-Haq, Duncan's less favorable than Choudhury's. Choudhury also has much to say about the three outstanding political leaders of Pakistan prior to Zia—Jinnah, Ayub Khan, and Z. A. Bhutto. Duncan has fascinating comments on Benazir Bhutto, whom Choudhury hardly mentions, since his manuscript was completed before Benazir came to power as a result of the elections of November 1988.

Both authors are quite gloomy about Pakistan's political future. In an epilogue, written just after Zia's death, Choudhury expresses the view that "ultimately the choice in post-Zia Pakistan may be between a left-oriented civilian government [and] a new martial law regime." In the long run, Duncan foresees continuing failure in nation building in Pakistan unless at least two trends—the "growing cynicism" that "is leading people to turn away from the regular institu-

tions of government" and "the breakdown of law and order"—are reversed.

NORMAN D. PALMER

University of Pennsylvania
Philadelphia

ELWARFALLY, MAHMOUD G. *Imagery and Ideology in U.S. Policy toward Libya, 1969-1982.* Pp. ix, 220. Pittsburgh, PA: University of Pittsburgh Press, 1988. $29.95.

Colonel Muammar Qaddafi, Libya's volatile leader who came to power on 1 September 1969 as a result of a military coup, has been the object of American study for two decades. He has been variously appraised by successive administrations from the initial period of his stewardship. Foreign policy specialists under Nixon, Ford, and Carter sought to accommodate the colonel on a wide range of issues. His support for "liberation" movements worldwide, however, as well as his financial assistance to terrorist organizations, finally led the Reagan administration to adopt a posture of confrontation, with Reagan characterizing the colonel as the "Flaky Barbarian."

Mahmoud Elwarfally, a former Libyan diplomat and now a practicing member of the academic community, has prepared a balanced assessment of evolving U.S.-Libyan relations, one that seeks to provide a more objective assessment of the colonel, his motivations, perceptions, and policies. Using cognitive theory as his baseline for analysis, Elwarfally argues that distorted images and beliefs on the part of American policymakers have shaped their decisions vis-à-vis Qaddafi. At the information-processing stage, pre-established beliefs and images have constricted the boundaries—that is, the limitations—of policymaker comprehension of Qaddafi's purposes and goals. The result has been policy decisions that have distorted and eroded relationships.

In the instance of the United States and Libya, ties became frayed during the Reagan administration as a by-product of (1) the prevailing belief in Washington that Qaddafi was a major actor in supporting international terrorism; (2) the adoption of Reagan's so-called doctrine, which had as its basic strategy "rollback": "the Soviets have long made it their business to probe the Third World, seeking to add satellites to their orbit," and "the U.S. can no longer afford to watch passively as the Soviets consolidate their power"; and (3) the conviction that Libya had become a Soviet proxy. On such beliefs are adversarial relations built.

Professor Elwarfally concludes that we "may expect that U.S. behavior toward Libya will continue to be provocative and confrontational" as long as these images persist. Certainly, the recent record would appear to support his judgment. The construction of a chemical-weapons complex in Libya, Qaddafi's efforts to acquire a ballistic-missile delivery system of intermediate range, and his search for other, more lethal forms of weaponry are a source of concern in Washington. How the Bush administration will respond is a matter of widespread speculation in the United States and the Middle East.

WILLIAM H. LEWIS

George Washington
University
Washington, D.C.

NYANG'ORO, JULIUS E. *The State and Capitalist Development in Africa: Declining Political Economies*. Pp. xi, 178. New York: Praeger, 1989. $39.95.

Nyang'oro begins this book with an overview of the contemporary crisis of production in cereals, export agriculture, and industry in Africa. It is a stark reminder that orthodox theories of modernization, emphasizing comparative advantage and export agriculture and encouraged by the International Monetary Fund and the World Bank, have not served Africa well in the postindependence period. In addition to providing a critique of neoclassical economic orthodoxy, Nyang'oro rejects much of early dependency theory, which had a tendency to view external factors as the sole determinant of Africa's underdevelopment.

Nyang'oro argues for a new analysis of dependency that recognizes that the expansion of world capitalism has affected regions of the Third World differently and that much of Africa remains precapitalist, which he defines as a mode of production characterized by simple commodity production and resource-based agriculture. Such conditions present internal obstacles to the development of capitalism. Furthermore, he argues that the state reflects Africa's material conditions and therefore lacks the requisite institutions to sustain development programs. He thus characterizes the African state as patrimonial-bureaucratic and rejects terms such as "bureaucratic bourgeoisie" and "state bourgeoisie" because they assume a level of material development and a relationship to the mode of production that do not exist.

This is a well-written book that nicely summarizes the modernization and dependency frameworks of analysis. The discussion of capitalism and the state in Africa also provides a clear analysis of the debates between those who are attempting to characterize Africa's political economy. Nyang'oro's contention that the mode of production in Africa is predominantly precapitalist is slightly overstated, thus leaving the impression that the African peasantry is largely isolated from all market forces. This is hardly the case, as Mahmood Mamdani and others have argued. Furthermore, his call for state leaders who are progressive and willing to collaborate with the private sector relies too fully on a voluntarist conception of political leadership. The constraints on political choice are too real to put so much stock in individual agency and will. His argument could have been considerably strengthened by a discussion of particular governments with such potential or actual progressive tendencies and with specific cases of successful collaboration between the government and the private sector in Africa.

CATHERINE V. SCOTT

Agnes Scott College
Decatur
Georgia

TAYLOR, ALAN R. *The Islamic Question in Middle East Politics*. Pp. ix, 150. Boulder, CO: Westview Press, 1988. $29.95. Paperbound, $14.95.

Alan R. Taylor's *Islamic Question in Middle East Politics* is the latest in a long line of works attempting to make some sense of Islamic fundamentalism for Western readers. Like most books on the subject, Taylor focuses on normative phenomena.

The basis of the book is that Islamic fundamentalism is a product of the inability of secular nationalism to create new and more responsive political systems in the Arab world in the twentieth century. The nationalists of the Arab world based their politics on the belief that two forces prevented the Arab world from achieving greatness: the domination of the West and the tradition of Islam. In order to modernize and free the Arab world and bring it into the twenti-

eth century, these forces had to be defeated. Nationalism was the program of choice to accomplish these goals in the Middle East. While Taylor ventures no comprehensive explanation of what the nationalist program was, he stresses that nationalism ultimately failed because it did not fully embrace the liberal democratic tradition on which it was based and of which Western nations so fully took advantage for their own development.

Taylor sees that by the 1960s Arab nationalism had largely been discredited because of a long list of failures: the breakup of the United Arab Republic, the inability of nationalist regimes to deal effectively with the existence of Israel, the Yemeni revolution, and the 1967 war. These failures seriously undermined the credibility of nationalist regimes and the movement in general. When this was combined with the increasing internal repression in these states, the scene was set for an alternative movement to rise to challenge the dominant nationalist ideology in the region.

For Taylor, the only viable alternative to nationalism in the Middle East is fundamentalism. He discounts Marxism out of hand—with no explanation of why—and focuses his attention on the Islamic perception of the postindependence Arab state. The 1928 founding of the Muslim Brotherhood is identified as the beginning of neofundamentalism, though Taylor does give the reader a perceptive and insightful account of the early roots of Islamic political influence.

The book's title refers to the question of what role can and should Islam play in "the restructuring of the Middle East's ideological orientation and institutional framework." Taylor is highly critical of Islamic fundamentalism and its current trend toward ideological rigidity. For him, the humanistic and idealized tradition of Islam with its cultural greatness, its eclecticism, and its understanding of the nature of nature and humans is the Islam that needs to be embraced to return Muslims to greatness. It is this Islam, not the radical ideological sloganeering of the Iranian Revolution or the Shia movements in Lebanon, that is, for Taylor, the true Islam, the Islam that has a preeminent place in Islamic society and politics. Moreover, Taylor argues, such a perspective is desperately needed today because the form that neofundamentalism has taken is primarily destructive—it aims at destroying the value systems and institutions that have been created by contact with the West. He considers its leaders not men of God but brutal, repressive despots who are bound to repeat the mistakes of the nationalists—Taylor draws comparisons between Khomeini and the Shah to make his point. They are men who seek the narrowest possible definition of what is true to Islam, and they do this to serve their own ends.

Taylor therefore feels that a resurgent Islam harking back to the more universal and humanistic tenets of Islam is the answer to neofundamentalism. Such a conclusion is not new nor is it necessarily correct, for Taylor is convinced that the ideals of Western society—such as the concept of liberalism—can and should play an important role in rescuing the Middle East from neofundamentalism and the mistakes of the nationalists. This conclusion is remarkably similar to conclusions drawn in the colonial period, when it was generally considered that the only thing wrong with the Arab world was that it was not Western enough. Taylor therefore fits into a long history of Western scholars who are determined to inculcate the Middle East with Western ideals. The only difference between Taylor and others of this tradition is his couching his views in Islamic terms—he has found what he thinks is a sound Islamic tradition of westernism in Islam, and he is

certain that it is this and only this tradition that will aid the Arab world.

T. Y. ISMAEL

University of Calgary
Alberta
Canada

VOGEL, EZRA F. *One Step Ahead in China: Guangdong under Reform.* Pp. viii, 510. Cambridge, MA: Harvard University Press, 1989. $29.95.

However hopeful they may be, the tumultuous changes sweeping the Communist world are surprising and confusing. Because they are largely unprecedented, social scientists have been unable to forecast them and have no models to predict their outcomes confidently. It is important therefore to focus our close attention now on those places that have taken the earliest lead in economic and political reforms to look for clues about what may happen elsewhere. One of the pioneers in the process of reform was the People's Republic of China, and within China the region that consistently has moved one step ahead since the reforms were launched in 1979 has been the southern province of Guangdong. Ezra Vogel's book comprehensively chronicles the reform process in Guangdong, analyzing both the promises it holds and the obstacles it faces. It is an extremely useful and timely book.

Vogel was ideally situated to write a major work on the reforms in Guangdong. His 1969 *Canton under Communism* was the most comprehensive and solidly grounded study published about the Guangdong region under Communist rule. Since China's opening to the West, Vogel has become known by and gained the confidence of many provincial officials of Guangdong. In 1987, they invited him to Guangdong to conduct seven months of fieldwork there. They gave him exceptional opportunities to travel, observe, and interview local officials throughout the region. In extraordinarily rich detail—perhaps too much detail to bring a compelling argument into sharp focus—Vogel was able to portray the variety of social changes that have swept the Guangdong region over the past decade.

It is indeed a region rather than a province that is the object of Vogel's study. His book takes in Hong Kong and the newly established province of Hainan Island as well as the province of Guangdong. In Vogel's perspective, it is mainly economics rather than politics that explosively drives social change in contemporary China. Hong Kong, Guangdong, and Hainan are parts of a "newly industrializing region," in the words of John Kamm, who contributed an excellent chapter, "Reforming Foreign Trade," to Vogel's book. The material and indeed the spiritual center of this region is Hong Kong, which provides much of the capital, technology, managerial skills, and images of the good life that drive other parts of the region to produce and consume. What mainly determines the pace of social change in this region is not political structures but the extent of an area's integration into the markets centered in Hong Kong.

The newly industrializing region of Guangdong is approaching an economic takeoff similar to that reached by newly industrializing countries like South Korea and Taiwan in the 1970s. Vogel enthusiastically and vividly describes the increases in wealth and the quickening pace of economic development coming to even peripheral areas in the Guangdong region. He also notes serious problems that may make it difficult for the region to achieve the successes in economic development of the so-called little tigers of East Asia.

In the end, the problems have to do with the interplay between economics, politics, and culture. As Vogel notes, economic development in late-developing countries requires a considerable degree of government coordination and of voluntary self-sacrifice to build the infrastructure necessary for an effective economy. The governments of many of the newly industrialized countries of East Asia were able to achieve this by calling upon an intense nationalism bolstered by a fear of communism. But the Communist Party in China has largely lost the ability to inspire dedicated service to the common good. Economic development in the Guangdong region has been driven by the intense desire of individuals to cast off the rigid, now meaningless restraints imposed upon them during the Maoist era and to get rich by pursuing the opportunities opened up by a market economy. As a result, the process of development in Guangdong has been dynamic but chaotic. Necessary infrastructural investments have not been made. Important resources have been squandered through government corruption.

Throughout his book, which was mostly written before the brutal crackdown on protesters in Beijing on 4 June 1989 but which acknowledges the crackdown in a brief preface, Vogel remains optimistic that the positive forces for economic development can overcome the obstacles. The book seems aimed as much at the provincial officials who invited its author to Guangdong as at a Western audience. While Vogel honestly notes serious problems in Guangdong, he seems to phrase his account in such a way as to urge the officials to build on their positive achievements and not to be discouraged by their difficulties. If Vogel's primary reference group in China had been dissident intellectuals rather than reform-minded local officials, his book might have had a much darker tone.

It is still hard to know whether there will ultimately be a tragic or a triumphal outcome to the changes that began to sweep China in the past decade and that now sweep over most of the Communist world. By showing us the opportunities and dangers encountered by a region that went one step ahead down the path to reform, Vogel has given us an important resource for rational discussion about what we can possibly hope for and realistically need to fear about the future.

RICHARD MADSEN

University of California
San Diego

EUROPE

BURSTIN, BARBARA STERN. *After the Holocaust: The Migration of Polish Jews and Christians to Pittsburgh.* Pp. xv, 219. Pittsburgh, PA: University of Pittsburgh Press, 1989. $19.95.

The heart of this work is the presentation and analysis of interviews with 60 Polish Christians and 60 Polish Jews who came to Pittsburgh after leaving Poland during or immediately after World War II.

First, the interviewees' past in Poland before World War II is set forth; next, the experience of both groups under Nazi occupation; then, exploration of the attitudes of both groups who after the war did not return to Poland or remain there. Following this, efforts of the American Jewish and American Polish Catholic communities to bring these Jews and Catholics to the United States are presented; next, the efforts of the Pittsburgh Jewish community to resettle the refugees; after that, how the refugees reacted to the reception they received in Pittsburgh; then, the present experience of the refugees; and, finally, a record of a meeting arranged in 1987 between six Polish Jews and six Polish Christians.

Extracts from the interviews with these survivors are scattered liberally through these chapters. The actual words of these individuals who were there bring the book to life.

Readers whose lives are bound up with intellectual and artistic activities are probably familiar with the migration of people like themselves to the United States during the Holocaust, as described in works such as Laura Fermi's *Illustrious Immigrants.* Burstin's book broadens this view by interviewing survivors from all occupational levels. In a world where the well-educated control access to publication, it seems important to have the voices of people at all levels heard and recorded. Burstin's contribution here is most useful.

Burstin's 120 interviewees are, of course, a statistically insignificant part of the World War II and postwar resettlement. What makes them special is that they are representative of the longstanding enmity between Polish Catholics and Polish Jews.

Six of the Polish Christians and six of the Polish Jews were brought together by Burstin for a dialogue, an event described in the postscript, in the hope that such dialogues would be helpful in reconciling the two groups. Considering the recent dialogue over the Carmelite convent at Auschwitz, it is evident that not much reconciliation has taken place.

Certainly, as one who from the outside encountered in 1945-46 bits and pieces of the refugee experience—the refugee trains decorated with green branches, the disoriented refugees appearing at the gates of American military installations, the rounding up of babies born to Russian slave-laborers in Germany for transporting back to the Soviet Union—I could not help but share then, as I do now, Burstin's compassion for her subjects. I wish I could share her optimism for intergroup understanding.

This is a book, then, that can be recommended for offering both an oral history of the Holocaust and a perspective on current world events.

FREDERICK B. LINDSTROM

Arizona State University
Tempe

IRVINE, WILLIAM D. *The Boulanger Affair Reconsidered: Royalism, Boulangism, and the Origins of the Radical Right in France.* Pp. viii, 239. New York: Oxford University Press, 1988. $34.95.

Appointed minister of war as a reward for his successful army reforms and passionate calls for revenge on Germany, General Georges Boulanger—protégé of Georges Clemenceau—orchestrated the chauvinistic military display at Longchamp on Bastille Day 1886 that catapulted him to national popularity. When he appeared to make Bismarck back down in the Schnaebelé incident the following spring, frightened civilian politicians excluded him from the government, a move that only enhanced his standing with a public fed up with scandals and incompetence in Paris.

In still another blunder the government forced Boulanger into retirement, making him eligible for election to the Chamber of Deputies. The general promptly won a seat and began to agitate for revision of the constitution. Precisely what changes he had in mind remained vague enough to permit almost every political faction in France to believe *"le général Revanche"* was secretly on its own side and only awaited a clear nationwide mandate to act.

This is where William Irvine comes in with new answers to the old question,

Who supported Boulanger? On the basis of some new evidence and—more important—a reexamination of materials long available, Irvine concludes that conservatives in general and royalists in particular constituted the financial and electoral heart and soul of Boulangism: "Without their active intervention there would have been no Boulanger affair."

It was indeed a *mésalliance* of the first magnitude. Boulanger's mass following came from the Left and the Center; republicans and Socialists assured each other that, in accepting royalist funding of his campaigns, Boulanger was merely taking from the royalists the rope with which he would hang them.

Whether the general saw it quite that way is another matter. When candidates—mostly Leftists—who were identified with him won smashing victories in Paris in January 1889, all France expected Boulanger to mount a white horse and march on the Élysée Palace, there to do—who knew what? Royalists anticipated a restoration to result from their heavy financial contributions.

Lacking the stuff of dictators, however, Boulanger failed to move after his greatest triumph. Able to tolerate almost anything but indecisiveness in politicians, the French quickly forgot the general, who committed suicide on his mistress's grave in September 1889.

Irvine has argued a convincing case for the royalist content of the Boulanger movement, a classic example of the conservative Right attempting to use a man of the people for its own ends. Mussolini and Hitler would offer similar candidacies, with quite different outcomes, a generation later. This is a splendid, highly instructive book.

WOODFORD McCLELLAN

University of Virginia
Charlottesville

JACKSON, ALVIN. *The Ulster Party: Irish Unionists in the House of Commons, 1884-1911.* Pp. viii, 359. New York: Oxford University Press, 1989. $69.00.

O'LEARY, CORNELIUS, SYDNEY ELLIOTT, and R. A. WILFORD. *The Northern Ireland Assembly, 1982-1986: A Constitutional Experiment.* Pp. vi, 270. New York: St. Martin's Press, 1989. $39.95.

Beyond a shared interest in the north of Ireland, these two books have little in common. Jackson examines the evolution of the Unionist party grouping in the House of Commons at the turn of the century. The book by O'Leary and his colleagues is a case study of a constitutional experiment almost a century later. Despite the differences in period, settings, and focus, however, a common atmosphere hangs over both, the brooding fear, suspicion, and intransigence of a culture deeply resistant to change.

Since 1972, when Westminster took over responsibility for the administration of Northern Ireland, the province has been administered by a system of direct rule, a sort of proconsular arrangement headed by a secretary of state and ministers appointed by Westminster. The subsequent years of direct rule are littered with the wrecks of attempts to restore to Northern Ireland a legislative and executive forum acceptable to both Unionists and Nationalists. All had foundered between the Scylla of Unionist insistence on majority rule and the Charybdis of the Nationalist—and British—requirement that both traditions share power in any devolved administration.

The Northern Ireland Assembly, which attempted to break the political log jam between 1982 and 1986, was another doomed voyage. It merits attention, according to O'Leary, Elliott, and Wilford, "because it represented the most recent attempt to promote an internal solution to the problems of governing Northern Ireland." Within a year of the Assembly's collapse, however, the British and Irish governments had signed the Anglo-Irish Agreement, apparently abandoning the search for internal settlement in favor of an international deal above the heads of the embattled communities. Only time will tell whether the Assembly will remain a dim memory of irrelevant theater or a constructive guide to a future settlement.

The Assembly's most likely monument is the six statutory committees—and the seven nonstatutory ones—it established to scrutinize departments of government and to introduce some measure of accountability to ministers and civil servants. The committees were without precedent in Northern Ireland and were designed to explore the possibility of power sharing below cabinet level. Their activities occupy about half the book and are impeccably researched. Nevertheless, two obstacles prevent a proper assessment of the Assembly experiment. First, as O'Leary and his colleagues pointed out, the committees were very "dependent upon the willingness of the Executive to assist and support the Committees in their pursuit of open government." The other obstacle is more fundamental. Both nationalist parties, the Social Democratic and Labor Party and Sinn Fein, refused to participate at all in the Assembly, thus ruling out its value as an experiment in power sharing. Power can only be shared if the antagonists agree to share it. The authors, however, are careful to make no exaggerated claims for the Assembly's success, and their book is likely to be the definitive work on the subject.

Alvin Jackson's scholarly review of Unionism's emergence as a parliamentary force in the years between 1884 and 1911 will be appreciated by historians. Until comparatively recently the origins of Unionism have been neglected, leaving a lopsided and half-understood version of Irish history. Jackson's close-grained study adds to a growing body of new research that has helped to remedy the imbalance. The book's greatest strength is its careful delineation of party organization during periods of political routine.

The price for such detail, unfortunately, is that it may obscure more general developments for the nonspecialist reader. Hence Jackson argues convincingly against the McNeill hypothesis that "Ulster militancy evidently only truly developed after August 1911," but one is left wondering if the hypothesis is worth the argument. One strong theme is the danger of reading too much into Unionist disunity. Divided they certainly were, and still are, but even more striking is their willingness to unite under external threat. Edward Saunderson, the landlord-leader of the Ulster party, unashamedly defined the sole basis for their unity as follows: "that is, that we should never permit hon. Gentlemen opposite (the Nationalists) to rule over us."

If there is a dominant theme in these two very different books, it is the unwillingness of either side to be ruled by the other.

JOHN DARBY

University of Ulster
Ireland

RENSENBRINK, JOHN. *Poland Challenges a Divided World*. Pp. ix, 246. Baton Rouge: Louisiana State University Press, 1988. $19.95.

This is a book about the origins, significance, and impact of Solidarity. The book is divided into three parts. The first part can be said to be a diary of sorts, chronicling John Rensenbrink's perspectives on Poland and Solidarity before, during, and after a five-month stay in Poland in 1983. His major point is that he, like so many

others, misunderstood what Solidarity was all about. In particular, Solidarity is best seen, in his view, as patient, not pushy; systemic, not particularistic, in its concerns; and permanent, not transitory, in its effects. The rapid changes in Poland since this book was written, of course, bear him out. The strikes of 1988, the round table between the government and the opposition, the election of June 1989, and the formation in August 1989 of a Solidarity-led government all suggest that this was a singular movement of singular power.

In the second part of the book, Rensenbrink moves from personal reflections to an analysis of the origins of Solidarity. He addresses seven factors, weaving together in admirable fashion the structural consequences of state socialism with what might be termed Polish-specific factors. In the former case, he notes the degree to which, for example, socioeconomic development, the fusion in effect between politics and economics, and the creation of a " 'society' shorn of its own self-organization" worked together to create a society united by its redundant experiences in the polity and the economy and by its opposition to the party-state in Poland. As for factors specific to Poland, he highlights such influences as the role of the Church as the carrier of the Polish nation and the long and distinguished constitutional history of Poland. When combined, these factors explain what is the crux of Solidarity, in Rensenbrink's view, that is, its nonviolent strategy for renewal, its subjectivity, its legalism, and its religious and national basis.

In the final section of the book, Rensenbrink addresses the question of whether Polish history is in fact fated to repeat its past of fostering many rebellions but producing little in the way of genuine liberation. He is an optimist. It is not just that Solidarity can be seen as a major step in the direction of building a society that in turn will be able to fashion at some future point an appropriate and just state. It is also that there is, in his view, nothing inherently permanent about the postwar division of Europe.

The strengths of this book are many. In particular, I found Rensenbrink's treatment of Solidarity as a product of state socialism, its architects to the contrary, a particularly useful way to look at what seems to be a very surprising phenomenon—that is, a massive mass movement developing in a system structured on the principle of preventing such. Moreover, as the events since the fall of 1988 suggest—that is, since this book was written—optimism, with respect to the Soviets and with respect to the durability of Solidarity, seems to have been well placed. I also think that he has defined Solidarity well by emphasizing its qualities as a social movement.

There are some weaknesses here, however. The origins of Solidarity can be found not just in the power of society but also in the economic crisis that had hit Poland by the end of the 1970s and, even more important, in the weakness, the divisiveness, if not the outright incompetence, of the party-state apparatus in Poland. The international economy and the party-state apparatus, in short, are as responsible for the development of civil society in Poland since 1956 as the push from Polish publics. Second, while the role of Solidarity as a giant magnet for Polish frustrations and hopes is crucial —as are the many sides of Solidarity, which cannot be captured in the term "union"—these characteristics should have made Rensenbrink more sensitive to the limitations on what Solidarity could do underground and aboveground, in opposition and now in government. Finally, as recent events testify, it is wrong to see Solidarity as a movement concerned with amending socialism. To get what it wanted, Solidarity in the end had to replace state socialism. To have done anything less would have been to reject the accords signed in Gdansk in August 1980.

VALERIE BUNCE

Northwestern University
Evanston
Illinois

ZEMTSOV, ILYA and JOHN FARRAR. *Gorbachev: The Man and the System.* Pp. xvii, 462. New Brunswick, NJ: Transaction Books, 1989. $29.95.

KLUGMAN, JEFFRY. *The New Soviet Elite: How They Think and What They Want.* Pp. x, 237. New York: Praeger, 1989. $24.95.

Kremlinology, understood as that branch of Soviet studies that focuses on political maneuver and resulting policy formation within the Soviet leadership, has probably done more for academic employment than it has to advance our understanding of the Soviet Union. The recent contribution by Zemtsov and Farrar to this genre, while displaying significant analytical acuity, illustrates why this should be so.

The book is, first of all, a massively detailed examination of Soviet policy —domestic, foreign, and military—in the period since Gorbachev assumed his present role. It is certainly a useful compendium of factual data covering all aspects of Soviet policy in the first two years of Gorbachev's ascendancy, with each major topic buttressed by a convenient chronology. But Zemtsov and Farrar are also experienced observers, and their treatment of the dramatic developments of the period, conjectural by necessity, is careful and often insightful.

But there is something wrong when drama is made to seem dull, when innovation is converted into routine. A part of the difficulty is a matter of timing: the book covers about as much of the Gorbachev period as has elapsed since the writing was finished, and it follows that Zemtsov and Farrar have taken a large risk in poising such a substantial body of analysis on such a slender basis. But that fact merely intensifies a more basic problem. This genre is habituated to skepticism, especially in the face of what may seem just another set of ideological claims, and the usual reaction is to deflate apparent rhetoric by recourse to what seem to be the long-term regularities of Soviet conduct. Kremlinology thus tends toward conservative analysis, even a debunking kind of analysis—which makes it useful and appropriate during times of stagnation but just as unhelpful when genuine change is afoot. And that is a severe charge, for it means that a whole branch of scholarship is valuable only when we do not much need it and self-defeating when we do. It does seem a shame, as one contemplates the serious effort and sober intention embodied in this book, that it could not contribute more to the current rethinking precipitated by Gorbachev.

Klugman's book is a very different sort of exercise, an attempt at a psychology of organization that is novel only because Soviet bureaucracy is its context. We have not had any great amount of close study of this subject, and the Soviet literature is apparently also rather thin. But the interviews that Klugman conducted in the Soviet émigré community enable him to offer considerable insight into Soviet career patterns, motivations, and the socialization that undergirds this fundamental feature of life in the Soviet Union. The material is often quite dry and the treatment sometimes repetitive, but it would not be too much to say that we have, in this study, the anatomy of the institutional obstacle course confronting a reforming leadership. It is a much more

pertinent reminder of the immensity of Gorbachev's task than are the reflexes of conventional Kremlinology.

LYMAN H. LEGTERS
University of Washington
Seattle

UNITED STATES

BROOKINGS TASK FORCE ON CIVIL JUSTICE REFORM. *Justice for All: Reducing Costs and Delay in Civil Litigation.* Pp. ix, 49. Washington, DC: Brookings Institution, 1989. $6.95.

The authors of this task force report declare that the "American system of civil justice is under attack: from clients . . . federal and state legislators . . . from judges . . . . and from many attorneys." Certainly, anyone who has ever encountered the civil justice system in even minor ways can think of numerous reasons why this is the case: justice is expensive, the courtroom is often the worst forum for resolving disputes because rigid rules result from decisions, litigation creates sluggish justice with remedies that come too late, judicial solutions are not real solutions to problems—any malpractice complainant can confirm that —and so on. But most of our concerns are with the justice system in general, and few of us will take the trouble to think about specific ways of improving the civil justice system. In addition, talk of procedural remedies is, for all but the college-educated, abstract at best, opaque at worst.

But fashioning specific, procedural remedies is precisely the problem the Task Force on Civil Justice Reform has set for itself. The Federal Rules of Civil Procedure are supposed to ensure the "just, speedy, and inexpensive determination of every action," but we all know that whatever system is in place, certainly this is not the end result we daily witness in the courts. Otherwise, we would not have the complaints we do about the system.

This is a book that every person who has ever been involved in any way with a civil lawsuit ought to read because it illuminates procedural problems with the system that allow "justice delayed" to become "justice denied." This book also reflects the truism of Kurt Lewin: "If you want to truly understand something, try to change it." It is because this task force is composed of seasoned attorneys and law professors, as well as advisers who sit on the federal bench, that it is really an excellent contribution to the literature on judicial reform. Further, it is short enough to be read in an hour or so, despite the fact that the suggested reforms in civil procedure might require hours of contemplation.

Almost everyone has heard many stories about "justice delayed." Yet at the same time, how often do we think to examine the justice system from a managerial perspective to promote the efficient resolution of disputes? That is what is required to put an end to the cases that continue until they become seven-year lawsuits, settlements that do not really settle anything, judges who put civil suits on indefinite hold, and so on. It would be impossible to even mention all of the procedural remedies suggested, but here is just one made by the task force to speed up management of cases through the system: "Permit in each district's plan only narrowly drawn 'good cause' exceptions for delaying trials and discovery deadlines." In addition, "where continuances and extensions are requested with excessive frequency or on insubstantial grounds, the court should adopt one or a combination of the following procedures": "cross-reference" requests for extensions by the name of the lawyer requesting them; require attorneys to have requests for extensions endorsed by the litigants; and summon and discipline lawyers who persistently request continuances.

Disputants should be present when serious settlement questions are at stake, judges should resolve motions early if they are likely to have an impact on the discovery to be conducted, a system for tracking cases should be developed in each district, expensive discovery should be avoided by careful scrutiny of discovery requests, and so on. For the person seriously interested in reducing the costs and delay of civil litigation, this book is probably the best primer on the subject one could read. For the person who wants simply to understand how to change procedures so that procedural barriers do not frustrate speedy resolution of issues, this is also must reading. Despite the fact that the recommendations have not been implemented, almost every one of them seems intuitively correct to one who has only modest acquaintance with the civil justice system in this country.

STEPHEN W. WHITE

Auburn University
Alabama

COGAN, FRANCES B. *All-American Girl: The Ideal of Real Womanhood in Mid-Nineteenth-Century America.* Pp. x, 298. Athens: University of Georgia Press, 1989. $35.00. Paperbound, $14.95.

All-American Girl is an ambitious and contentious book. Its aim is to recover a lost nineteenth-century ideal of womanhood and to present it, in all its substance and complexity, as a historical model for modern American women. In so doing, it takes to task most current women's historians and questions the scholarly validity and usefulness of many of the methodologies and theoretical assumptions behind the so-called new feminist, cultural, and social histories.

Cogan charges that, beginning with Barbara Welter, most contemporary women's historians have caricatured the universe of role models and ideals of womanhood available to nineteenth-century women by starkly dividing them between those that were shaped by and submissive to the patriarchal order and those that were resistant to that order and thus protofeminist. Her intent is to challenge that caricature, and she does so by devoting her book to illustrating the existence of a third, middle-of-the-road, and very popular ideal, one that she labels the ideal of real womanhood.

As Cogan describes it, the ideal of real womanhood was one that valued femininity and accepted that women occupied a separate sphere but that also promoted physical fitness, critical intelligence, self-sufficiency, familial and communal responsibility, economic competency, and a realistic view of marriage. As such it was neither antifeminist nor protofeminist but rather an emotionally and rationally satisfying model of behavior and belief that provided a survival ethic and a substantial measure of worth for middle-class women who had to balance their senses of self-autonomy with very real and valued ties of duty to family and community. Indeed, Cogan argues, such a balancing act much more accurately describes the average nineteenth-century middle-class woman's experience than do the caricatured images of women as doormats to duty or rebels for self.

To recover this lost ideal and illustrate its basic tenets, Cogan searches through a wide variety of popular literature: domestic novels, magazine short stories, editorials, and advice and etiquette books. For the most part, she interprets these works literally, deliberately avoiding what she sees as the dangers of deconstruction and subtextual criticism.

In the richness of detail provided, Cogan's literal reading and use of a wide variety of sources are seductive. So, too, are the simplicity and common sense of her assertion that an alternative ideal of womanhood existed between the images of the submissive doormat and the protofeminist rebel. Yet there is a disturbing disingenuousness to all this. While offering her book as a corrective to what she claims is women's history's caricature of nineteenth-century ideals of womanhood, Cogan ends up caricaturing the writings of other women's historians. Few such historians would acknowledge or even recognize the simple split vision she ascribes to them. Hence, although *All-American Girl* is a valuable and frequently finely nuanced study of a major nineteenth-century ideal of womanhood, it is neither as new nor as groundbreaking as it claims to be.

RICHARD A. MECKEL

Brown University
Providence
Rhode Island

CRABB, CECIL V., Jr. *American Diplomacy and the Pragmatic Tradition.* Pp. 302. Baton Rouge: Louisiana State University Press, 1989. $37.50.

Cecil V. Crabb, Jr., is the author of more than a dozen books on U.S. foreign policy including one of the standard texts in the field, *American Foreign Policy in the Nuclear Age.* In his new book, he offers an interpretation of twentieth-century American foreign policy that holds that the pragmatic worldview explains customary American viewpoints and conduct in foreign affairs "better than any other competing theory of American diplomatic behavior."

Crabb believes their collective experiences made Americans particularly receptive to the pragmatic school of philosophy when it emerged late in the nineteenth century. He identifies its tenets in a well-grounded examination of the work of the three principal American pragmatic philosophers, Charles Peirce, William James, and John Dewey. Succeeding chapters attempt to draw out the linkages between pragmatism and American foreign policy behavior using illustrative examples, especially from the administrations of Franklin Roosevelt, Truman, Kennedy, and Reagan. Among the tenets of pragmatism Crabb sees as having special relevance are experience as the best test of truth, the priority of the environmental context as opposed to a priori principles in diplomatic decision making—hence the crisis orientation of American diplomacy—the belief in evolutionary change, and the belief in a pluralistic universe.

Crabb asserts, in chapter 5, that often-noted characteristics of American foreign policy such as public apathy, deference to the president, distrust of diplomacy, unilateralism, isolationism, and multilateralism may be accounted for by America's pragmatic orientation. So, too, can the pluralistic quality of the internal environment of American foreign policy decision making, mentioned in chapter 6. The evidence presented to support these claims, however, is more suggestive than conclusive because Crabb does not consider alternative explanations systematically.

Crabb identifies 14 pragmatic guidelines of American diplomacy from his analysis. These are much less specific than the "fourteen points" of an earlier era. For example, "in the pragmatic world view, American foreign policy operates in a highly pluralistic external environment, consisting of a wide range of uniform and unique, recurrent and random, and predictable and unpredictable forces that combine variously to affect the well-being of American society." The lack of precision is inherent in the nature of pragmatism, as Crabb recognizes early on: "pragmatism has always suffered from what sometimes appeared to be an extraordinarily high level of semantical imprecision and confusion, stemming from seeming contradictions among some of its primary tenets." Given this, one may continue to question whether pragmatic principles are better predictors of American foreign policy than those offered by other theoretical perspectives. Explicit comparison with the behavior of other nations also would help to establish the claim for the distinctiveness of pragmatism's influence on American foreign policy.

Crabb's argument will not sit well with those who are convinced that American foreign policy has been driven either by the interests of dominant economic groups or by crusading ideological commitments. He ignores the arguments of the former, and although he finds evidence of occasional crusades, he believes that they have been tempered by the sometimes hard lessons of experience. Even if his case is not fully convincing, Crabb's interpretation is thought provoking, especially in his conclusion, which assesses the pitfalls, profits, and payoffs of pragmatic diplomacy.

RICHARD FLICKINGER

Wittenberg University
Springfield
Ohio

FITZGERALD, MICHAEL W. *The Union League Movement in the Deep South: Politics and Agricultural Change dur-*

ing Reconstruction. Pp. x, 283. Baton Rouge: Louisiana State University Press, 1989. $25.00.

Fitzgerald's book is a well-researched study of the Union or Loyal League movement in Alabama and Mississippi during the years 1866-69. Arguing that the League has been misunderstood both by conservative Dunning School historians of Reconstruction and by later revisionists, Fitzgerald provides a useful corrective.

In the years just after the war ended, League membership and enthusiasm was greatest among unionist whites in the mountain counties of north Alabama. They defended political rights for freedmen and occasionally even established biracial leagues. But as the dream of confiscation and redistribution of plantations faded and racism reasserted itself, whites played a lesser role.

For freedmen the League represented more than a mere Republican organization. It was a way of breaking the social and economic power of planters. Blacks used the leagues to apply economic pressure on whites to end intrusive supervision of their work and lives and to push for more favorable agricultural arrangements. In time whites used violence in the style of the Ku Klux Klan against the League and by 1869 had destroyed the organization.

By comparing the League in Alabama and Mississippi Fitzgerald provides some interesting insights. The greater success of the Alabama League resulted from centralized organization, initial white support in the mountain counties, and a military governor sympathetic to freedmen's rights, none of which prevailed in Mississippi.

Internally leagues differed substantially. Urban leagues tended to focus on labor conditions, employment, and segregation of public facilities, and they used strikes and boycotts as weapons. The presence of military garrisons, black newspapers, and a concentrated black population made them more radical. Rural leagues consisting of isolated black farmers who were more vulnerable to terrorism experienced a more tumultuous history. Moderates and radicals, blacks and whites vied for control of the leagues. Ultimately Fitzgerald sees the League as the only realistic course open to freedmen trying to change basic economic relationships, and he believes the lack of support from Congress and the Republican Party led to its demise.

One of the few flaws in this book is Fitzgerald's tendency to take sources at face value. For instance, he cites the rabidly anti-Republican Tuscaloosa *Monitor,* edited by Klansman Ryland Randolph, on the motives leading Greene County Republican planter Charles Hays to join the League. Hays joined, thought Randolph, because he cynically desired to acquire black laborers for his plantation. Fitzgerald cites this source in a section on the economic motivation for white planters to join the League. But citing Randolph as a source on Hays is like citing Stalin on the motivation of Churchill. In fact, Hays was one of the more loyal Republican congressmen, putting up money as bond for freedmen and risking his life on numerous occasions at public rallies throughout the Black Belt. Surely Hays could have found a safer source of labor.

Despite such minor qualifications, this is a splendidly researched book that substantially enlarges our understanding of how blacks tried to control their own destiny in the first years of freedom.

WAYNE FLYNT

Auburn University
Alabama

SMITH, STEVEN S. *Call to Order: Floor Politics in the House and Senate.* Pp.

xvi, 269. Washington, DC: Brookings Institution, 1989. $31.95. Paperbound, $11.95.

In keeping with the current trend in political science of refocusing attention upon institutional questions, Steven Smith has produced a careful and convincing study of the impact of institutional changes in Congress over the past two decades. The heart of the analysis can be summarized as follows. Our picture of the modern Congresses of the 1960s and earlier is one that emphasizes a decentralized power structure wherein the committees—and, increasingly, subcommittees—perform the legislative tasks, leaving the members at large free to service constituency interests and thereby —particularly in the House—assure reelection. Legislative activity thus consists largely in credit claiming and taking popular positions on the floor of Congress.

This picture began to change markedly in the 1970s. New issues, many of them volatile and polarizing; increasingly heavy demands made by constituents and pressure groups; and a growing sense of member frustration resulted in a number of reforms designed to reassert member sovereignty in Congress. Smith's analysis is devoted to explaining the extent to which and the means by which legislative decision making came more and more to be an activity that takes place on the floor of Congress. Since the pace of change has overtaken the explanatory analysis of students of the process, an important part of Smith's report is devoted to the counterrevolution that has set in during the present decade, particularly in the House of Representatives.

One thing that has not changed is that the playing-out of these institutional changes has occurred in different ways in the two houses. Bicameralism remains significant. To make the central point, the modern Senate has always been a more individualistic, decentralized, unpredictable body where members are disinclined to defer to committee subsovereignties. During most of the period under review, it was even more so. The big news of change comes from the House. Here, largely through the mechanism of offering floor amendments to committee-prepared legislation, individual members have, for nearly two decades, been asserting their legislative rights. In explicating these changes, Smith provides an elaborate array of tables and figures incorporating an imaginative variety of empirical indicators. Yet the tale of institutional revolution is barely spun before it becomes necessary to take account of a moderate turning back of the clock, particularly in the House.

Briefly—and brevity does not do justice to the meticulous documentation of the argument—what happened, especially in the House, was that many members—as leaders, as committee members, and as ordinary back-benchers—came to feel overwhelmed by the excess of individualism and the consequence of such excess in gumming up the legislative process. Once again, participatory democracy needed to be balanced with a measure of self-restraint. The nature of the restraints includes so-called special rules that inhibit absurdly excessive amendment sprees and increasing resort to omnibus legislative texts, packaging many substantive targets of individual member intervention and thus restricting opportunities for micromanagement of committee—especially Budget and Appropriation —decision making. Even the last stage of conference-committee activity seems to be being reclaimed as a vehicle of decentralized committee strategic assertiveness.

We are thus left in a state of uncertainty and even tentativeness in assessing prospects for longer-term institutional stability or equilibrium. Yet we come to that state with a much greater appreciation of the complexities of institutional change, owing to the careful analysis offered by Steven Smith.

CHARLES E. JACOB

Rutgers University
New Brunswick
New Jersey

SOLEY, LAWRENCE C. *Radio Warfare: OSS and CIA Subversive Propaganda.* Pp. x, 249. New York: Praeger, 1989. $24.95.

For anyone who, like me, is both a World War II buff and interested in international propaganda, this is a fascinating book. It retells the fairly well-known story of the origins of the Office of Strategic Services (OSS) under British tutelage. But Lawrence Soley provides some fresh detail and weaves in enough background history of World War II to give the narrative coherence and make it interesting reading.

Briefly, Soley, who has written before on psychological warfare and propaganda, describes how just before World War II, Britain hurriedly reassembled some of its World War I psychological warriors, establishing a propaganda agency at Electra House. In 1938 the powerful medium of radio was added. Radio could reach friend and foe alike, could not be stopped at the borders, and often could be camouflaged to sound like a crony rather than the serpent that it was.

It was from the British that Colonel William J. ("Wild Bill") Donovan learned the tricks of subversive propaganda or psychological warfare. Starting before the United States entered the war, Donovan labored hard to get political leaders and especially military field commanders to recognize psychwar as a modern weapon of warfare. He also had to struggle to distance himself and his operation from mere propaganda or overt information, which was the responsibility of Elmer Davis's Office of War Information.

Several interesting things emerge from the book. Although many have attributed the invention of disinformation to the Soviet Union, during the two world wars it was Britain that was most active in using deception, fabrication, and rumor. In spite of the fact that the United States has always been far ahead of other countries in commercial public relations, in the use of communication to help win wars, Americans have been Britain's pupils—often slow learners at that. And probably most important, despite much effort, the evidence points to only minimal successes of psychwar.

Soley never misses an opportunity to name and to give the professional background of every major—and occasionally minor—member of the psychwar caste that he can uncover. While he has made excellent use of research data, he tends to be somewhat repetitive and given to *obiter dicta* on members of his caste. Thus he lists postwar incidents to "prove" that General Eisenhower had "little devotion to democratic principles" as president of the United States.

In much of chapter 6 on Soviet psychwar, one is sidetracked to a discussion of the establishment of national freedom committees and shadow governments in a book supposedly on radio warfare. Also, too much space in the same chapter, and elsewhere throughout the book, is devoted to the Red scare and the House Un-American Activities Committee in the United States.

On the whole, however, this is a solid, well-documented book that makes good and interesting reading.

L. JOHN MARTIN

University of Maryland
College Park

SOCIOLOGY

BARNOUW, ERIK, ed. *International Encyclopedia of Communications*. 4 vols. Pp. xxvi, 462; vi, 506; vi, 490; vi, 455. New York: Oxford University Press; Philadelphia: University of Pennsylvania, Annenberg School of Communications, 1989. $350.00.

Any attempt to encapsulate the amorphous and still-emerging discipline of communications is bound to realize, at best, ephemeral success. Sundry reference works—handbooks, guides, dictionaries, encyclopedias—covering the full spectrum of communication studies have proliferated in recent years, inspired in no small part by the marketing strategies of a few publishing houses and enterprising scholars. Publication of the *International Encyclopedia of Communications*, the most inclusive such reference, perhaps marks the attainment of a certain maturity in a field long racked by its own self-doubts and one still disparaged by external critics.

As with most encyclopedias, its expansive scope is at once a strength and a weakness. All levels of communication—from interpersonal to mass—are amply represented, along with the communicative aspects of institutions and social phenomena, including art, architecture, religion, and many others. The four volumes bring together specialties that rarely, if ever, meet: entries on plant and animal communication appear, figuratively at least, alongside those on journalism and mass media. As a practical matter, however, botanists and animal behaviorists probably will not consult the *Encyclopedia*. Social scientists will find such entries useful only if developing the most transcendent biologically based theories of communication. Still, given the nature of encyclopedias, such an odd amalgam is perhaps unavoidable.

Modeled on the *International Encyclopedia of the Social Sciences,* this work's entries are organized around persons, processes, concepts, institutions, technologies, events, research methods, and geographic areas. Readers likely will find the *Encyclopedia* most useful for its coverage of the intangible features of the field and less useful for the tangible ones. For instance, before the *Encyclopedia,* discussions of processes and concepts usually had to be dug out of specialized works; now students of the field can turn to this set of succinct, lucid explications. In contrast, the *Encyclopedia*'s entries on institutions such as newspapers and advertising, no matter how well developed, will stand as poor substitutes for readily accessible books on the subjects.

Grand, collaborative works on the scale of the *Encyclopedia* inevitably suffer from some unevenness. To their credit, the editors have minimized stylistic and organizational inconsistencies. Harder to standardize are the contributors' approaches, some of which are idiosyncratic and do not always—as in the case of the entry on postal systems—build on the latest or best works. The editors pay more than lip service to the "international" in the title; entries were written by an eclectic group of distinguished scholars from around the world, many based in fields outside communication. Likewise, the work strives to cover subjects from a global perspective, though some contributors were better able to meet that expectation than others.

The *Encyclopedia*'s features and format make it a user-friendly work. Most important, a thorough index and a well-developed system of cross-references directs readers to kindred entries. Broad topics are divided into logical, digestable subparts. Photographs and line drawings enliven the pages and nicely complement the text. And, not least, entries conclude with selected bibliographies.

The *International Encyclopedia of Communications* should be added to the collections of university, departmental, and large public libraries. Graduate students and faculty working in unfamiliar terrain will welcome its convenient overviews. Undergraduates will discover the efficiency of consulting the *Encyclopedia* when writing term papers—indeed, some may be tempted to begin and end their research in these four volumes.

RICHARD B. KIELBOWICZ

University of Washington
Seattle

CURRAN, PATRICIA. *Grace before Meals: Food Ritual and Body Discipline in Convent Culture.* Pp. xiv, 174. Champaign: University of Illinois Press, 1989. $22.95.

Although Curran's book about the food rituals of two convent cultures—the Dominican Sisters of Mission San Jose in California and the Sisters of Notre Dame de Namur in Massachusetts and California—suffers from trying to do too much, it also makes very interesting reading. Much of the book is devoted to detailed description of the religious rituals that accompany dining in the two communities, told as only an insider like Curran can tell them. Those unfamiliar with convent life will be fascinated by both the history of those practices and their current manifestations. The rituals practiced in various ways at various times include such penances as begging food, kissing feet, and eating in a kneeling position or at a special, low penance table; the reading of spiritually inspiring books and tracts during meals; as well as general attitudes about the relationship between feeding the body and feeding the soul.

Readers cannot help but be reminded of the scholarship on anorexia among nuns that suggests a relationship between religious women's eating disorders and their devotion to service and to spiritual perfection. This part of Curran's book is ominous in tone, and one fears for the health of women whose lives are so completely focused upon seeking approval from both their earthly and their heavenly superiors (see Rudolph Bell, *Holy Anorexia,* [1989]).

Having been lured into this critical stance, however, the reader is somewhat surprised to find that Curran is not particularly critical of monastic eating rituals, despite her clear understanding of their troubling nature. Rather, she is more interested in exploring the differences between the two convent cultures, which are rooted in their respective Jesuit and Dominican heritages, as well as historical changes in specific rituals. For instance, she notes that the Dominican sisters continue to regard their silence in the refectory, or dining room, as a form of penance, while the Sisters of Notre Dame have allowed conversation since the 1960s. The Dominicans kneel in the doorway only to atone for confessed faults whereas the Sisters of Notre Dame eat kneeling on a regular basis.

The result is a book that, despite its fascinating subject matter, has a weak point of view. Curran reveals her fondness and respect for both convent cultures even as she acknowledges the emotional costs of their dining rituals for modern nuns. As a result, the reader is unlikely to share her enthusiasm for the premises of those rituals—the Christian view that eating represents both "opportunity and danger."

Curran's attitude toward the gender questions embedded in the issue of eating is also ambiguous. While noting that the meaning of food rituals could vary for the two sexes—men must learn to humble

themselves in order to overcome traditions of male cultural dominance, while
women's use of the same symbols "merely
reaffirm[s] the reality of [their] lowly status"—she denies that gender played a
role in the differences that emerged in
male and female convent cultures.

The book's best chapter is chapter 3,
"Christian Food Beliefs." Here the quality of Curran's scholarship shines as she
recounts the details of Christian attitudes toward food. Scattered throughout
the book are her descriptions of personal
interviews with practicing nuns in two
generations of the two convents. These
are also interesting and important, but
she undercuts her research by choosing
not to base her analysis on her findings.

SALLY L. KITCH

Wichita State University
Kansas

EDELSTEIN, MICHAEL R. *Contami-
nated Communities: The Social and
Psychological Impacts of Residential
Toxic Exposure.* Pp. xviii, 217. Boulder,
CO: Westview Press, 1988. $29.95.

What happens to people when they
think they have been deliberately exposed to toxic waste? In this book Michael
Edelstein says they get angry and confused; lose trust in the government; begin
to think of their homes not as refuges
from the world but as dangerous; feel
they have no control over their lives; become pessimistic about their health; and
change the way they think about the environment. These conclusions are not
very surprising, and Edelstein does not
incorporate them into a new and insightful analysis of community response to
toxins. Nevertheless, *Contaminated Communities* is worth reading for its memorable description of one community's
experience with contaminated ground-

water and for its general discussion of
toxic-waste experiences.

The community in question—Legler, a
section of Jackson, New Jersey—became
the site for a new municipal landfill in
1971. Although residents objected to the
odor, noise, traffic, litter, and dust the
landfill brought, they learned to put up
with it. But everything changed in 1978
when leachate from the dump began to
seep into the surrounding groundwater
and the Board of Health announced that
wells in the area were contaminated. For
the next two years, the citizens of Legler
had to take their drinking and cooking
water from city-supplied 17-gallon jugs.
Neither esthetically pleasing nor convenient, the jugs were a constant reminder
that the well water was "poisoned."

Edelstein compares Legler to Love
Canal and to a number of lesser-known
instances of contamination. He says that
in cases of toxic exposure the state "dis-
ables" citizens because it communicates
so poorly with them. Thus, instead of
collaborating, government and citizens
become antagonists. But communities
are "enabled" if they develop community
organizations. Such organizing follows
from the fact that "normal lives are severely disrupted by the exposure incident, victims are isolated from their
normal relational and institutional networks, individual families cannot solve
their problems alone, and a group of prox-
imate victims share the same conditions."
Edelstein recognizes that these community organizations are usually not-in-my-
backyard groups, but he supports them
as legitimate responses to the fear of toxic
exposure and as powerful avenues for
citizen participation.

Among the interesting observations
that Edelstein makes along the way are
the following. The feelings people have
about their homes are important indicators of how they will respond to toxic
exposure. In most toxic exposures, people

are in a "double bind [because they are] neither sufficiently at risk to warrant definitive action by government nor sufficiently free of risk to allow for a return to life as usual." One reason the community organizations are hard to sustain is that they are originally only temporary, "created quickly in response to a toxic crisis [but] forced to persist long beyond initial expectations."

Contaminated Communities rests firmly on the assumption that hazardous chemicals cause human disease. Unfortunately for this book, but perhaps fortunately for us humans, there is at the present time virtually no epidemiological evidence to support this assumption. Lack of evidence does not necessarily mean a chemical is safe, but the book would have been much stronger had Edelstein discussed this issue and analyzed communities' responses to exposure in light of it. Perhaps his avoidance explains why he never tells us what chemicals were found in Legler's water, why his point of view at times wavers between the citizens' and the bureaucrats', why in the section on responsibility for exposure he does not take a position, and why his concluding chapter on environmental pollution has almost nothing to do with the rest of the book.

SYLVIA N. TESH

Yale University
New Haven
Connecticut

HOFFMAN, LILY M. *The Politics of Knowledge: Activist Movements in Medicine and Planning*. Pp. x, 290. Albany: State University of New York Press, 1989. $54.50. Paperbound, $17.95.

Must professionals inevitably thwart social change? Or can they be change agents—activists? In addressing these questions, Lily Hoffman draws upon her qualitative study of 19 case histories of activist organizations extant from 1960 to 1979, 8 in city planning and 11 in medicine, professions chosen due to their differences in degree of institutionalization.

The book is divided into three parts. The first presents basic conceptual issues, the developmental history of each profession, and the social and political contexts of the post-World War II era, especially the early 1960s' spawning of the urge for activism. The case material follows and is presented neither around chronology as a whole nor case by case but rather around Hoffman's conceptions of the activists' strategies, each conception constituting a chapter: "Delivery of Services," "Empowering People," "Transforming the Work Place," and "Transforming Society." In the final two chapters is a synthesis of observations and conclusions.

In her examination of the interplay between the various strategies and what she terms the "central dilemmas of professional work—claims to knowledge, ideals of service, and autonomy," Hoffman offers her conceptualizations, with bolstering references, of the linkages between what happened—or, more often, what did not happen—and the strains between activism and professionalism. Yet these insights remain scattered, and attempts to garner a conceptual whole remain tenuous. Not so with her last two chapters, especially the last, where she incisively deals with the "problem of professional knowledge" and deftly draws out the range from the folly of professionals who rejected their claims to exclusive knowledge when that was precisely what was wanted, to their defensive retreat into such knowledge by developing new, albeit radical, theoretical perspectives.

Does the book answer the questions posed at the outset? A varied readership, which the book deserves, will have varied answers. I had some nagging questions as to whether failure was due only to professionalism.

Avowed major foci of the activist efforts were improvements in the lot of the poor and minorities. Repeatedly, the recorded failures were related to rejection by these intended constituencies. Was race an issue that warranted singular attention beyond that of other status differentials, including class and professionalism? The data from the case histories do not reveal such attention. Hoffman does make several references to black power yet never defines it, as she also never defines "Left," "New left," "Medical left," and so on. Yet the failure to define or elaborate on just what black power meant to these groups is an omission that beclouds understanding of the effects of race on the outcomes of the activist efforts, over and above professionalism. The reported data would not indicate that the activists understood such distinctions very well.

A related concern centers on organizing, an essential tool in all of the strategies used. There is scant reference to the organizing literature, not that it would offer missed panaceas. Yet the chapters on the data give ample evidence of ineptitude: for example, medical organizing of black mothers without consulting black physicians in the area who eventually defeated the effort. Such ineptitude, spawned either by amateurism or by professionalism, is just that and it fails.

Despite these possible shortcomings, the book should prove of use for the data presented, for Hoffman's incisive interpretations, and as a compendium of exemplars for use by a broad range of professionals and relevant social scientists and by students who want to be—or whose teachers still want them to be—activist professionals.

JEANNE M. GIOVANNONI

University of California
Los Angeles

KIRSCH, GEORGE B. *The Creation of American Team Sports: Baseball and Cricket, 1838-72.* Pp. xiv, 277. Urbana: University of Illinois Press, 1989. $27.50.

With the publication of *The Creation of American Team Sports,* the latest release in the University of Illinois's Sport and Society series, George Kirsch joins the growing ranks of social historians who have been scrutinizing America's sporting heritage. Of course, these Johnny-come-latelies must compete with a host of popular writers who have already staked out much of the territory, a lamentable circumstance brought on by academia's long-standing rejection of such supposedly frivolous pursuits. But winds of change are wafting away such snobbery and are enabling historians like Kirsch to indulge pent-up passions for sports study.

The title of Kirsch's book is misleading, however. The word "creation" suggests creators, but these play no part in the narrative. Rather the subtitle tells the tale, for this is a study of the concomitant rise of organized cricket and baseball in the young America of 1838-72. With personalities and splendid performances relegated to the background, Kirsch's 10 chapters focus more on changing social conditions wrought by advancing urban industrialism that speeded the rise of these competing field sports.

Thanks to established British antecedents, cricket first emerged as a formally organized sport in America. By 1860, indeed, organized cricket teams outnumbered baseball clubs, but for reasons such as continuing British control of the game, lengthy contests, and limited spectator appeal, cricket lost out to baseball in the struggle for dominance.

Drawing on comprehensive research, Kirsch laboriously traces the growth of each sport. Baseball evolved from informal games like rounders, one-old-cat, and townball, and, spurred by cricket's example, reached levels of formal organization by the 1840s. During that decade the New York version of baseball play came to dominate over other forms of the game. By 1861 some 75 clubs belonged to the National Association of Base Ball Players, an important matrix organization, whose counterpart was lacking in American cricket, that embraced the New York game and codified rules of play. With elite teams like the Brooklyn Atlantics popularizing the game and with Civil War soldiers spreading the game to the hinterlands, a veritable baseball mania swept America in the post-Civil War era. Thus by 1870 baseball was acclaimed as our national game while cricket became a peripheral sport, rooted mainly among upper-class aficionados. In developing this thesis, Kirsch analyzes the forces shaping the growth of both sports and further illuminates our understanding of the players, clubs, and spectators. He concludes his narrative with the professional baseball players' launching of the first commercial league in 1871.

While serious students will welcome this work, general readers may find it heavy going. Tendentious phrases like "structural characteristics for players and spectators," "modernization," or "time conscious society" will bore some readers. Others will chafe at Kirsch's belaboring of the obvious, as when he writes that "there is evidence that superior players did not always apply the most rational and scientific principles to the sport"

or "joining a baseball club had members sacrificing individual freedom to group obligations." Some informed readers will bridle at his handling of concepts like social class, values, leisure, and play. Baseball historians will shudder over a lead sentence identifying A. G. Mills as the fourth president of the National League, and the mislabeling of the photos of the Brooklyn Atlantics and the Brooklyn Eckfords. Those photos are two of six taken from Spalding's *America's National Game* and not credited to that source.

Nevertheless, such criticisms ought not to detract from the book's importance both as a study of the symbiotic growth of the two field sports and as a contribution to the history of American baseball.

DAVID Q. VOIGT

Albright College
Reading
Pennsylvania

LIEBERSON, STANLEY and MARY C. WATERS. *From Many Strands: Ethnic and Racial Groups in Contemporary America.* Pp. xiv, 289. New York: Russell Sage Foundation, 1988. $29.95.

This book is one of the volumes in the Census Monograph Series prepared for the National Committee for Research on the 1980 Census of the United States. Within the stated objectives of the series, the book is successful. It consists of eight chapters. The opening chapter gives an overview of the methods used in the census to collect ethnic-ancestry data. Chapter 2 summarizes the ethnic and racial composition of the United States in 1980. The following five chapters focus on white ethnic groups, analyzing the changes and trends of their spatial patterns, cultural differences, economic attainment, and intermarriage. The last chapter is the conclusion.

The identification of an ethnic group is based on different traits, and no two ethnic groups establish their identity in exactly the same way. The 1980 census of the United States introduced for the first time an ethnic-ancestry question in addition to the question concerning the race of the population, and thus there is a certain amount of overlap between them. Lieberson and Waters point out, for example, the obvious discrepancy in the American black response: 26.5 million people reported themselves as black on the race item, but only 21.0 million identified themselves as Afro-American or black on the ancestry item. Lieberson and Waters solved this problem through a simple and pragmatic approach: all persons were classified as black if they either checked off "Black or Negro" on the race item or described themselves as such on the ancestry item. The authors described in detail their methods and approaches in dealing with other types of discrepancies, such as those between birthplace and ethnic ancestry.

From Many Strands contains a vast amount of ethnic data, which are presented in 51 tables. The data include a selection of socioeconomic and demographic indicators of various ethnic groups not only from 1980 but also from earlier years. This timely information about the ethnic and racial composition of the United States is a welcome addition to the selection of books available for use in many university political and social science courses. The inclusion of massive amounts of data in the text, however, sometimes made reading boring. Many of them could have been represented by maps and diagrams, which are effective means of displaying the changes in and spatial distribution of cultural traits. This failing is probably forgivable since the total lack of maps and diagrams may

not be considered serious shortcomings from the sociologist's point of view. Overall, the book is a very useful reference for both teachers and students.

DAVID CHUENYAN LAI

University of Victoria
British Columbia
Canada

RIESS, STEVEN A. *City Games: The Evolution of American Urban Society and the Rise of Sports*. Pp. xii, 332. Urbana: University of Illinois Press, 1989. $29.95.

Nearly two decades ago Steven Riess and a few other scholars pioneered the serious study of sport in American society. He is currently editor of the *Journal of Sport History* and one of the leading specialists in a field that has grown rapidly over the past ten years. *City Games* is a comprehensive study of the complex interaction between the development of modern forms of sport and the rise of cities in the United States from 1820 to the present. Riess has written an interpretive survey in which he synthesizes a vast body of secondary works with his own original research. The result is a volume that is clear, informative, thoughtful, and thorough.

In his introduction Riess argues that the evolution of the city has been the most important influence on the development of organized sport and recreational athletics in America. He develops this central thesis by exploring three dimensions of urbanization that profoundly shaped American sport. These are the city's physical structures and spatial patterns, social and political organizations, and value systems. For Riess, American cities did not simply provide the settings for sport; they also profoundly shaped its growth and were in turn influenced by trends in athletics.

City Games divides the development of sport in urban America into three eras, each of which featured distinctive spatial patterns dictated by that period's dominant mode of transportation. The opening chapter, "Sport in the Walking City, 1820-1870," examines premodern and early modern sport during the Civil War era. The bulk of the book—nearly 200 pages—concentrates on "sport in the industrialized radial city, 1870-1960." This is the strongest section of the work, for it covers many of Riess's favorite research topics. Here he examines the role of social class, ethnicity, race, political machines, and criminal organizations in shaping American sport. He also includes a very fine review of spectators and the commercialization of professional sport during that period. The volume concludes with a sketchy summary, "Sport in the Suburban Era, 1945-80," which surveys the geographic and economic trends of professional leagues since World War II. Riess uses examples from all regions but concentrates on the largest cities, especially New York City, Boston, and Chicago. He refers to many major and minor sports but focuses on his specialties of baseball, boxing, and horse racing. Tables, maps, and several dozen well-chosen illustrations enhance the text and the extensive footnotes.

The strengths and weaknesses of *City Games* stem from its dual character as both textbook and monograph. It succeeds very well as a comprehensive reference work that includes coverage of a wide variety of ideas, issues, groups, organizations, and sports. In an age when historians are often criticized for overspecialization, this volume provides both the scholar and the general reader with an excellent overview of an important

subject in American history. On the other hand, Riess's attempt to compress an enormous amount of material into a little over 300 pages results in a certain degree of oversimplification of fascinating and complex questions, especially for the years before 1870 and after 1945. But, on the whole, this book should be required reading for all who are interested in the dynamic interplay between sport and the urbanization of the United States.

GEORGE B. KIRSCH

Manhattan College
Riverdale
New York

SCHNEIDER, MARK. *The Competitive City: The Political Economy of Suburbia.* Pp. xii, 249. Pittsburgh: University of Pittsburgh Press, 1989. $34.95.

Bryan Jones observes that studies of the policy process at the national level stress the autonomy of the political system, while studies of local policymaking correct this bias by stressing the dependence of governments on outside forces. Schneider's very useful study is a case in point. His conceptual and empirical analysis of suburban governments argues that economic settings severely constrain local budget decisions. He uses public-choice theory to examine what he calls the "local market for public goods" and concludes that suburban governments are even more constrained than other studies have shown, that they have little autonomy in this market and are severely limited in their capacity to improve their tax base. Further, there is marked stability in existing distributions of wealth, with the result that local communities can make only marginal changes in their economic well-being. Moreover, these constraints are welcome, since he also assumes, bureaucrats and politicians, as economic actors, desire to increase their budgets beyond what is desired by consumers.

Schneider directly addresses the role of political actors by including in his basic model bureaucrats and politicians, the sellers of public goods, along with consumers and producers, the buyers of public goods. In doing so, he amends the influential Tiebout model, which bases government budgets solely on consumers' demand for services and their budget preferences. Using public-choice assumptions that political actors behave like "economic man," Schneider assumes that bureaucrats desire to maximize their budgets and that politicians are motivated to provide services in order to be reelected. In the local arena, however, these actors are constrained from expanding their budgets and services by structural factors such as competition between jurisdictions, the paucity of suppliers, the monopoly position of many local governments, and regulation.

Schneider usefully amends another tendency in much economic analysis. While all of the actors share an interest in an expanded tax base, he makes a point of distinguishing between different groups and deducing how each would determine the benefits and costs it would receive from various budget packages. For example, instead of talking about producers or business as a single interest, as is frequently done in economic models, he distinguishes between manufacturers and those who provide services and analyzes how members of each group view government budgets in light of their economic situation. He characterizes each community according to its demographic and economic characteristics, such as income, poverty, housing status, race, population growth, density, and type of business. Relying on census-type data, he first extrapolates the budget preferences in a

community based on its demographic and economic characteristics. He then correlates this preferred budget package with fiscal information about actual expenditures and the extent of competition in a region. His purpose is to determine if competition holds down expenditures, and he concludes that it does.

Critics will note that because he relies wholly on aggregate census data, Schneider cannot go even further than he does in distinguishing between the preferences of different groups or in adding some historical realism to his economic theory. In order to develop a predictive model, he assumes that consumers and producer groups are driven solely by economic considerations. As he admits, this approach omits residents' estimates of "physical amenities, proximity to employment, availability of housing and so forth." It also omits geographic and cultural factors, with the result that one cannot ask whether consumers in New York make the same assessments as do consumers in Houston.

Schneider offers some provocative suggestions about future directions for research, and in the process he notes some problems in continuing to rely on narrowly defined economic models. For example, he finds that the local government arena often resembles an oligarchy rather than a competitive market. Further, there is evidence that individuals are more apt to express their interests through voice rather than exit, again qualifying traditional market assumptions. These findings have led to some interesting propositions about the roles that policy entrepreneurs play in interpreting budget choices to residents, propositions that will require more exploratory, empirical study.

The study's systematic application of public-choice theory to suburban policymaking both confirms the major research in the field and significantly amends the theory. For those who value a parsimonious and predictive model that can be tested with aggregate data, Schneider's work is both useful and important. For those who wish for more historical and contextual realism, particularly about the roles of bureaucrats and politicians, the study offers a number of interesting propositions for further research.

LOUISE G. WHITE

George Mason University
Fairfax
Virginia

SNYDERMAN, MARK and STANLEY ROTHMAN. *The I.Q. Controversy: The Media and Public Policy.* Pp. xiii, 310. New Brunswick, NJ: Transaction Books, 1988. $24.95.

Amid comprehensive and exhaustive reviews of innumerable studies grappling with continuing problems of defining and measuring the elusive concept of intelligence and its scope, the constant emerging challenge in reading this book is to find and identify precisely what Mark Snyderman and Stanley Rothman are trying to say about the subject. It is, of course, helpful and enlightening to be provided a lengthy and learned restatement of the history of the various instruments developed by the early pioneers —Binet, Wissler, Terman—down to the more recent practitioners—Jensen, Herrstein, Kamin—in the protracted quest for a valid and reliable I.Q. test. While this effort is being made, Snyderman and Rothman repeatedly emphasize their view that there is "some relationship" between genetic endowment and intelligence. Their approval of Jensen's position is overwhelming even though they inject the caveat that "Jensen believes that individual differences in I.Q. are largely determined by the genes."

From this stated premise a solid clue is provided about Snyderman and Rothman's real intent when, much later on, they quote yet another supportive source:

[Although] Noam Chomsky makes quite a legitimate point that some groups have less innate capacity for making it in our society, [this] need not serve as justification for discriminating against them or allowing them to remain poor. Indeed we might come to just the opposite conclusion. We might decide to allocate more resources to such groups simply because of their greater need.

Such a sad litany of pejorative, ill-chosen, symbolic words. Surely if there is "less innate capacity," there must be, in their view, greater innate capacity; if society "might decide to allocate more funds to such groups," society might, and often does, decide to allocate those funds to other priorities; the use of the words "their greater need" easily condemns the poor to the lowest label and track in our society.

Snyderman and Rothman need not be too anxious or concerned. Affirmative action is gone; some school boards routinely ignore court orders; Head Start is only reaching a small portion of the youngsters in need of the program; tracking systems in schools are endorsed and applauded because some students are going to be future world leaders while others are going to be workers. One recent headline, disconcerting to some and encouraging to others, strikes a different note: "Black students improving faster than White students [on a standardized statewide test]."

For some strange and inexplicable reason, the authors come thoroughly unglued in the final chapter, "The New Sociology of Science." Here they identify and bitterly complain about those groups in our society, appearing on the scene in the 1960s and 1970s, who are called the real culprits in this whole controversy. The list includes the following: the liberal press, a biased and uninformed "elite"; media personalities, seekers of sensational topics only; universities and academics; environmentalists—one wonders if the irony is noticed by Snyderman and Rothman; civil rights activists who dared to question and confront the societal implementation of the in-place value system; and social service professionals who are responsible for "liberal and cosmopolitan ideas." These are the enemies who constitute an elite "alienated from the remnants of American Puritanism and the idea of a meritocratic society." Quite a burden for those groups but there it is.

Snyderman and Rothman continue adrift when they claim, "In the social sciences, at least, a favorable review in the *New York Times* or the *New York Review of Books* is, in some cases, a more significant source of recognition and reward than that offered by professional journals." Perhaps they might supply more information on this use or misuse of faculty evaluation instruments to support such an outrageous statement.

The last chapter aside, this book is comprehensive and informative on the I.Q. controversy. It is also insensitive, irresponsible, and dangerous.

JOHN J. LENNON

University of Arkansas
Little Rock

USEEM, BERT and PETER KIMBALL. *States of Siege: U.S. Prison Riots, 1971-1986.* Pp. 278. New York: Oxford University Press, 1989. $29.95.

Useem and Kimball's *States of Siege* has already come into its own as one of the better studies on prison riots. It is a richly detailed case study of seven riots —Attica, Joliet, New Mexico, three Michigan prison riots, and West Virginia Penitentiary—that is well written and well documented.

The book begins with a brief introduction outlining the major issues and concepts central to studying riot behavior. Included are a definition of the term "riot"; the stages a riot passes through, namely, pre-riot, initiation, expansion, siege, and termination/recapture stages; and four theories that explain the causes of riots—deprivation, resource-mobilization, breakdown, and collective-behavior theories. Given the centrality of these concepts to the area, the treatment afforded these elements is far too brief. Some of these issues are expanded upon in chapter 9 and in appendix A.

The second chapter is devoted to an analysis of the historical context behind riots of the 1970s. This chapter fails to capture or explore the many intricacies of this era, 1950-75, and is offered as a token attempt to place riots within a broader social-economic-historical context. The same may be said of chapter 5—4 pages long—which examines the historical context impinging upon riots of the 1980s.

The chapters examining individual prison riots are more thorough and well done, and they make engrossing reading. These chapters point to the many situational factors that contributed to each riot. While rich in detail, they lack connections to riot theories and to the historical context in which these riots emerged. Such links are of vital importance to improving existing theory. Appendix A begins this task by linking deprivation and breakdown theories, but Useem and Kimball leave many issues open to debate.

The major conclusion offered concerning the cause of prison riots is disappointing, possibly because it appears obvious:

Several years ago we suspected that . . . riots could [not] be predicted. We suspected that a riot could be sparked by a random event at . . . any . . . prison, at . . . any time. . . . Our data suggest that . . . riots . . . have taken place not in any old prison, . . . but in prisons with a particular . . . pathology. The key factor has not been organization of inmates but the organization of the state (p. 218).

On a positive note, this conclusion draws our attention to structural-organizational issues and downplays the all too common assertion that riots are related to inmate pathology. In other words, inmates do not riot because they are depraved or evil; their behavior appears to be associated with the conditions in which they are kept:

Most prisoners we talked with carried on normal, rational conversations. . . . Whatever led them to commit their crimes . . . they are not visitors from a different moral universe. They do not argue that crime is good. . . . they . . . take seriously our understanding that the Constitution should be obeyed. . . . When they break our rules, we punish them. When we break our own rules, they punish us (p. 231).

In this way, Useem and Kimball at once humanize inmates—something most criminology has been incapable of achieving —politicize riot behavior, and yet make it part of the normal environment of the prison. From such conclusions, we could rephrase the question concerning riots from, Why do riots occur? to Why don't more inmates riot? In short, we should not be surprised that inmates riot; we should be surprised when they do not.

In sum, Useem and Kimball's attempt to normalize prison riots hits the mark. But, while it may be true that administrative disorganization contributes to riot behavior, this disorganization cannot be isolated as the sole cause of riots. Riot behavior, like criminal behavior, must be studied within contextual models that emphasize opportunities and motivations. Inmates would not seize upon the opportunities administrative disorganization created unless they were motivated to do so. The source of these motives could be linked to any number of conditions. For example, inmates are largely drawn from the marginal classes. Maximum-security inmates have lived a

life, both inside and outside the prison, that was founded in powerlessness. As a result, they are alienated and freed from bonds to social order. Given these facts, could we expect any amount of state organization to control the spirits of demoralized men; men who have been made less than human; men who have lost control of their labor, their lives, the time and space their bodies occupy, and the forms of power, knowledge and control exerted over their bodies?

While Useem and Kimball's book represents some of the best research into the problem of prison riots, we still have a long way to go before we can understand the processes that create prison riots. This book marks a beginning in the attempt to develop a new view of inmates, their behaviors, and the situational and power contexts in which they find themselves and in which prison riots emerge.

MICHAEL J. LYNCH

Florida State University
Tallahassee

ECONOMICS

HALPERIN, RHODA. *Economies across Cultures: Towards a Comparative Science of the Economy.* Pp. ix, 226. New York: St. Martin's Press, 1988. $39.95.

Although Halperin uses three examples of cross-cultural comparisons to bolster her analysis, this is on the whole a book that presents Halperin's theoretical perspectives on economic anthropology. The majority of the book deals with three different approaches to economic anthropology. Halperin attempts to synthesize existing paradigms in order to develop a cross-cultural science of the economy. She maintains the primacy of the institutionalist model—Polanyi's substantivism— while integrating Weber's and Lukac's interpretation of Marx. In doing so, she uses the formal deductive model building of neoclassical economics, pointing out that Polanyi and Marx constructed models, too.

Marx's dialectical materialism provides a framework for looking at comparative cultures, as does Polanyi's analysis of redistributive, reciprocal, and market exchange. Halperin argues for a blending of these two analyses of production and exchange. Where her analysis seems contradictory to the intent of the two theoreticians on whom she relies is where she endeavors to develop a science of the economy by separating economics from politics and society. Marx tried to establish dialectical materialist analysis as the science of political economy, not economics. A central idea of Polanyi's analysis is that the neoclassical economists were mistaken in applying their theory to premarket societies where the economy is buried in society (*The Great Transformation* [Boston: Beacon Press, 1957], p. 46). In separating the economy from society in her analysis, Halperin seems to have taken a position in opposition to one of Polanyi's major perspectives on economic anthropology. If the economy is submerged in social relationships, then a description of those social relationships would seem necessary for understanding the economy.

In her cross-cultural comparisons, Halperin compares economic processes in structurally similar societies using a process that she calls "controlled comparison." One example looks at the organization of labor among band-level hunter-gatherers. Here she has controlled for type of society but has varied the ecological conditions. In another example, she looks at the organization of land and labor among the peasantry in Mexico in different historical periods. Both type of society and culture are controlled here. Finally, she analyzes age and the organi-

zation of labor in a variety of both capitalist and precapitalist societies. This latter, more generalized analysis does not seem parallel to the first two, controlled analyses.

In a world where studying economies across cultures is increasingly urgent, Halperin has developed her thoughts on a theoretical framework for a comparative science of the economy. She finds that the institutional paradigm has the greatest potential for a comparative science. She develops formal models, with institutions and processes being the units of analysis. She believes that processes of material livelihood are analytically identifiable and separable from the social formations that provide the context for the economy.

NAN WIEGERSMA

Fitchburg State College
Massachusetts

LOCKE, ROBERT R. *Management and Higher Education since 1940: The Influence of America and Japan on West Germany, Great Britain, and France.* Pp. xiii, 328. New York: Cambridge University Press, 1989. $59.50.

Victory in World War II opened vast new frontiers for the American economy. Rather than a feared return to the trauma of the Great Depression, virtually all important economic sectors in the United States experienced a boom; growth was strong enough to sustain domestic prosperity while simultaneously helping to rebuild Europe and Japan. Understandably, the reputation of American management soared along with this economic performance, and the self-confidence of those who proclaimed the efficacy of a new science of management reached similar heights. Industrial and financial leaders in Western Europe and Japan eagerly studied American management tech-niques and training. Yet by the 1970s something had gone wrong. Americans were lamenting slumping productivity, so-called stagflation, and other economic ills, while Japan and West Germany, risen from their ashes, had emerged as economic miracles. Foreign regard for American managers, and the system of education that produced those managers, declined accordingly. The changes in economic performance and managerial prestige have been dramatic, easily one of the most important chapters of recent history. In *Management and Higher Education since 1940,* business historian Robert Locke has sought to explain the stellar postwar rise of American manage-ment science and its subsequent, but equally remarkable, fall from interna-tional grace.

Locke's scope is ambitious: he surveys the relationships between postwar man-agement science techniques, pioneered by American business schools, and man-agement and higher education in Great Britain, France, and West Germany. For comparative purposes, he also discusses Japanese reactions to American manage-ment approaches. The initial focus of Locke's work is the rise of "the new para-digm" of business studies, "the applica-tion of science to the solution of man-agerial problems," after World War II. For at least two decades, operations re-search and econometrics, with associated linear programming and other quantita-tive analyses, dominated management ed-ucation in the United States. Economic and political leaders placed enormous faith in these approaches, which fostered management as a distinct profession with skills generic to different production and business circumstances. The new par-adigm virtually swept away the former reliance on learning management tech-niques on the job and in a specific field or business.

There was a great deal to the new management science. Locke concedes that it produced some interesting theo-retical work and a body of good scholar-ship. He argues with telling effect, however, that the new paradigm was in-herently flawed; specifically, it seldom al-lowed business leaders or government planners to bridge the gap between the-ory and practice when confronted with novel or changing circumstances. Major attempts to use mathematics decision modeling to predict rates of growth, prof-itability, consumption rates, and the like often resulted in spectacular failures. The inability of the planning-programming-budgeting-system effort to provide realis-tic policy assessments during the Viet-nam war was a major case in point, but there were plenty of other examples.

While there are different views on why econometrics has fallen short of many postwar expectations, Locke insists that the chief problem is cultural. In this, he is certainly right. While certain aspects of American management science were useful to nations with different cultural and business traditions—Japan and West Germany, for instance, have made good use of American models of produc-tion and inventory control—many other crucial facets were not. Managerial moti-vation, styles of labor relations, and per-ceptions of corporate loyalty are im-portant factors that defy easy statistical analysis. Rather, these were cultural elements, which have little or no place in American econometrics or operations research and which vary widely across borders.

In fact, quantitative models of eco-nomic behavior are themselves culturally derived. They assume a rational "eco-nomic man" in the Anglo-American his-torical tradition of individualism, one who reacts only to hard data and acts to maximize economic performance. But what happens to such models, Locke asks, without "economic man"? In Japan, history has ingrained communal loyalties; German *Technik* has kept theory tied closely to practice within given fields. Thus, while profits are important, Japanese take corporate loyalties seriously and Germans are concerned with product quality as a tenet of professionalism. Such perspectives are alien to the management science taught at most American business schools and are at marked variance with the individual career emphases found among British and American managers as well as the loyalties of French managers to the managerial elite graduated from the *grandes écoles*. For Locke, then, it was no surprise to find that Japan and West Germany, the nations that adopted the fewest innovations from the new American paradigm, have emerged as international economic leaders. Similarly, without following the American lead, the Germans instituted the most effective management education in Europe, an education reflecting traditional German concern for collective motivation, *Technik*, and professional pride.

Robert Locke's study is informed by a fine research effort and by a careful and insightful use of the literature. His arguments are persuasive and, if anything, his conclusions are conservative. Locke's text, however, is both a curse and a blessing. Perhaps the nature of the subject set the tone of the narrative, but much of the prose was enough to cure the insomnia of even the most ardent student of management science. The text plods on for pages, Locke seemingly loath to sacrifice even a single note card; but then—almost out of the blue—he will summarize essential points with clarity and genuine insight. *Management and Higher Education* is hardly light reading, but it is a significant book. No other monograph places management education in such an important context and suggests so strongly that the United States reassess the efficacy of the

management sciences, as currently practiced, as tools in economic and public policy planning.

MARK EDWARD LENDER

Kean College of
New Jersey
Union

USEEM, MICHAEL. *Liberal Education and the Corporation: The Hiring and Advancement of College Graduates.* Pp. xxvii, 216. Hawthorne, NY: Walter De Gruyter, 1989. $35.95. Paperbound, $16.95.

There has been increased interest in the relationship between business and the liberal arts. The impetus comes from corporate concern about management at a time of international competition and economic restructuring, student concern about jobs in a stagnant economy, and the concern of higher education with declining liberal arts enrollments. This study by Michael Useem, author of *The Inner Circle: Large Corporations and the Rise of Business Political Activity in the U.S. and U.K.,* falls under this rubric. Drawing upon research supported by the Corporate Council on the Liberal Arts and the President's Committee on the Arts and the Humanities, Useem surveys corporate hiring and promotions in over 500 major corporations to compare the advantages of liberal arts, business, and engineering graduates in corporate America.

Useem finds that although almost half of the companies sought liberal arts graduates, demand differed by both market and institutional factors. Financial services offer more opportunity than manufacturing and functional areas such as marketing and sales and do better than production. Size matters in that larger corporations are more likely to recruit formally on campus. Given the importance of the financial services sector and the trend to corporate growth, these findings suggest greater future opportunity for liberal arts graduates.

Preferences become "educational cultures" because of the tendency of managers to favor those with similar backgrounds. But Useem also finds that the more senior the manager, the stronger his or her interest in liberal arts. Frontline supervisors need new employees who can make immediate contributions, but senior management is responsible for long-range planning and creative vision.

Useem recommends changes in liberal arts as well as business education and corporate culture. Rather than look abroad for models of leadership, he suggests we tap some of our own cultural creativity by crossing arbitrary disciplinary boundaries. From the liberal arts, with their traditionally negative view of business, we need understanding of business organization and culture, an effort in which Useem has been in the forefront.

While this book's narrow focus reflects its origins and objective—to inform the choices of students, educators, and corporate employers—it does raise larger questions about the fit between the restructuring service economy and education. Whereas the major division in the interwar and immediate postwar period was between the arts and the sciences, the new divide seems to be between business—the useful arts—and the liberal arts. We learn from this study that it is the changing role of the corporation—not just the demand for jobs or students —that fuels interest in bridging the gap. Corporations are increasingly active in every area of American life. They also employ anthropologists to study corporate cultures, philosophers to deal with ethics, and art historians to catalog their collections. What is missing in Useem's book is an attempt to understand why these changes are occurring and a critical examination of this interface.

For example, corporate America's concern with education extends to the three Rs as well as higher education. Business is promoting efforts to enrich primary education to get better workers at the bottom as well as the top of the corporation. While these efforts represent opportunities to be sure, they can also be seen as attempts to shift the costs of change from the corporate sector to the public and the individual.

LILY M. HOFFMAN

New School for
  Social Research
New York City

OTHER BOOKS

AGIBALOVA, YE and G. DONSKOY. *History of the Middle Ages.* Translated by Natalia Belskaya. Pp. 280. Moscow: Progress, 1988. $10.95.

ALIMOV, YURI. *The Rise and Growth of the Non-Aligned Movement.* Pp. 230. Moscow: Progress, 1987. Paperbound, $6.95.

ANNIS, SHELDON. *God and Production in a Guatemalan Town.* Pp. xii, 197. Austin: University of Texas Press, 1987. $27.50.

ARDAGH, JOHN. *France Today.* Pp. 647. London: Penguin Books, 1988. Paperbound, $7.95.

BAPTISTE, FITZROY ANDRE. *War, Cooperation, and Conflict: The European Possessions in the Caribbean, 1939-1945.* Pp. xiv, 351. Westport, CT: Greenwood Press, 1988. $39.95.

BARRERA, MARIO. *Beyond Aztlan: Ethnic Autonomy in Comparative Perspective.* Pp. xii, 209. New York: Praeger, 1988. No price.

BECK, EMILY MORISON, ed. *Sailor Historian: The Best of Samuel Eliot Morison.* Pp. xxxvii, 431. Boston: Houghton Mifflin, 1989. Paperbound, $11.95.

BECKLES, HILARY McD. *Natural Rebels: A Social History of Enslaved Black Women in Barbados.* Pp. 197. New Brunswick, NJ: Rutgers University Press, 1990. $35.00. Paperbound, $13.95.

BELL, CORAL. *Dependent Ally: A Study in Australian Foreign Policy.* Pp. x, 230. New York: Oxford University Press, 1988. Paperbound, $16.95.

BENEWICK, ROBERT and PAUL WINGROVE, eds. *Reforming the Revolution: China in Transition.* Pp. vii, 255. Pacific Grove, CA: Brooks/Cole, 1989. $36.50.

BENJAMIN, GERALD and CHARLES BRECHER, eds. *The Two New Yorks: State-City Relations in the Changing Federal System.* Pp. xviii, 557. New York: Russell Sage Foundation, 1988. $55.00.

BERGLUND, STEN et al. *East European Multi-Party Systems.* Pp. 126. Helsinki: Finnish Society of Sciences and Letters, 1988. Paperbound, no price.

BOSTON, THOMAS D. *Race, Class and Conservatism.* Pp. xix, 172. London: Unwin Hyman, 1988. Paperbound, no price.

BOSWORTH, BARRY P., ANDREW S. CARRON, and ELISABETH H. RHYNE. *The Economics of Federal Credit Programs.* Pp. xii, 214. Washington, DC: Brookings Institution, 1987. No price.

BOSWORTH, BARRY P. et al. *Critical Choices: What the President Should Know about the Economy and Foreign Policy.* Pp. viii, 184. Washington, DC: Brookings Institution, 1989. Paperbound, $6.95.

BREINES, WINI. *Community and Organization in the New Left, 1962-1968: The Great Refusal.* Pp. 187. New Brunswick, NJ: Rutgers University Press, 1989. Paperbound, $13.00.

BROWN, JANET WELSH, ed. *In the U.S. Interest: Resources, Growth, and Security in the Developing World.* Pp. 228. Boulder, CO: Westview Press, 1990. Paperbound, $19.85.

BROWN, LESTER R. et al. *State of the World: A Worldwatch Institute Report on Progress toward a Sustainable Society.* Pp. xvi, 256. New York: W. W. Norton, 1989. No price.

BROWNE, CHRISTOPHER with DOUGLAS A. SCOTT. *Economic Development in Seven Pacific Island Countries.* Pp. vii, 219. Washington, DC: International Monetary Fund, 1989. Paperbound, $18.00.

BRUNO, MICHAEL et al., eds. *Inflation Stabilization: The Experience of Israel, Argentina, Brazil, Bolivia, and Mexico.* Pp. xi, 419. Cambridge: MIT Press, 1988. $27.50.

BURLATSKY, FYODOR. *From Geneva to Reykjavik.* Translated by Sergei Chuklai. Pp. 206. Moscow: Progress, 1987. Paperbound, $2.95.

CASSIRER, ERNST. *The Question of Jean-Jacques Rousseau.* 2d ed. Edited and translated by Peter Gay. Pp. 146. New Haven, CT: Yale University Press, 1989. Paperbound, $7.95.

CHANDHOKE, NEERA. *The Politics of U.N. Sanctions.* Pp. xi, 300. New Delhi: Gitanjali, 1988. $35.00.

CHERNIKOV, G. P. et al. *Fundamentals of Scientific Socialism.* Pp. 205. Moscow: Progress, 1988. $7.95.

COHEN, G. A. *History, Labour, and Freedom: Themes from Marx.* Pp. xiii, 317. New York: Oxford University Press, 1989. $65.00. Paperbound, $24.95.

Comparative Study of South and North Korea, A. Pp. 315. Seoul: National Unification Board, 1988. No price.

COOK, BRIAN J. *Bureaucratic Politics and Regulatory Reform: The EPA and Emissions Trading.* Pp. 192. Westport, CT: Greenwood Press, 1988. $37.95.

COSTNER, HERBERT, ed. *New Perspectives in Liberal Education.* Pp. 192. Seattle: University of Washington Press, 1989. $12.50.

CROVOTZ, L. GORDON and JEREMY A. RABKIN, eds. *The Fettered Presidency: Legal Constraints on the Executive Branch.* Pp. xx, 335. Lanham, MD: American Enterprise Institute, 1989. Paperbound, $14.95.

DANZIGER, SHELDON and JOHN F. WINE. *State Policy Choices: The Wisconsin Experience.* Pp. xvii, 294. Madison: University of Wisconsin Press, 1988. Paperbound, no price.

DAVIES, PHILIP JOHN and FREDERICK A. WALDSTEIN, eds. *Political Issues in America Today.* Pp. vi, 240.

Manchester, UK: Manchester University Press, 1987. Paperbound, $29.95.

DE VOTO, BERNARD. *The Year of Decision: 1846.* Pp. xxv, 538. Boston: Houghton Mifflin, 1989. Paperbound, $11.95.

DESARIO, JACK PAUL, ed. *International Public Policy Sourcebook.* Vol. 1, *Health and Social Welfare.* Pp. xiv, 344. Westport, CT: Greenwood Press, 1989. No price.

DICKIE, PHIL. *The Road to Fitzgerald.* Pp. xi, 293. Queensland, Australia: University of Queensland Press, 1988. Paperbound, $9.95.

DORSEY, GRAY L. *Jurisculture: Greece and Rome.* Pp. ix, 78. New Brunswick, NJ: Transaction Books, 1989. No price.

DOWTY, ALAN. *Closed Borders: The Contemporary Assault on Freedom of Movement.* Pp. xvii, 270. New Haven, CT: Yale University Press, 1987. Paperbound, $12.95.

DRAPER, ALAN. *A Rope of Sand: The AFL-CIO Committee on Political Education, 1955-1967.* Pp. x, 166. New York: Praeger, 1989. No price.

DREIJMANIS, JOHN, ed. *Karl Jaspers on Max Weber.* Translated by Robert J. Whelan. Pp. xxiv, 216. New York: Paragon House, 1989. $18.95.

ELAZAR, DANIEL and CHAIM KALCHHEIM, eds. *Local Government in Israel.* Pp. xxxiv, 426. Lanham, MD: University Press of America, 1988. Paperbound, $23.75.

ENGEMAN, THOMAS S., EDWARD J. ERLER, and THOMAS B. HOFELLER, eds. *The Federalist Concordance.* Pp. xiv, 622. Chicago: University of Chicago Press, 1988. Paperbound, $19.95.

FAURIOL, GEORGES A. and EVA LOSER. *Guatemala's Political Puzzle.* Pp. xix, 127. New Brunswick, NJ: Transaction Books, 1988. $24.95.

FEDERAL INSTITUTE FOR EAST EUROPEAN AND INTERNATIONAL

STUDIES, ed. *The Soviet Union 1986/1987: Events, Problems, Perspectives.* Pp. xi, 373. Boulder, CO: Westview Press, 1989. $40.00.

FEIGE, EDGAR L., ed. *The Underground Economies: Tax Evasion and Information Distortion.* Pp. xi, 378. New York: Cambridge University Press, 1989. No price.

FERGUSON, YALE H. and RICHARD W. MANSBACH. *The Elusive Quest: Theory and International Politics.* Pp. viii, 300. Columbia: University of South Carolina Press, 1988. $29.95.

FLAMM, KENNETH. *Creating the Computer: Government, Industry, and High Technology.* Pp. xi, 282. Washington, DC: Brookings Institution, 1988. $28.95.

FOSLER, R. SCOTT, ed. *The New Economic Role of American States: Strategies in a Competitive World Economy.* Pp. 336. New York: Oxford University Press, 1988. $29.95.

FREDDI, GIORGIO and JAMES WARNER BJORKMAN, eds. *Controlling Medical Professionals: The Comparative Politics of Health Governance.* Pp. 250. Newbury Park, CA: Sage, 1989. $45.00.

FRIEDELBAUM, STANLEY H., ed. *Human Rights in the United States: New Directions in Constitutional Policymaking.* Pp. xxi, 200. Westport, CT: Greenwood Press, 1988. $39.95.

FRITSCH-BOURNAZEL, RENATA. *Confronting the German Question: Germans on the East-West Divide.* Pp. 150. Oxford: Berg, 1988. $28.00.

GABRISCH, HUBERT. *Economic Reforms in Eastern Europe and the Soviet Union.* Pp. vii, 214. Boulder, CO: Westview Press, 1989. Paperbound, $25.00.

GIBBONS, WILLIAM CONRAD. *The U.S. Government and the Vietnam War: Executive and Legislative Roles and Relationships.* Pt. 3, *January-July 1965.* Pp. xviii, 489. Princeton, NJ: Princeton University Press, 1989. Paperbound, $12.50.

GIERSCH, HERBERT, ed. *Macro and Micro Policies for More Growth and Employment: Symposium 1987.* Pp. vii, 369. Tübingen, Germany: Mohr, 1988. Paperbound, $56.00.

GILLESPIE, MICHAEL ALLEN and MICHAEL LIENESCH, eds. *Ratifying the Constitution.* Pp. xiv, 417. Lawrence: University Press of Kansas, 1989. $19.95.

GODSEY, FRED. *A Gathering at the River: Stories from a Life in the Foreign Service.* Pp. ix, 205. Menlo Park, CA: Markgraf Publications Group, 1989. $28.95.

GORBACHEV, MIKHAIL S. et al. *USSR/US Summit, Washington, December 7-10, 1987.* Pp. 144. Moscow: Novosti Press, 1987. Paperbound, $1.95.

GORDON, WENDELL and JOHN ADAMS. *Economics as Social Science: An Evolutionary Approach.* Pp. 254. Riverdale, MD: Riverdale, 1989. Paperbound, $25.00.

HAAS, MICHAEL, ed. *Korean Reunification: Alternative Pathways.* Pp. xx, 152. New York: Praeger, 1989. No price.

HABERMAS, JÜRGEN. *On the Logic of the Social Sciences.* Translated by Shierry Weber Nicholsen and Jerry A. Stark. Pp. xiv, 220. Cambridge: MIT Press, 1988. $22.50.

HARRISON, ALEXANDER. *Challenging De Gaulle: The O.A.S. and the Counterrevolution in Algeria, 1954-1962.* Pp. 192. New York: Praeger, 1989. $39.95.

HERROD, JEFFREY. *Power, Production, and the Unprotected Worker.* Pp. xviii, 347. New York: Columbia University Press, 1987. $40.00.

HEYMANN, PHILIP B. *The Politics of Public Management.* Pp. xv, 196. New

Haven, CT: Yale University Press, 1989. Paperbound, $9.95.

HINSHAW, ARNED L. *Heartbreak Ridge: Korea, 1951.* Pp. 172. New York: Praeger, 1989. $19.95.

HOLLINGER, DAVID A. and CHARLES CAPPER, eds. *The American Intellectual Tradition.* Vol. 1, *1620-1865.* Pp. xiii, 393. New York: Oxford University Press, 1989. Paperbound, $14.95.

HOLLINGER, DAVID A. and CHARLES CAPPER, eds. *The American Intellectual Tradition.* Vol. 2, *1865 to the Present.* Pp. xii, 276. New York: Oxford University Press, 1989. Paperbound, $12.95.

HUDSON, YEAGER and CREIGHTON PEDEN, eds. *Philosophical Essays on the Ideas of a Good Society.* Pp. xv, 347. Lewiston, NY: Edwin Mellen Press, 1988. $59.95.

JAMES, ESTELLE, ed. *The Nonprofit Sector in International Perspective: Studies in Comparative Culture and Policy.* Pp. xv, 384. New York: Oxford University Press, 1989. $55.00.

JOHN, ROBERT. *Behind the Balfour Declaration: The Hidden Origins of Today's Mideast Crisis.* Pp. 107. Costa Mesa, CA: Institute for Historical Review, 1988. Paperbound, $8.00.

JUVILER, PETER and HIROSHI KIMURA. *Gorbachev's Reforms: U.S. and Japanese Assessments.* Pp. xxi, 178. Hawthorne, NY: Walter de Gruyter, 1988. $36.95. Paperbound, $14.95.

KARNIG, ALBERT K. and PAULA D. McCLAIN. *Urban Minority Administrators: Politics, Policy, and Style.* Pp. xvi, 166. Westport, CT: Greenwood Press, 1988. No price.

KÄSLER, DIRK. *Max Weber: An Introduction to His Life and Work.* Pp. x, 287. Chicago: University of Chicago Press, 1989. $45.00.

KAUTSKY, KARL. *The Materialist Conception of History.* Pp. lxx, 558. New

Haven, CT: Yale University Press, 1988. $55.00.

KAZUKO, ONO. *Chinese Women in a Century of Revolution, 1850-1950.* Edited by Joshua A. Fogel. Pp. xxvi, 255. Stanford, CA: Stanford University Press, 1989. $35.00.

KEELEY, EDMUND. *The Salonika Bay Murder: Cold War Politics and the Polk Affair.* Pp. xvii, 395. Princeton, NJ: Princeton University Press, 1989. $24.95.

KEENER, FREDERICK M. and SUSAN E. LORSCH, eds. *Eighteenth-Century Women and the Arts.* Pp. xv, 301. Westport, CT: Greenwood Press, 1988. No price.

KINZO, MARIA D'ALVA G. *Legal Opposition Politics under Authoritarian Rule in Brazil.* Pp. xiii, 234. New York: St. Martin's Press, 1988. $45.00.

KOLODZIEJ, EDWARD A. and ROGER E. KANET, eds. *The Limits of Soviet Power in the Developing World.* Pp. xx, 531. Baltimore, MD: Johns Hopkins University Press, 1989. $47.50.

KOZLOV, I. and V. POMINOV. *The World Energy Problem.* Translated by Igor Kochubei. Pp. 232. Moscow: Progress, 1987. Paperbound, $3.95.

KRAVCHENKO, VICTOR A. *I Chose Freedom.* Pp. xix, 458. New Brunswick, NJ: Transaction Books, 1989. Paperbound, $24.95.

KREPON, MICHAEL. *Arms Control in the Reagan Administration.* Pp. xxvii, 314. Lanham, MD: University Press of America, White Burkett Miller Center of Public Affairs, 1989. $32.50.

LABEDZ, LEOPOLD. *The Use and Abuse of Sovietology.* Pp. 372. New Brunswick, NJ: Transaction Books, 1989. No price.

LANOUE, DAVID J. *From Camelot to the Teflon President: Economics and Presidential Popularity since 1960.* Pp. xii, 125. Westport, CT: Greenwood Press, 1988. $33.95.

LaPALOMBARA, JOSEPH. *Democracy Italian Style.* Pp. xii, 308. New Haven, CT: Yale University Press, 1989. Paperbound, $10.95.

LARSON, DEBORAH WELCH. *Origins of Containment: A Psychological Explanation.* Pp. xvi, 380. Princeton, NJ: Princeton University Press, 1985. Paperbound, $12.95.

LEE, CHUNG H. and SEIJI NAYA, eds. *Trade and Investment in Services in the Asia-Pacific Region.* Pp. xii, 216. Boulder, CO: Westview Press, 1988. $34.50.

LEE, SU-HOON. *State-Building in the Contemporary Third World.* Pp. xiii, 191. Boulder, CO: Westview Press, 1988. $30.00.

LINDEN, RONALD H. *Communist States and International Change: Romania and Yugoslavia in Comparative Perspective.* Pp. xviii, 201. Winchester, MA: Allen & Unwin, 1987. $39.95.

LINNEMANN, HANS, ed. *Export-Oriented Industrialization in Developing Countries.* Pp. xii, 467. Athens: Ohio University Press, 1987. Paperbound, $25.95.

MAHLER, GREGORY. *Contemporary Canadian Politics: An Annotated Bibliography, 1970-1987.* Pp. xiv, 400. Westport, CT: Greenwood Press, 1988. No price.

MAIER, HENDRIK M. J. *In the Center of Authority: The Malay Hikayat Merong Mahawangsa.* Pp. 210. Ithaca, NY: Cornell University, Southeast Asia Program, 1988. Paperbound, $14.00.

MANDEL, ROBERT. *Conflict over the World's Resources: Background, Trends, Case Studies, and Considerations for the Future.* Pp. viii, 148. Westport, CT: Greenwood Press, 1988. No price.

MARE, GERHARD and GEORGINA HAMILTON. *An Appetite for Power: Bethelezi's Inkatha and South Africa.* Pp. vii, 261. Bloomington: Indiana University Press, 1987. $35.00.

MARTIN, MICHAEL T. and TERRY R. KANDAL, eds. *Studies of Development and Change in the Modern World.* Pp. xii, 458. New York: Oxford University Press, 1989. Paperbound, $19.95.

MARTINEAU, HARRIET. *How to Observe Morals and Manners.* Pp. lx, 265. New Brunswick, NJ: Transaction Books, 1989. Paperbound, $19.95.

MASTNY, VOJTECH, ed. *Soviet/East European Survey, 1987-1988.* Pp. viii, 413. Boulder, CO: Westview Press, 1989. Paperbound, $27.95.

MAYNTZ, RENATE and THOMAS P. HUGHES, eds. *The Development of Large Technical Systems.* Pp. 299. Boulder, CO: Westview Press, 1988. Paperbound, $32.50.

McCLESKEY, CLIFTON. *Political Power and American Democracy.* Pp. 178. Pacific Grove, CA: Brooks/Cole, 1989. Paperbound, $17.75.

McKENZIE, RICHARD B. *The American Job Machine.* Pp. 275. New York: Universe Books, 1988. $24.95.

McKNIGHT, STEPHEN A. *Sacralizing the Secular: The Renaissance Origins of Modernity.* Pp. xi, 131. Baton Rouge: Louisiana State University Press, 1989. $25.00.

MEIER, GERALD M. *Leading Issues in Economic Development.* 5th ed. Pp. xvi, 560. New York: Oxford University Press, 1989. Paperbound, $29.95.

MENON, RAJAN. *Soviet Power and the Third World.* Pp. ix, 261. New Haven, CT: Yale University Press, 1989. Paperbound, $13.95.

MESA-LAGO, CARMELO, ed. *Cuban Studies.* Vol. 18. Pp. 257. Pittsburgh, PA: University of Pittsburgh Press, 1988. $24.95.

MILLER, ARTHUR S. *The Secret Constitution and the Need for Constitutional Change.* Pp. x, 179. Westport, CT: Greenwood Press, 1987. $29.95.

MLADENKA, KENNETH R. and KIM QUAILE HILL. *Texas Government: Politics and Economics.* 2d ed. Pp. xix,

324. Pacific Grove, CA: Brooks/Cole, 1989. Paperbound, $18.75.

OTT, J. STEVEN. *Classic Readings in Organizational Behavior.* Pp. xii, 638. Pacific Grove, CA: Brooks/Cole, 1989. Paperbound, $23.75.

OTT, J. STEVEN. *The Organizational Culture Perspective.* Pp. 228. Pacific Grove, CA: Brooks/Cole, 1988. Paperbound, $20.75.

PASTOR, MANUEL, Jr. *The International Monetary Fund and Latin America: Economic Stabilization and Class Conflict.* Pp. xvi, 228. Boulder, CO: Westview Press, 1987. Paperbound, $23.00.

PESSEN, EDWARD. *Riches, Class, and Power: America before the Civil War.* Pp. xxi, 378. New Brunswick, NJ: Transaction Books, 1990. Paperbound, $19.95.

PHILLIPS, DENNIS. *Ambivalent Allies: Myth and Reality in the Australian-American Relationship.* Pp. x, 228. New York: Penguin Books, 1988. Paperbound, $7.95.

PORTES, ALEJANDRO et al., eds. *The Informal Economy: Studies in Advanced and Less Developed Countries.* Pp. viii, 327. Baltimore, MD: Johns Hopkins University Press, 1989. $39.50. Paperbound, $16.95.

REAMS, BERNARD D., Jr. and STUART D. YOAK. *The Constitutions of the United States: A State by State Guide and Bibliography to Current Scholarly Research.* Pp. xix, 554. Dobbs Ferry, NY: Oceana, 1988. $60.00.

RICHTER, LINDA K. *The Politics of Tourism in Asia.* Pp. x, 263. Honolulu: University of Hawaii Press, 1989. $24.00.

ROETT, RIORDAN and FRANK SMYTH. *Dialogue and Armed Conflict: Negotiating the Civil War in El Salvador.* Pp. 56. Washington, DC: Johns Hopkins University, 1988. Paperbound, $7.00.

ROSE, RICHARD. *The Postmodern President: The White House Meets the World.* Pp. ix, 350. Chatham, NJ: Chatham House, 1988. Paperbound, $17.95.

SALAMON, LESTER M., ed., assisted by Michael S. Lund. *Beyond Privatization: The Tools of Government Action.* Pp. xvi, 265. Lanham, MD: Urban Institute Press, 1989. Paperbound, $14.75.

SCHOENHALS, KAI P. *The Free Germany Movement: A Case of Patriotism or Treason?* Pp. 176. Westport, CT: Greenwood Press, 1989. $39.95.

SCHULZ, BRIGITTE H. and WILLIAM W. HANSEN, eds. *The Soviet Bloc and the Third World: The Political Economy of East-South Relations.* Pp. ix, 246. Boulder, CO: Westview Press, 1989. Paperbound, $34.50.

SCHWARTZMAN, EDWARD. *Political Campaign Craftsmanship: A Professional's Guide to Campaigning for Public Office.* Pp. xl, 326. New Brunswick, NJ: Transaction Books, 1989. Paperbound, $19.95.

SCOTT-STEVENS, SUSAN. *Foreign Consultants and Counterparts: Problems in Technology Transfer.* Pp. xvii, 229. Boulder, CO: Westview Press, 1987. Paperbound, $25.00.

SEABROOK, JEREMY. *The Leisure Society.* Pp. 195. New York: Basil Blackwell, 1988. $49.95.

SEGAL, GERALD et al. *Nuclear War and Nuclear Peace.* 2d ed. Pp. xiv, 173. New York: St. Martin's Press, 1988. $39.95.

SIU, PAUL C. P. *The Chinese Laundryman: A Study of Social Isolation.* Pp. xlii, 311. New York: New York University Press, 1987. $47.50.

SKIDMORE, THOMAS E. and PETER H. SMITH. *Modern Latin America.* 2d ed. Pp. xii, 436. New York: Oxford University Press, 1989. Paperbound, $14.95.

SMALL, MELVIN and J. DAVID SINGER. *International War: An An-*

thology. 2d ed. Pp. xv, 419. Pacific Grove, CA: Brooks/Cole, 1989. Paperbound, $20.25.

SPANIER, JOHN and ERIC M. USLANER. *American Foreign Policy Making and the Democratic Dilemmas.* Pp. xiv, 397. Pacific Grove, CA: Brooks/Cole, 1989. Paperbound, $20.25.

SULZBERGER, C. L. *Paradise Regained: Memoir of a Rebel.* Pp. 157. New York: Praeger, 1989. Paperbound, $12.95.

SUPER, JOHN C. *Food, Conquest, and Colonization in Sixteenth-Century Spanish America.* Pp. viii, 133. Albuquerque: University of New Mexico Press, 1988. $24.95. Paperbound, $11.95.

TAUBMAN, WILLIAM and JANE TAUBMAN. *Moscow Spring.* Pp. 304. New York: Summit Books, 1990. Paperbound, $9.95.

TINLING, MARION. *Women into the Unknown: A Sourcebook on Women Explorers and Travelers.* Pp. xxvi, 356. Westport, CT: Greenwood Press, 1989. No price.

TIRADO, ISABEL A. *Young Guard! The Communist Youth League, Petrograd 1917-1920.* Pp. xii, 264. Westport, CT: Greenwood Press, 1988. $39.95.

TOMA, PETER A. *Socialist Authority: The Hungarian Experience.* Pp. xxvii, 288. New York: Praeger, 1988. $49.95.

TURNER, HENRY ASHBY, Jr. *The Two Germanies since 1945.* Pp. viii, 228. New Haven, CT: Yale University Press, 1987. Paperbound, $9.95.

TURNER, W. BURGHARDT and JOYCE MOORE TURNER, eds. *Richard B. Moore, Caribbean Militant in Harlem: Collected Writings 1920-1972.* Pp. ix, 324. Bloomington: Indiana University Press, 1988. $57.50.

VILLARREAL, ROBERTO E., NORMA G. HERNANDEZ, and HOWARD D. NEIGHBOR, eds. *Latino Empowerment: Progress, Problems, and Prospects.* Pp. xxiv, 152. Westport, CT: Greenwood Press, 1988. No price.

VOELTZ, RICHARD A. *German Colonialism and the Southwest Africa Company, 1894-1914.* Pp. x, 133. Athens: Ohio University Press, 1988. Paperbound, $10.00.

WEISBAND, EDWARD, ed. *Poverty amidst Plenty: World Political Economy and Distributive Justice.* Pp. xiv, 270. Boulder, CO: Westview Press, 1989. $49.00.

White Paper on South-North Dialogue in Korea, A. Pp. 571. Seoul: National Unification Board, 1988. Paperbound, no price.

WILSON, TOM. *Ulster: Conflict and Consent.* Pp. xvii, 330. New York: Basil Blackwell, 1989. $49.95.

WINHAM, GILBERT R. *Trading with Canada: The Canada-U.S. Free Trade Agreement.* Pp. ix, 81. New York: Priority Press, 1988. Paperbound, $9.95.

WRONG, DENNIS H. *Power: Its Forms, Bases, and Uses.* Pp. xvi, 326. Chicago: University of Chicago Press, 1988. Paperbound, $14.95.

INDEX

Of Special Interest!

WRITING ACROSS LANGUAGES AND CULTURES
Issues in Contrastive Rhetoric

edited by ALAN C. PURVES,
State University of New York, Albany

Differences in cultural background are an obstacle not only for those who are learning to write in a foreign language but also for scholars who want to compare across cultures the criteria used for evaluating student writing. **Writing Across Languages and Cultures** brings together outstanding international contributors who explore the differences among student compositions written in their native language, compositions written in a second language, and the criteria that are used by monolinguists in judging compositions by students from other cultures. Based on original research and theory, these innovative pieces present a framework for understanding and contrasting the varying structure of texts and the aspects involved in writing various types of texts for culturally diverse audiences.

This book is an essential resource for teachers of composition and English as a Second Language (ESL), as well as for researchers in rhetoric, linguistics, anthropology, and psychology.

Written Communication Annual, Volume 2
1988 / 312 pages / $36.00 (c) / $17.95 (p)

SAGE PUBLICATIONS, INC.
2111 W. Hillcrest Dr.
Newbury Park, CA 91320

SAGE PUBLICATIONS LTD
28 Banner Street
London EC1Y 8QE, England

SAGE PUBLICATIONS INDIA PVT LTD
M-32 Market, Greater Kailash I
New Delhi 110 048 India

New from Sage!

THE WRITING SCHOLAR
Language and Conventions of Academic Discourse

edited by WALTER NASH, University of Nottingham, England

There is a popular image of academic writing as obscure, convoluted, replete with jargon. Some academic writing conforms to the popular image, while others transform the image. Academic discourse is clearly influenced by many factors, conventions, and motives.

This collection, by internationally-noted researchers and theorists in the field, brings varied insights to bear on the question of what happens, linguistically and psychologically, when academics set out to report facts, explain phenomena, propound hypotheses, argue, persuade and rebut. The focus of these chapters centers on the Western tradition of academic writing that was established in Classical times and has been perpetuated in academic institutions in the United States and Europe ever since. The contributors look critically at assumptions and principles underlying academic writing, examining in detail the language and "voice" of the writer, as well as the texture of academic language.

The Writing Scholar offers valuable insight into academic writing with practical applications for instructors in composition, rhetoric, and text linguistics, along with avenues for further research.

Written Communication Annual, Volume 3
1990 (Spring) / 320 pages / $36.00 (c)

SAGE PUBLICATIONS, INC.
2111 W. Hillcrest Dr.
Newbury Park, CA 91320

SAGE PUBLICATIONS LTD
28 Banner Street
London EC1Y 8QE, England

SAGE PUBLICATIONS INDIA PVT LTD
M-32 Market, Greater Kailash I
New Delhi 110 048 India

The ANNALS of the American Academy of Political and Social Science

English Plus: Issues In Bilingual Education

Special Editors: Courtney B. Cazden and Catherine E. Snow

Bilingual education is a controversial public issue. Often identified in the American mind with the use of Spanish in the public schools, it actually involves the use of any of several dozen different languages of both indigenous and immigrant groups.

The first article in **English Plus: Issues in Bilingual Education** attempts to place both English-only and bilingual education within a language-planning framework. General discussion articles follow in four sections:

- Historical and International Contexts
- Policy Statements
- Legislation, Litigation and
  Role of Evaluation Research
- Research on Public Attitudes

The final section presents case studies of English-Plus programs in existing schools or school systems.

This issue presents an in-depth discussion of the complexities involved in bilingual education.

The ANNALS Volume 508
March 1990
paper — $13.95 individual / $15.95 institution
cloth — $22.95

SAGE PUBLICATIONS, INC.
2111 W. Hillcrest Dr.
Newbury Park, CA 91320

SAGE PUBLICATIONS LTD
28 Banner Street
London EC1Y 8QE, England

SAGE PUBLICATIONS INDIA PVT LTD
M-32 Market, Greater Kailash I
New Delhi 110 048 India